Bones of
Contention

Bones of Contention

The Archaeopteryx Scandals

PAUL CHAMBERS

JOHN MURRAY
Albemarle Street, London

A catalogue record for this book is available from the British Library

ISBN 0-7195-6054-3

Typeset in 11.5/13.5 pt Bembo by Servis Filmsetting Ltd, Manchester

Printed and bound in Great Britain by
Butler & Tanner Ltd, London and Frome

To Rachel, my wife, best friend and pillar of support. This book would not have been possible without your encouragement, help and cajoling. My love for you is without limit.

Contents

Preface		ix
Acknowledgements		xii
Note on Scientific Conventions		xiii
1.	The Doctor's Lucky Find	1
2.	The Missing Link	14
3.	The Feathered Enigma	23
4.	The Hard Bargain	45
5.	Evolutionary Rivals	68
6.	The Eagle has Landed	82
7.	Making Sense of it All	94
8.	The Toothed Birds	116
9.	A Second Specimen	140
10.	The Origin of Birds	151
11.	The Wilderness Years	166
12.	Dinosaurs of a Feather	174
13.	The Demon Fossil	194
14.	A New Flock of Fossil Birds	210
15.	*Archaeoraptor* – The Piltdown Bird	235
	Epilogue	251
	Sources	254
	Index	265

Preface

The small feathered fossil named *Archaeopteryx* has probably been at the centre of more bitterness and confrontation than any other single scientific object. This rancour began in 1861 and is just as vigorous today.

I first came face to face with this fossil some years ago when I was working on a children's television series about dinosaurs. The script demanded that we film the two most photogenic *Archaeopteryx* specimens, one of which is in the London Natural History Museum and the other in Berlin's Humboldt Museum.

In London our filming trip was an elaborate process. The *Archaeopteryx* was locked in a safe in a secure and environmentally controlled room. It could only be handled by staff and the fossil was not at any time allowed to leave its sturdy trolley. The children we had with us were kept at a safe distance between takes.

Filming in Berlin was a different matter entirely. The Humboldt Museum had only just emerged from decades of East German under-funding and was at the time awaiting new government money to repair damage done to the building during World War Two. Their *Archaeopteryx*, arguably the most valuable of the specimens, was kept in a wooden cabinet next to a draughty window. It was dragged out by hand and left on a nearby table while the camera crew stood around drinking coffee. This contrast in the treatment of the two *Archaeopteryx* specimens, both of which are considered to be the prize exhibits of their respective museums, amused me at the time. It also sparked my curiosity about this strange fossil.

As a former palaeontologist (albeit one specializing in ancient plankton) I thought that I knew all about the *Archaeopteryx*. It was half-bird, half-reptile. It was the 'missing link' that had proved Darwin to be correct and also proved that birds were descended from dinosaurs. This is certainly how most popular dinosaur books portrayed it. Even specialist textbooks did not add much more than this, they just expressed it in more technical terms. The *Archaeopteryx* appeared to be an open and shut case.

However, there was something about this fossil that appealed to me. Perhaps it was because it had been discovered at the height of the Victorian era, a period of history which fascinates me. Perhaps it was the beauty of the *Archaeopteryx* fossils themselves and the fact that I had managed to see the two best specimens for myself. Whatever it was, I was sufficiently intrigued to start digging into its past.

As I casually nosed my way through various library archives a bizarre story started to emerge. It quickly became apparent that beneath the few solid paragraphs allocated to this fossil in various books and magazines lay a seething and explosive history which had pitted scientist against scientist, nation against nation, science against religion and caused many other cataclysmic collisions. It was almost as if the *Archaeopteryx* were cursed and anybody who tried to understand it would end up getting their fingers burnt. Careers had been ruined, rich people bankrupted and esteemed organizations made to look ridiculous. The *Archaeopteryx* also seemed to be able to support several mutually exclusive causes at once. Perhaps most surprising of all was that this was not just a case of historical rivalry. The bitterness it engenders is, if anything, worse today than it was when the first *Archaeopteryx* was discovered in 1861. All this is quite an achievement for a creature that died 150 million years ago.

As I pieced together the history of the *Archaeopteryx* I became less interested in the hard science and more and more fascinated with the effect that this humble fossil could have on individuals and even whole communities. This is the *Archaeopteryx*'s most amazing quality.

This book is not just about science but about the iconic status of one fossil and how it could change people's lives and create improbable, unpleasant and even dangerous situations. To a degree this has meant delving behind the calm façade of the scientific community and into the turmoil that lies behind. In some cases it reveals a scientific world riddled with split loyalties and personal feuds. At other times it shows the deductive process at its most brilliant and the way in which discovery of just one new fact can instantly change the thinking of a generation.

To me the life and times of the *Archaeopteryx* is one of the great scientific stories of our age.

Paul Chambers

Acknowledgements

The writing of this book was by no means a solo effort. Many, many others have played a vital part in its genesis.

I should especially like to thank the following people who provided help with the scientific and historical research: Sankar Chatterjee (Museum of Texas Technology University), Alan Feduccia (University of North Carolina), Alexandra Freeman (BBC Science Unit), Alan Lord (University College London), Larry Martin (University of Kansas), Ilja Nieuwland (Groningen University, Netherlands), Mark Norell (American Museum of Natural History), Dave Unwin (Humboldt Museum, Berlin), Günter Viohl (Jura-Museum, Eichstätt) and Chandra Wickramasinghe (University of Wales).

I would also like to thank the following institutions whose libraries provided me with invaluable support: University College London, Imperial College London, Cambridge University, Natural History Museum (London), British Newspaper Library (Colindale), Marylebone Library and The British Library at St Pancras.

Finally, a big thank-you to all those who have provided practical and emotional support especially my agent Sugra Zaman of Watson Little Ltd., Grant McIntyre and Caro Westmore of John Murray Ltd., Simon Butler, Karen Pulford, Karen Ings, Ian Coles, Alex Freeman, Tim Haines and my parents and other family members. My apologies if I have inadvertently missed anybody. Thank you all.

Note on Scientific Conventions

It was my aim that this book should be as readable as possible and that it should not be some form of textbook on the evolution of birds. To this end I made a number of compromises so as to keep the text relatively free of complicated terms, complex techniques or over-long discussions. It should therefore be noted that for the most part geological dates and ages quoted in the text are based on the latest data. I have only used generic names and not species names except where absolutely necessary. Likewise, whenever possible bones and body parts are referred to by their common names. Most arguments have been boiled down or are quoted on their strongest pieces of evidence.

I do not claim to have included every last contribution to the scientific debate surrounding the *Archaeopteryx*. Instead I have focused on key incidents and/or individuals. For those who wish to delve further into the complex science behind the history of the *Archaeopteryx*, a bibliography is included, which lists works that cover this in more detail.

I

The Doctor's Lucky Find

THE SPRING OF 1861 was particularly mild in northern Europe. Throughout the unseasonably warm weather Queen Victoria was celebrating the twenty-fourth year of her reign while her country swelled under the financial rewards of an industrial revolution and the benefits of owning the largest trading empire on Earth. Similar industrialization had developed across much of the rest of northern Europe, especially in Britain's two great rivals, France and Germany. The world's other great industrial power, the United States of America, was using its engineering skills to power a bloody and divisive civil war, fought ostensibly over the issue of human rights for slaves. This was a crucial time for the western world as science, industry and social reform all began to pull together in what would be regarded for decades afterwards as a 'golden age' when these societies broke away from their medieval roots and moved towards the modern era.

Despite the massive advances taking place around them, neither world politics nor the weather is likely to have overly affected quarry workers in the district of Solnhofen in Germany. There were, and still are, a great many quarries peppering the landscape around the rural town of Solnhofen all exploiting a band of Jurassic limestone that snakes its way through the Bavarian countryside, occasionally outcropping on hillsides and in valleys. Mining methods here have remained unchanged in over 300 years and the backbreaking work continues, day in and day out, through sunshine, rain, wind and snow. In the 1860s a job in the Solnhofen quarries was poorly paid and required little formal skills or training, just physical strength and a keen eye, but in a region which had thus far seen few benefits from the Teutonic industrial revolution the work was steady, all year round and welcomed by those who could get it.

Every day large blocks of fine-grained, jaundiced-looking limestone would be levered out from high up the quarry face and then lowered to the ground. Those below would split the blocks along their fine bedding planes to produce cardboard-thin sheets of rock. Each slab of limestone would then undergo a tortuous quality control process, passing from the workers at the quarry face to one or more inspectors. From there it would be taken by porters to the stonecutters who shaped each slab before sending it to the stackers, who would store it ready for sale.

As each man received each new piece of rock he would look at its uniformity and roughness and give it a grade of quality. By the time it reached the stacking pound, every rock fragment could have been examined by as many as a dozen people, each giving their opinion on its intended use and hence its ultimate price.

The flattest, smoothest slabs were allocated the highest grade and were destined for use in the lithographic printing industry. The rougher, thicker slabs would be used for roofing or flooring tiles, and the lowest quality of all for general building material. Blocks of Solnhofen limestone have been found even on the floors and roofs of 2,000-year-old Roman villas, which demonstrates the long-standing importance of the stone from this region.

Since the Middle Ages the Solnhofen quarries have been known for far more than just the building quality of their rocks. The thin, easily split limestone layers also contain some of the best-preserved fossils known anywhere in the world. Fossils are not a common find in the quarries, but when they do occur each one is so complete and so perfect in its detail that once in the hands of the palaeontologist it inevitably produces some new revelation about the 150-million-year-old Jurassic world from which it came.

Even before the days of organized science, the Solnhofen fossils were a valued prize in the manor houses and stately homes

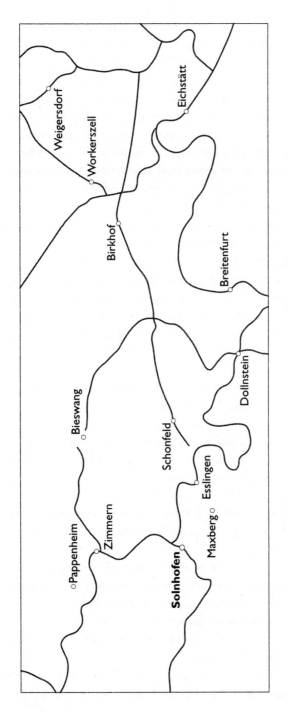

Solnhofen and its quarries

of Europe but by the 1860s they were being sought after by the newly founded museums and universities of Europe and America. High prices could be commanded and consequently the owners of these privately run quarries demanded that all fossil finds be reported to the managers so that their sale could be added to the profits. With a dozen pairs of eyes scanning each piece of stone, few fossils escaped attention. Quite how far down the line of command the fossils would get was another matter entirely. Many disappeared long before they reached the stone-cutters' shed, smuggled home in knapsacks to be sold on the black market.

During one of the mild spring days of 1861, the exact date being long ago lost to history, a worker in the Ottmann Quarry, just north of Solnhofen, prised a thin sheet of limestone from a larger block that had been pulled to the ground from 20 metres up the rock face. Briefly he scanned the rock's fresh surface, checking for weak spots, mineral veins or other imperfections that could affect its quality. On this occasion he saw the series of faint, but regular, marks and imprints which indicated the presence of a fossil. In its unprocessed state, the rock revealed only the faintest traces of the ancient life preserved within it: a few semicircular curves that indicated where some bones lay and a series of imprinted symmetric patterns that could have been anything at all. The fossil was modest in size, about 30 centimetres or so at its widest, but the markings did not form themselves into any apparently meaningful shape.

The quarry worker must have been unsure as to what type of petrified animal he had found. Many other fossils from the quarry were clearly recognizable as having once been fish, insects or crabs, similar in form to their living counterparts. He had probably also seen a great many other fossils which looked like nothing alive on Earth, such as the pterosaurs or 'flying lizards' with their giant leathery wings and the tightly curled ammonite shells. His fossil did not resemble any of these.

The quarry workers knew that the more unusual the fossil, the more it would be worth financially. Many excited scientists had visited Solnhofen in search of its fossils, sometimes paying extortionate prices. Only the previous year the quarry workers had watched in stunned silence as a bizarrely mustachioed English lord had paid the equivalent of several years' of their wages for a few fossilized fish. No one could believe that he could waste so much money on a fish that could not even be eaten. The Solnhofen fossils meant big money.

Holding the newly discovered fossil in his hands, the quarryman had only a few seconds to make his decision. He could pass the fossil up the quality control line, in which case somebody else might pocket it, or he could hand it on to the quarry manager in person and get a grunted nod of thanks, while the quarry owner would have the pleasure of selling the specimen to some over-excitable museum professor. In the end, and almost without thinking, he chose the logical third option. Gently the quarryman clipped the excess rock from around the fossil, clamped the two halves of rock together again and stuck the whole lot under his coat. There was a risk that he would get stopped at the gate and searched but it was a remote one; in any case the fossil looked scrappy and not of the quality that would cause eccentric noblemen to reach for their wallets. This was, as far as he was concerned, a perk of the trade in recompense for the unpleasantness of working next to the muddy, wet and often dangerous rock face.

At the end of work on that day, what was to be the most important fossil discovery of the century, and possibly of all time, passed through the Ottmann Quarry gates smuggled inside the clothing of a low-paid quarryman. History does not record his name.

Three weeks later, thoughts of ancient life were probably not on the mind of Dr Carl Häberlein as he rose to answer a knock on the door of his modest but comfortable Bavarian house. The doctor took his time, his seventy-four years and portly figure were beginning to slow him down after what had been a full and active life in one of the remoter regions of the Bavarian state. A medical doctor by trade, Häberlein had recently retired from his job as District Medical Officer of his home town of Pappenheim. He had hoped to have given up his practice

Carl Häberlein, the German doctor who chanced upon the first
Archaeopteryx *specimen*

completely but he still had a daughter at home and his pension
was looking less than stable, given the regional political turmoil.
Much to his displeasure, he continued to see a selection of his
old patients at his distinctive white house on the outskirts of
Pappenheim.

Häberlein had been born locally and was raised in the nearby town of Solnhofen. He had trained in medicine at Munich before returning to set up his practice in Pappenheim in the early 1800s. He had been married twice, first to a woman about whom nothing whatsoever is known, and then, in 1813, to Katharina Friederika Weigel. The couple had a healthy family of two sons and nine daughters, three of whom were not to make it beyond their early years. After Katharina's death in 1848 the doctor had been left to bring up his considerable brood alone for thirteen years, with the assistance of a housekeeper.

The unexpected knock on the door may have suggested to Häberlein that he was required to give a medical consultation at short notice. The man on the doorstep was indeed a patient. Dressed simply, he was a manual worker from one of the local limestone quarries. Häberlein invited him through to the front room, sharply requesting him to sit down on a wooden chair reserved for those whose soiled clothes might leave marks on the upholstery. The man had come with what was apparently a chest infection, probably picked up in one of the local smoke-filled beer cellars and exacerbated by working outdoors in the cold, damp air. By the sound of his breathing and coughing, the infection had got a good hold: the quarryman should have seen Häberlein a week ago but, in a region where wages were low, a visit to the doctor was a last resort. Häberlein had, however, always been a popular choice for the quarry workers because he was one of the few reliable fences in the local stolen fossil trade.

The poverty around Pappenheim had long ago led to the creation of an alternative economy based not on cash but on a barter system where objects or labour were offered in lieu of hard currency. A hard-up carpenter might mend a broken door for a butcher in return for meat, or a woodsman exchange logs with a blacksmith for a new knife. Häberlein's participation in the system was more esoteric – his passion was for the Solnhofen fossils but he did not like to pay cash for them. Instead the penniless quarrymen willingly swapped their fossils for his medical services.

On this particular day Häberlein found himself being offered what at first looked to be quite a scrappy piece of Solnhofen limestone. The halves of rock were muddy and the fossil inside very indistinct. One of the pieces of rock had also been broken along one corner, catching the edge of the fossil. This was doubtless a consequence of the quarryman's attempt to get the specimen out of his quarry unseen. Nonetheless, a few delicate pieces of bone were visible and from these Häberlein knew he was dealing with a rare fossil. The bones were clearly designed to support the weight of a land animal, not a marine reptile or fish. Instinct suggested that it might be some form of pterodactyl, a leathery winged flying reptile whose remains were occasionally found in the Solnhofen limestone and whose fossils could command huge sums.

Only a few years previously Häberlein had sold several Solnhofen pterodactyl fossils to the nearby Munich Bavarian State Collection for the extortionate sum of £900, the equivalent of several years' worth of his wages. The old doctor was not locally noted for his good humour and charity: he took the fossils not out of pity for the wretched quarry workers, but because he could exchange them for hard cash.

As he turned the slab backwards and forwards in his hands, letting the half-light from the window catch its surface and highlight its topography, Häberlein could clearly make out the distinctive shape of a long and straight backbone and, below it, some leg bones. Concentrating harder, he fancied that he could see further features surrounding the main body which appeared to radiate from the bones of the fossil itself. Could it be that an outline of the pterodactyl's wings had been preserved? If so, then this would be a very rare and valuable specimen indeed, and one that Häberlein had to have.

As a seasoned negotiator, Häberlein never once let his enthusiasm for the new fossil show. His lips remained thin, his eyes fixed and his expression unemotional. This was a man who could drive a hard bargain, especially when the odds were stacked in his favour, as they invariably were. The coughing quarryman, to whom the fossil had no fixed worth, agreed to Häberlein's suggestion that he be treated free that day and then allowed to visit him a further four times. It was more than the quarryman had hoped for and certainly more than he had received in exchange for the other fossils he had brought to the doctor's house. After receiving advice and a prescription, he returned to the warm spring air outside little knowing that he had just set in motion a train of events which would shake the scientific world for a century and a half.

To call Häberlein a palaeontologist would be like calling an accountant a professor of mathematics. In the dim and distant past he had taken to collecting, cleaning and studying fossils for interest's sake alone, but this stopped abruptly when he realized the commercial potential of his hobby.

His first sales were to local collectors and fetched a useful amount of pin money. However, as the early Victorian world awakened to the joys of geology, the demand increased, driving the price of the rarer Solnhofen fossils through the roof. Häberlein had long ago given up any pretence that he was a true palaeontologist, although in recognizing and preparing Jurassic fossils he was probably as good as any of the curators in the natural history museums of Europe. No, much as Häberlein had once been fond of his fossils, he now preferred the cash. Having had such a large family to feed, clothe and educate (not to mention his own love of rich food and fine wines), this should not perhaps be surprising.

Having shown his patient the door, Häberlein was itching to get a better look at his latest acquisition. Aside from his medical knowledge and bartering skills, Carl Häberlein was also a master of the fine art of fossil preparation. Separating a delicate, often degraded, fossil from its rock matrix requires several key skills, the most notable of which are a precise hand, an eye for detail and a superhuman degree of patience.

Even in the modern world of electric micro-drills and chemical preparations, each tiny piece of rock must still be individually removed so as not to disturb the fossil within. The whole process can take anything from a day to several years, depending on the size of the fossil and the toughness of the rock in which it lies. Fortunately the Solnhofen limestone is so fine grained and its fossils so perfect that they are relatively easy to process. Sometimes they emerge from between the limestone layers already fully exposed, with little further work needed. But this is rarely the case and certainly did not apply to Häberlein's new find. Even allowing for the relative ease with which a Solnhofen fossil can be prepared, a quick look at some of the specimens that have passed through Häberlein's hands reveals him to have been a patient and gifted worker with an artistic eye for detail. Häberlein's pterodactyls stand proud from their matrix. Just enough rock has been chipped away to reveal their bones and wings, but not so much that the fossil becomes indistinct compared to the mantle of yellowing rock around it. His fossil insects and crabs sit raised on gentle platforms, as though they had died yesterday and been mounted on cork by a patient naturalist. His petrified fish were so exquisitely cleaned that their last meals (invariably other fish) are still visible inside the delicate ribcages.

Often Häberlein spent whole weekends and evenings at his living-room table with a small chisel and hammer. A sea of tiny rock chips would build around him as his workings slowly revealed the finest details of an animal that had died over 150 million years ago. His housekeeper must have cursed him as she swept up the dozens of tiny pieces of rock from the floor surrounding his work table. And his teenage children, who had to walk barefoot through the house, would occasionally stand on a sharp rock fragment missed by the housekeeper. However, and as we shall see later on, at least one of Häberlein's considerable brood was sufficiently interested in his father's lucrative hobby to adopt it for himself.

With the new fossil on his workbench, Häberlein gently wiped each side with a damp cloth to remove any dirt from the surface. This revealed to him which of the two slabs contained the actual bones. The other slab, called the counterpart, would contain merely an imprint of the fossil. The fact that the quarryman brought both halves of rock with him suggests that he had a knowledge of fossil collectors' preference to have both the fossil and its counterpart.

Having selected the half with the fossil in it, Häberlein began to work. His first task was to glue the broken corner of the slab back into place. This is a time-consuming process, with the glue taking several hours to set properly. In the meantime the fossil cannot be moved. Häberlein used the opportunity to assess his new acquisition as it lay on his workbench. The two slabs had a shape almost identical to that of the continent of Africa and were only about 50 centimetres across at their widest point. The visible bones were clustered in the centre of the slab around what was instantly recognizable as a long series of tail bones trailing downwards in a straight line. Häberlein could tell that some of the lower bones were unquestionably from the leg of a land animal whilst some of the higher bones were probably from its arms. There was no sign of the all-important head or indeed of any hands or feet but these might yet lie buried in the limestone. The overall effect made it look like something a cat had killed.

Based on his astute geological knowledge, Häberlein knew that his Jurassic fossil could only be from a very select group of land animals. The presence of arms and legs meant that it could be a dinosaur, a pterosaur, an amphibian or a small reptile such as a lizard. Fossil mammals were not known from the Solnhofen and birds were, at that time, not thought to have arrived on Earth until some time after the dinosaurs' extinction.

Given that only one dinosaur had ever been found in the Solnhofen and that small reptiles were exceedingly rare, Häberlein stuck with his original thought that his fossil was that of a pterosaur. After all, it had light bones and a tail just like the other Solnhofen pterosaurs in his collection. This, however, looked like a species that he had not encountered before, raising the old doctor's hopes that it might carry a more inflated price. After warning his daughter not to touch the drying fossil, Häberlein went to bed, pleased with his day's work.

It was only the next morning, when he started to work on the fossil in an invasive manner, with a hammer and chisel, that Häberlein began to understand the importance of his new specimen.

Only a brief amount of work was needed for Häberlein to see that this fossil was no pterodactyl. The leg and tail bones were wrong, and other key bones of a pterodactyl's skeleton were nowhere to be found. Instead, Häberlein realized that he was dealing with a small and compact animal which had claws on its feet and arms and a massively long tail. Everything pointed to it being a primitive reptile of some sort but it was not of a kind that he had ever seen before. Unfortunately, Häberlein's workings still revealed no sign of a head and so exactly what type of reptile he was dealing with was going to be impossible for him to tell.

With its basic shape revealed, Häberlein saw that he was looking at an animal which was lying either face up or face down (it is difficult to tell which) in the centre of the rock. The arms and legs were spread apart as though the animal had adopted a 'star shape' just before it died. The long and distinctive tail bones that emerged from between the legs pointed in a straight line to the bottom of the slab. Apart from the missing head and hands, and some of the ribs not being quite in place, the specimen was a good one. Having discovered the extent of his fossil, it was now time for Häberlein to work his artistic magic, making the fossil sit neatly on its own prepared surface.

It was at this point that Häberlein received his greatest surprise. As he tapped gently at the layers of rock with a miniature hammer and chisel, he noticed that a pattern was emerging from underneath which corresponded to the faint outline that he had initially assumed to be a pterosaur's wing. As more of the rock was removed, the pattern became increasingly distinctive. It seemed to consist of long straight structures with fine divisions running across them. In fact, they looked for all the world like the feathers of a bird.

Fossilized feathers? Surely not! The oldest known fossil bird was nearly 100 million years younger than the Solnhofen limestone and every popular science textbook positively denied that any birds had been alive during the era of the dinosaurs. Then there was the reptilian skeleton. A feathered bird in the Jurassic might just be conceivable – after all, new fossil discoveries were being made all the time – but a feathered reptile? There was simply no such animal known to science. There must be some mistake.

In disbelief, Häberlein started work on the long lizard-like tail bones. Even after just a few minutes he could see that the tail too had feathers. If anything they were more obvious and distinctive than those on the arms, radiating outwards to form what must in life have been a very long and magnificently plumed tail.

The Solnhofen limestone had once again lived up to its reputation for producing extraordinary finds. There, attached to the arms and tail of the new specimen, were the unmistakable impressions of feathers. Every barb on every quill was visible and the radiating pattern of feathers looked identical to that on a modern bird. Except that this wasn't a bird – it had a long reptilian tail and sharp dinosaur-like claws on its arms. No modern bird had such features. Then there was the problem of the fossil's Jurassic age. Could birds really have been around that early in geological history?

Häberlein's hopes were raised. As more and more of the fossil was revealed over the following days he knew that what he had was nothing less than a scientific enigma – a reptile with feathers. A single glance at the fossil would reveal as much to any right-minded scientist. Häberlein was certain that the feathered fossil would be of great scientific value. However, it was the commercial value that interested him more.

2

The Missing Link

CARL HÄBERLEIN HAD chanced upon his enigmatic feathered reptile during the spring of 1861. Almost exactly a year earlier an event had taken place which would have great bearing on how the Victorian scientific community would greet the news of his discovery. This event would ensure that his fossil received a baptism of fire.

It was the 30th of June 1860. The weather was hot but even so nearly a thousand people crammed themselves into the confined space of the Oxford University Museum lecture room. The audience was a *mélange* of cassocked clergymen, suited and booted professionals, well-dressed students and their lecturers and even, to the surprise of many there, a few women. For its time, this was a rare combination of people even for a learned university town such as Oxford. The organizers had expected only a few dozen. By the start of the proceedings the lecture room was packed with people squeezed in wherever there was space to sit or stand. They fanned themselves with hats, fans and sheets of paper in an effort to move the fetid air away from their faces.

The rattle of background voices died away as the chairman, the Reverend Robert Stevens Henslow, took to the narrow stage and prayed silence from the crowd. The guest speaker, the noted American biologist Dr John W. Draper, was invited on stage, and after light applause he began to deliver his paper to an expectant audience. His first few sentences were stumbling and delivered in a dry, monotone which made him sound more as if he was asking for directions from a stranger than offering a serious scientific opinion.

Within a few minutes the tense air of expectation melted away like morning mist. Far from being provocative, the speech was a long and tedious one which, given that its title was 'On the Intellectual Development of Europe, considered with reference to the views of Mr. Darwin and others, that the progression of organisms is determined by law', should perhaps not have come as such a surprise. But the majority of the crowd were not there for the pleasure of listening to Dr Draper's theory on European development. The doctor must have sensed that he was surplus to the proceedings when, at the end of what is noted as having been 'a long, boring paper', the crowd politely applauded him back to his seat before quickly resuming the fanning of their faces again. The desultory talk and the general lack of interest displayed by most in the hall seemed to be contradicted when, within moments of Dr Draper's finishing, several members of the audience rose to their feet to comment on what they had heard. Perhaps the talk had not been so dull after all.

The first person to take the floor was a clergyman, the Reverend Richard Cresswell, who stood silent for few seconds as though waiting for a class of naughty schoolboys to quieten down. Then, before anyone could catch their breath, Cresswell launched straight into a vocal and savage diatribe against Charles Darwin's *The Origin of Species*, a controversial book which had been in print for only a matter of a few months. The Reverend sparked the crowd into life once more. The mention of Darwin's name and his *Origin of Species* sent cheers and howls through the lecture room.

Dr Draper looked bemused. He had touched lightly upon *The Origin of Species* during his talk, and then only in an illustrative manner. He knew how controversial Mr Darwin's book had proved to be and had not wanted his ideas on the European peoples to be overshadowed by a debate on 'evolution by natural selection', Darwin's central thesis. But it was too late. Draper's talk had been hijacked by others with their own agenda and it was now very clear that these people had not gathered to talk about the niceties of the European peoples. Instead they were going to use this meeting to thrash out the validity or otherwise of *The Origin of Species* and its bearing on science.

The Reverend Cresswell sat down to cheers from the crowd, his anti-Darwinian piece said. Another man stood up and launched himself straight into what was obviously another prepared talk, this time in favour of Darwin. A barrage of shouting and abuse from the floor all but drowned his voice. The scene became rowdier still until the chairman halted proceedings, declaring that the floor was for 'those with arguments and not for mere declamation'.

The crowd quietened and the invitation to speak was offered to the Bishop of Oxford, one Samuel Wilberforce, better known to many in the hall as 'Soapy Sam' because of his slipperiness when engaged in an argument. For several days prior to the meeting, Soapy Sam had let it be known that he would use Draper's talk as an opportunity to 'smash Darwin' once and for all. Word of his intention had quickly travelled along the university grapevine, drawing Darwin's supporters and detractors out of the woodwork and creating the excessively large crowd now present. Oxford University was very anti-Darwin and the chance to see Wilberforce take the theory of natural selection to pieces was one that could not be missed.

The hopes of many of Darwin's enemies were pinned on Soapy Sam because, as a former mathematician and noted philosopher, he was considered one of the few members of the clergy who had both the skill and knowledge needed to tackle the pro-Darwinians. He was a fierce debater and an eminent intellectual who had an understanding of both scientific doctrine and Christian theology. Even prior to *The Origin of Species'* publication Soapy Sam was an avowed anti-evolutionist, but the promotion of Darwin's ideas had caused him to become more vocal still on the subject. He was a man on a mission.

Once on the floor, Soapy Sam launched straight into a diatribe against evolution in general and Darwin's theory in particular. His considerable skills as an orator and the logical way in which he dealt with his subject easily carried the mostly anti-Darwinian crowd along with him. After general comments on the nature of evolution, the Bishop picked on what was then acknowledged to be *The Origin of Species'* weakest point: the lack of solid proof that a plant or animal could transform itself from one species into another.

'If,' the Bishop argued in his resonant voice, 'one animal group can transform into another totally separate animal group, then there should surely be some representatives which have shared characteristics from the group of animals it is evolving from and the group of animals toward which it is evolving. There should be fossils of animals that link the major animal groups. If mammals are evolved from reptiles, then where is the beast that has the features of both a reptile and a mammal? Is it that these animals have yet to be discovered as fossils, as Darwin claims, or is it, as I believe, that they never existed at all? Where,' Wilberforce demanded to know, 'are these missing links?'

A huge cheer went up from the assembled mass. A small chorus of students mimicked the Bishop by asking each other loudly if they knew of the whereabouts of the missing link. Soapy Sam had captured the crowd. Buoyed with confidence, his talk and mannerisms became exaggerated and his tone more aggressive.

He thumped his fist hard on the table as he shouted that 'A rock-pigeon is what a rock-pigeon has always been!' A none too subtle reference to Darwin's love of pigeon-breeding, the results of which had been used as central evidence in *The Origin of Species*. As the roars of approval got louder, Soapy Sam became more and more confident. His talk began to stray from its carefully prepared theme. Feeling he had successfully proved his point about *The Origin of Species*, he decided instead to pick on some of the noted pro-Darwinists in the audience.

Had Darwin himself been there he would no doubt have received a lashing. But ill health and a dislike of controversy had kept him well away which, judging by Wilberforce's behaviour, was probably just as well. If, however, Soapy Sam was looking for a prominent target to hit then there, in the front row, was one of Darwin's most celebrated and vocal supporters, the young and gifted Thomas Henry Huxley, a medical doctor turned biologist

Thomas Huxley, a vocal supporter of Charles Darwin's theory of evolution through natural selection

and, more lately, palaeontologist. Soapy Sam's rhetoric swelled with his ego as he began laying into the silent figure of Huxley. The remarks became more personal, no longer touching on Darwin's scientific work but on that of Huxley.

If there had ever been any pretence that this discussion was about Draper's theory of European development then by now it had totally gone. Soapy Sam launched into an attack on the idea that humans were descended from apes, a theory that Darwin had chosen to avoid in *Origin of Species* but which Huxley had been promoting vigorously for some months. With the crowd's encouragement the Bishop's talk rose to its now unplanned finale.

He looked Huxley squarely in the eye and said: 'Would my learned colleague be kind enough to tell me whether it is on his grandmother's or his grandfather's side that he is descended from an ape?'

In a time when one's ancestry was all important, this was a horrendous insult. It drew forth a barrage of loud cheering and laughter. Wilberforce sat down again accepting the audience's applause and laughter, his piece said.

Huxley, who had worn a dispassionate expression throughout the proceedings, was seen to sit upright in his seat and say loudly, 'The Lord hath delivered him into my hands.' Following his ill-treatment at the hands of Soapy Sam, Huxley was immediately invited to reply on behalf of those few people present who favoured Darwin.

For some years Huxley had had the reputation of being a powerful, witty and sarcastic speaker and he had previously used these gifts to demolish some of the greatest names in science both on paper and in person. However, his involvement in defending *The Origin of Species* had not gone well, with his one previous talk on the subject ending in lacklustre reviews and few new converts to the cause. As he began to speak it looked as though on this occasion he would not fare much better. He began by stating that the Bishop's talk was full of old or disproved facts and that it lacked any scientific credibility whatsoever. One by one, Huxley began to take on the many points of contention raised by Wilberforce. Since there were few real scientists in the room and the audience was by now baying for a fight, not a list of dry facts, the tactic was a bad one.

Huxley tried in vain to explain that the missing links were undiscovered, not because they never existed but because of the imperfection of the geological record, but his voice was drowned out by quips and jeering. He knew that to claw back respect in front of this assembled rabble he was going to have to stoop to the Bishop's level. More and more frustrated by the hecklers, his notoriously quick temper and lightning wit gave rise to a master-stroke which undoubtedly saved him from defeat.

'I assert,' Huxley said above the still noisy crowd, 'that a man has no reason to be ashamed of having an ape for a grandfather. If there were an ancestor whom I should feel shame in recall-ing, it would rather be a *man*, a man of restless and versatile intellect, who, not content with an equivocal success in his own sphere of activity, plunges into scientific questions with which he has no real acquaintance, only to obscure them by an aimless rhetoric, and distract the attention of his hearers from the real point at issue by eloquent digressions and skilled appeals to relig-ious prejudice.'

Even in a society which valued aggressive and personal debat-ing, Huxley's assertion that he would rather be descended from an ape than from the biased Bishop Wilberforce was outrageous. The effect on the crowd was instantaneous. A roar of protest arose as Wilberforce's supporters made their feelings known. At the back one lady was so overcome that she fainted and had to be carried from the hall. Huxley's supporters, whilst shocked, cheered loudly and made a fuss of their hero, as the chairman tried in vain to restore order to the house.

In the remaining minutes one of Huxley's closest colleagues, the botanist Joseph Hooker, managed to wrap up the proceed-ings by achieving what Huxley had failed to do – namely demol-ish Wilberforce's arguments using succinct scientific reasoning. But by this point few people cared one way or the other. The crowd had received their pound of flesh and could return home happy at the sight of two supposedly learned gentlemen having verbally punched each other below the belt.

Soapy Sam, visibly shaken by the turn of events, declined to reply to Hooker's speech and so the meeting dissolved into the warm June air. As the sweating mass filed from the hall, most people remained on the side of Soapy Sam. *The Origin of Species* had only a few supporters world-wide and so neither Huxley's nor Hooker's rebuttal of Soapy Sam made much of an impact. Yet some sympathy was with Huxley, if for no other reason than that he had provided the crowd with the blood for which they had bayed.

Darwin and his small band of supporters had survived their first major trial by fire and, as *The Origin of Species* gained more and more converts, the Oxford debate would eventually be portrayed as a victory for those on the side of evolution. In reality it was at best a draw, most memorable for Huxley's lightning wit rather than any scientific revelation. That evening an impromptu party was held in Huxley's honour, the toast being to Darwin's book. History does not record whether the unfortunate Dr Draper, whose agreement to speak had sparked the whole affair, received an invitation.

The dust thrown up by Huxley and Soapy Sam attracted much publicity and was followed a few days later by a lengthy and expanded criticism of *The Origin of Species* in the *Quarterly Review*. Although this review was written anonymously it was sufficiently close to Soapy Sam's Oxford speech to make it plain who the author was. Like his talk, the Bishop's review went on at length (over six pages) about missing links in the fossil record. As far as the Bishop was concerned, Darwin's theory clearly stated that there should be fossils which link one animal group with another. Unless these fossilized missing links could be produced, *The Origin of Species* could only ever be a clever hypothesis not borne out by the facts.

Soon more and more of Darwin's critics followed Wilberforce's lead. Dozens of articles asked about the whereabouts of the missing link. It was an obvious chink in Darwin's armour, and Thomas Huxley and other pro-Darwinians could only lightly defend themselves against such attacks. The plain truth was that their critics were quite correct – among the hundreds of thousands of fossil specimens languishing in museum basements and cupboards, there was not one single missing link. Without this the Darwinian argument was beginning to stumble. Some evidence of a missing link had to be found – but where was it going to come from?

3

The Feathered Enigma

DR HÄBERLEIN WAS at first uncertain what to do with his new-found feathered enigma. Although it was not the best-preserved fossil in his collection (the flying pterosaurs and insects with their perfect wings had that privilege) it was certainly the most unusual. Over the years the doctor had seen many hundreds of fossils from the local quarries and thousands of others besides. None had looked anything like the strange beast that now lay fully prepared on his workbench. He was certain that he had in his possession an ancient animal that was totally new to science and one which somebody might be prepared to pay handsomely to own.

As a private collection, the diversity and quality of Häberlein's Solnhofen fossils were exceptional. Some compared his collection to that of another Solnhofen specialist, Count Munster of Munich, but Häberlein's close proximity to the quarries and his participation in the local bartering system meant that, in Häberlein's mind at least, his was the better of the two. His collection brought with it a certain notoriety: over the years Häberlein had built up many local and international contacts in the world of palaeontology. He would also occasionally receive distinguished academics or enthusiastic amateurs who willingly travelled off the beaten track in order to view his wealth of fossil treasures in Pappenheim.

In the late spring of 1861, Dr Häberlein received a visit from Mr O. J. Witte, a law councillor from Hanover, whose amateur interest in palaeontology led him to drop by when his work brought him to the Pappenheim district. Witte was far too poorly paid to be one of Häberlein's palaeontologist customers; instead he spent hours combing the riverbanks and road cuttings of Bavaria in search of new specimens. Over the years the two amateurs had become good friends, and they enjoyed nothing more than taking an early brandy while discussing the latest developments in the world of fossil-hunting.

Witte's unexpected visit gave Häberlein his first chance to show off the strange new fossil and it was not long before the slab was retrieved from a back room for his expectant visitor to view. The expression on Witte's face confirmed Häberlein's belief that he had found nothing less than the fossilized equivalent of the Holy Grail. The questions came thick and fast. Where did Häberlein find it? Did he know of any other examples? Were these really feathers and, if so, what were they doing on a long-tailed reptile?

Häberlein confessed that he did not know what type of animal it was. Perhaps it was a true bird or maybe a new type of flying reptile. Either way he felt sure that the find was going to be an important one to science. Witte agreed. He was still studying the fossil, trying to memorize its features. He would have dearly loved to borrow it to take to the Munich Bavarian State Collection but he knew from past visits that Häberlein would not let the specimen out of his sight unless he saw some cash up front.

An hour later Witte left the large house on the outskirts of Pappenheim to return to his hotel. He was still trying to make sense of what he had seen but he was impressed, mightily impressed.

Unlike Häberlein, who thought only of the uniqueness of his specimen, Witte had an inkling of the real scientific value of the feathered fossil. He was a religious man at heart and was strongly anti-Darwin. He was well versed in the turmoil taking place over the significance of the so-called 'missing link' and understood what the fossil could mean to supporters of *The Origin of Species*. All the same, Witte was a fair man and knew that, whatever the consequences, the world needed to know of Häberlein's discovery – but whom to tell, and what should he tell them?

★

Only days after leaving Pappenheim, Witte found himself as the guest of Johann Andreas Wagner, a professor of zoology and keeper of the Munich Bavarian State Collection. Although he was only an amateur palaeontologist, Witte was held in high esteem by Wagner, whose age and increasing frailty meant that he relied upon others to bring him news of recent fossil discoveries. For days Witte had been bursting to tell somebody of Häberlein's find and there could be no finer person than Wagner, whose academic career spanned decades and whose experience in the study of fossil animals from the Solnhofen quarries was considerable. Once he got going, Witte could not speak highly enough of Häberlein's discovery, although he was still unsure what to make of it.

Wagner listened patiently as Witte described the bizarre fossil to him, stressing the significance of the remarkably preserved feathers on the animal's arms and tail.

'On both the forelimbs and on the tail are an excellent coverage of feathers,' said Witte, 'which are indistinguishable from those of a living bird. Under any other circumstance I should have classified the animal as a bird; however, the skeleton is not fully like that of a modern avian and shows many differences. It has a long and feathered tail, more like that of a flying reptile than a bird. Even stranger was the appendage to the forelimbs, because this showed a sharp reptile-like claw extending from the front end of the forearm.'

He concluded: 'I am certain that the animal is new to science but I am unsure whether to call this androgyne creature a bird with a reptile's tail or a reptile with bird's feathers. The first one is to me as incomprehensible as the other. It could even be that this animal is somehow the link between the birds and the reptiles.'

Wagner had shown no emotion while Witte described the fossil, preferring to sit back and absorb his friend's news. However, the last comment about the fossil being a link between the birds and reptiles caused him to jolt in his chair. His mind instantly filled with horrifying possibilities. A feathered reptile from the Jurassic? A fossil with the characteristics of both a bird and a reptile? What Witte was describing was no less than Darwin's much sought-after 'missing link'!

If a respected amateur like Witte could suggest that Häberlein's fossil was this missing link, then there would surely be other lesser palaeontologists who would come to precisely the same conclusion.

Darwin's supporters, thought Wagner with alarm, would have a field day with this! Did not *The Origin of Species* predict the occurrence of just such a link between animal groups? Hadn't Darwin himself declared the birds to be the most isolated of the living groups of animals, with no readily discernible fossil ancestry? Although Wagner knew Witte's assessment must be wrong, the implications were serious. Häberlein's strange fossil had the potential to be a fully-fledged disaster to an anti-Darwinian such as himself. As Witte left the museum, Wagner struggled to decide what to do. Darwin's *Origin of Species* had been well received by a sizeable band of German scientists, making it more popular there than in most other European countries. It seemed that *Darwinismus*, as it quickly became known, had appealed to the Germans' materialistic side, offering a God-free mechanical explanation for the evolution of life on Earth. However, although it was popular in some parts of Germany, Darwin's supporters were still in a minority and the Munich Bavarian State Collection was a notable hotbed of anti-Darwinianism.

Professor Wagner, like a majority of English and American scientists, believed that the Bible offered the best explanation of the evolution of life. Publication of Darwin's book had come as a great shock to Wagner, who had already been involved in several heated debates on the issue of evolution and the Bible. *The Origin of Species* only served to increase the ferocity of his barbed attacks on fellow scientists.

Like many other anti-Darwinians, Wagner had quickly learned from the Soapy Sam debate of 1860 that the weak spot in the theory of natural selection was the so-called 'missing link' issue. Again and again Wagner had asked his opponents for solid evidence of the transmutation of one species to another. In reply he received the commonly used argument, and one first proposed by Darwin himself, that the fossil record is too imperfect to preserve every animal that has ever lived and that there must have been many ancient animals which have left no trace of their being, including the missing links. He now faced the possibility that the iconic missing link had been found.

Wagner decided that to raise the issue of this new fossil would be to draw attention to a possible weakness in his own argument against Darwin. The best solution to the problem would be to ignore it. If he starved the issue of the oxygen of publicity there was every chance that it would die an unnatural death.

Häberlein was old and his visitors infrequent so the fossil might yet escape the attention of other palaeontologists. Like the proverbial ostrich, Wagner buried his head in the sand, pretending that Witte's opinion of Häberlein's specimen was not an important one. It would not be long before his head would be forced into the daylight.

Palaeontology, like so many other scientific disciplines, seems to suffer from those curious twists of fate that Carl Jung termed synchronicity. Events, argued Jung, rarely operate in isolation and, in fact, often seem to work in co-operation. The Solnhofen quarries were about to add weight to this quasi-scientific notion.

Solnhofen fossils had been professionally collected for three centuries and had been desirable household ornaments for at least seventeen centuries prior to that. Many tens of thousands of fossils had been officially documented and yet, as first Häberlein, then Witte and now Wagner suspected, only one feathered fossil had ever come to light. Häberlein's was almost literally one fossil in a million.

Then, only a matter of weeks after Mr Witte had left Pappenheim, a small notice appeared in the *Neues Jahrbuch für Mineralogie, Geologie und Paläontologie*, a journal that was required reading for all German geologists. The comments were made in an informal letter from Professor Hermann von Meyer of Frankfurt, an esteemed geologist with a long-standing passion for Solnhofen fossils. His letter, written on the 15th of August 1861, informed the journal's readers that:

From the lithographic slate of the Solnhofen formation a fossil has been reported to me, which clearly exhibits a feather, which cannot be distinguished from that of a modern feather. In the organization of pterodactyls, of which we now know so much, there is nothing that indicates a feather coat in these animals; it therefore appears to represent the first remains of a bird from before Tertiary times. The feather, which possesses a blackish appearance, was approximately 60 millimetres in length, and the vane, which was gaping in places, was almost uniformly 11 millimetres wide. Its fibres on the one side of the shaft are only half as long as those on the other. Also, the reel, which was quite strong, is indicated. The end of the vane has a somewhat obtuse angle. The feather represents a downstroke or a turning feather.

Hermann von Meyer's discovery was an important one. On a small book-sized slab of Solnhofen limestone lay the perfect impression of a single, isolated feather. To look at it, the feather was indistinguishable from one taken from a living bird. Each barb was perfect. Some could even be seen to be separating from the central quill as if an invisible hand was ruffling it somehow. It looked soft and downy, as though it had only just fallen from a pigeon and landed in the mud. On the basis of its shape, von Meyer was even able to determine from whereabouts on the bird's body the feather had come.

A Jurassic feather from a Solnhofen quarry, the first proof that birds and dinosaurs shared the Earth with each other

The fossil had apparently been found during the previous year in unknown circumstances. It was so perfect that even the casual workers at Solnhofen quarries would have recognized it as a feather and it was presumably one such worker who had got the fossil noticed in the first place. In turn, a third party must have brought it to the attention of von Meyer during the August of 1861.

As it was identical to a modern feather, von Meyer had naturally assumed that the owner of this fossil must have been an ancient bird. To von Meyer this was the first solid evidence that dinosaurs and birds shared the Earth at the same time and, if the age of the Solnhofen limestone had been accurately gauged, they had done so for at least 85 million years. Although there were many who thought that fossilized birds would eventually be found in the Mesozoic era, few had thought that they would be found in the late Jurassic period. It was this significance that von Meyer played on. In one fell swoop the known fossil history of the birds had doubled its length of time. As a consequence several key geological textbooks would need updating.

In Hanover, Witte read von Meyer's published letter with keen interest. To him news of the feather meant far more than just a remarkable addition to the fossil record of the birds. Unlike his contemporaries, he had seen the fossilized animal from which von Meyer's isolated feather had presumably originated – and it was by no means certain that this animal was a bird in the conventional sense of the word. The next day Witte penned a letter to von Meyer, telling him of his recent meeting with Dr Häberlein and of the strange feathered creature in his possession. The description he gave of the feathered fossil was just as full as that given to Wagner, but this time his words fell on more fertile ground.

Hermann von Meyer received Witte's news with glee. He already intended to make a full study of the single feather; now he also had the opportunity to make a full description of the species of animal from which this single feather had probably come. Unlike Wagner, von Meyer was not worried about any Darwinian misinterpretations. He fully intended to act on Witte's news.

★

At this time von Meyer was just entering his sixty-second year and had spent a lifetime studying fossils, making many noted discoveries, especially in the very ancient Carboniferous period (about 360 to 290 million years ago). In more recent years he had become known as a minor authority on fossils from the Solnhofen limestone and had published several key academic papers on them.

He was also famous for the uncannily accurate drawings which often accompanied his scientific monographs. Even so, von Meyer always considered himself to be a poor artist, once remarking that he 'had no practice with the pencil, nor any experience in managing light and shade'. He would doubtless have liked to make a sketch and a full study of Häberlein's new fossil but first felt that it was important to release the news of the find to his colleagues. Based only on Witte's description to him, von Meyer penned a brief letter to *Neues Jahrbuch für Mineralogie*. It said:

> Additional to my writing of the fifteenth of last month, I can notify you that I have inspected the feather from Solnhofen closely from all directions, and that I have come to the conclusion that this is a veritable fossilization in the lithographic stone that fully corresponds with a bird's feather. Simultaneously, I heard from Mr *Oberichtsrath* Witte, that the almost complete skeleton of a feather-clad animal has been found in the lithographic stone. It is reported to show many differences with living birds. I will publish a report of the feather I inspected, along with a detailed illustration. As a denomination for the animal I consider *Archaeopteryx lithographica* to be a fitting name.
>
> Hermann von Meyer, 30th September 1861

Through this one letter, news of Häberlein's unique fossil at last entered the palaeontology community proper. Furthermore, and after thousands of years of silence, the Solnhofen quarries seemed to have thrown up two fossils crucial to the evolutionary history of the birds: a perfectly preserved feather and a strange feathered animal. So far von Meyer had only seen the

Era	Period	Epoch	Millions of Years	Evolutionary Events
Cenozoic	Tertiary		65 to 0	Mammals dominate the land while birds dominate the air Dinosaur extinction
Mesozoic	Cretaceous	Late	65–99	Marsh's 'toothed birds'
		Early	99–144	Flowering plants evolve; mammals diversify
	Jurassic	Late	144–159	Archaeopteryx is alive
		Middle	159–180	Evolution of the birds?
		Early	180–206	Dinosaurs rule the land
		Late	206–227	Dinosaurs and mammals evolve
	Triassic	Middle	227–234	Primitive crocodiles and pterosaurs evolve
		Early	242–245	Reptiles recover after the great extinction of 250 million years ago

A geological time scale

isolated feather but from Witte's description he felt sure that it must have come from Häberlein's creature. After all, how many different sorts of feathered animal could there be preserved in the Solnhofen limestone?

Although it was a little irregular, von Meyer had also taken it upon himself to give the same name, *Archaeopteryx lithographica*, to both his isolated feather and Häberlein's unseen animal. He clearly thought that he was dealing with an ancient bird, for the first name came from *arkhaios*, the Greek for 'ancient', and *pterux*, which means 'wing'. The second name, *lithographica*, was simply a reference to the fact that this 'ancient winged' animal had been found in the lithographic limestone of Solnhofen.

Having staked his scientific claim to Häberlein's fossil, von Meyer immediately wrote to the Pappenheim doctor requesting permission to view the *Archaeopteryx*, hoping that he might be the first to describe the fossil in detail. But von Meyer may have acted too soon. His published letter announcing the discovery of the *Archaeopteryx* finally stirred the hitherto reluctant Wagner into action. A scientific storm was brewing and it was about to break over the house of Dr Carl Häberlein of Pappenheim.

Von Meyer's letter did not go down at all well inside the Munich Bavarian State Collection. Wagner was angry that Witte should have contacted von Meyer at all, let alone offer him a description of the feathered fossil. Perhaps Witte had been frustrated by Wagner's lack of action on the matter. Either way, von Meyer had let the proverbial cat out of the bag and it was now up to Wagner to put it back inside again. He read again the notes made at his meeting with Witte, trying to decide how best to gain the upper hand once more.

If, thought Wagner, what Witte had said about the animal being half-bird and half-reptile was true then the Darwinians would have a mascot for their cause. Whether the animal was a true missing link or not, it would be viewed as a victory over the more bliblically oriented scientists.

The *Archaeopteryx* fossil, thought Wagner, must not be seen to be the missing link. He knew that von Meyer was already aware of the fossil's whereabouts and of Witte's opinion that it was a 'feathered reptile'. Although a religious man, von Meyer had remained relatively neutral in the debate about natural selection but he was known to have many contacts in Darwin's English circle, especially the dreaded Thomas Huxley, with whom he occasionally swapped letters. Von Meyer had already given Häberlein's animal a name: if he were to provide the first detailed description of the animal, and if this description in any way hinted at a reptilian affinity, the *Archaeopteryx* would be heralded as the missing link by Darwin, Huxley *et al*. Once this connection had been made, it would be nearly impossible to shift it from people's minds. Yet another battle would be won by the Darwinians. Wagner knew that he had to be the first to fully describe the *Archaeopteryx* and hence to claim the animal for the biblical scientists and not the atheists.

Although he was located in Munich, only a few days' journey from Pappenheim, Wagner's precarious health precluded him from making the journey to Häberlein's house. Instead he wrote to Häberlein requesting that he borrow the *Archaeopteryx* for a few weeks in order to describe it properly. Only a few years previously the Munich Bavarian State Collection had purchased Häberlein's whole Solnhofen fossil collection. Whilst Wagner had not been directly involved in this purchase, he hoped that it might soften the doctor's notoriously hard-nosed attitude towards those with an interest in studying his fossils. Wagner thought wrong.

Within the same week both Wagner and von Meyer received replies to their exploratory letters to Häberlein. In a curt and direct manner, the old doctor informed the learned scientists that he had decided to sell his entire collection of Solnhofen fossils, which included the *Archaeopteryx*, to the highest bidder.

Only those with an interest in purchasing the collection would be permitted to view the specimen and then only by prior arrangement. Furthermore, in no circumstances would Häberlein permit any visiting person to take notes, make sketches or photograph any of his specimens, especially the

Archaeopteryx. These were, he said, the only conditions under which any venerable person might be admitted into his house. No fossils would be allowed to leave the house unless, of course, they had been purchased along with the rest of the couple of hundred other Solnhofen specimens that comprised his collection. This news was a bitter blow to the scientists, both of whom had wished to claim the prize of being first to formally describe the *Archaeopteryx*.

Von Meyer did not have the backing of a museum and had no means of raising enough cash to make a realistic bid for Häberlein's Solnhofen fossils. The doctor's letter meant that he would not be allowed to view the *Archaeopteryx* unless somebody else first purchased it and then allowed him to examine it afterwards. Wagner was more hopeful. The fact that his Natural History Museum had previously traded with Häberlein meant that the obstinate doctor would take an approach from Munich seriously, although he knew the museum was unlikely to buy the whole collection. But at least Wagner should be able to get one of his staff into Häberlein's house on the pretext of making a bid. Whether the museum went on to buy the fossils was immaterial – getting somebody to view the fossil and to bring back a detailed description of the *Archaeopteryx* was the important thing. In the meantime, the conditions laid down by the doctor were such that few other scientists were likely to get a look in. Although time was still of the essence, Wagner felt that his position was secure.

For years there has been a minor debate amongst historians and scientists about the motive behind Häberlein's sudden decision to sell his collection and the severe conditions that he imposed upon those who wished to view the *Archaeopteryx*. In many early accounts of the sale of the fossil, Häberlein is portrayed as a money-grabbing mercenary, more interested in his bank balance than in furthering the interests of science. In later years this view changed, and Häberlein was seen as an astute businessman who had imposed the restrictions in order to create an air of mystery about the *Archaeopteryx* and so to raise its price. More recently still his actions have been viewed more charitably. This is mainly because of Gavin de Beer's assertion that Häberlein needed the money to allow one of his daughters to marry, although there is no contemporary evidence to support this.

This kind view of Häberlein gained further credence when in 1984 his great-great-grandson, Friedrich Hingkeldey, travelled halfway across Germany to deliver the only known photograph of Carl Häberlein to the Jura-Museum, just outside Solnhofen. Hingkeldey, who was ninety-one, had made the lengthy journey in order to plead that his long-deceased relative be viewed less as a mercenary capitalist and more as a poor doctor in search of a secure pension. However, having looked at the facts available, it is to my mind more probable that Häberlein was driven by his having stumbled upon a rather good way of extracting money from scientific institutions.

As mentioned, some years prior to the discovery of the *Archaeopteryx*, Häberlein had sold a collection of several hundred Solnhofen fossils to the Munich Bavarian State Collection for the sum of £900 (the equivalent of £41,000 or $66,000 today). At the time of the sale there was a great deal of scientific interest in the pterosaurs of the Solnhofen, which were often so well preserved as to show every wrinkle of skin on their bodies. In Germany there had been outrage at the sale of a stunning Solnhofen pterosaur fossil to an American museum in 1856. This specimen, probably the most famous pterosaur fossil of all time, is featured in books and newspaper articles to this day. For many years the German scientific community mourned the loss of what they believed was a vital piece of their national heritage. It is probably no coincidence that Häberlein decided to sell his collection to Munich at the height of this pterosaur mania.

If Häberlein had a particular love, then it was for pterosaur fossils. His letters to various people and institutions always stressed the number of complete pterosaurs he owned and their beauty, which no doubt had been enhanced by the doctor's masterful use of the hammer and chisel. Munich had approached Häberlein in 1855 with the idea of buying his magnificent pterosaur fossils for their collection. Häberlein, however, wanted to sell not just the valuable pterosaurs but his entire collection of several hundred fossils. 'But,' said the Munich museum, 'we do not need your other fossils, they are for the most part common and easily obtained elsewhere. Just give us the pterosaurs. We'll give you a good price!'

Häberlein could see their desperation and would not budge. He knew he could probably raise about £700 for the pterosaurs on their own but by throwing in dozens of more common fossils he could artificially inflate the price of the already expensive pterosaurs. The old man held out, insisting that the Munich museum buy the whole collection for £900, or nothing at all. In the end Munich capitulated.

As the doctor began to build up his collection of Solnhofen fossils again, he must have wondered whether the same trick would work twice. It is known that Häberlein had received many visiting palaeontologists at his home and yet, as far as can be ascertained, he was not selling his prized specimens to them. Instead he built up his collection to an enormous size. But if the same sales technique were to succeed again, he would have to have one or more specimens that were so valuable as to make somebody want to buy his entire collection, as Munich had had to do in order to obtain his pterosaurs. Häberlein must now have realized that he had in his hands a unique specimen. The *Archaeopteryx* could be used to sell his entire fossil collection.

Häberlein's stipulation that no notes, drawings or photographs should be made of any of his specimens can really only have been intended to preserve the monetary value of his prize specimen. During the 1860s it was quite common for palaeontologists to describe and interpret fossils using notes and drawings made by other scientists. Whereas modern science requires nothing less than first-hand evidence, 150 years ago the problems of travel, transport and the postal system made the viewing of some fossils difficult or even impossible. Remote opinions were considered as good as direct ones and a fossil could be described or even named without the scientist ever having been on the same continent as it, let alone in the same room. Indeed, von Meyer had already given a name to Häberlein's fossil based only on the briefest description from his friend Mr Witte.

Dr Häberlein, who was aware of the ins and outs of science, knew that at the very least his fossil was an enigma. After all, he himself did not really know what to make of the beast. From the excited attentions of Witte, von Meyer and Wagner, he must also have known that there was talk of the *Archaeopteryx* being the Darwinian missing link. The urgency with which people sought to view the fossil would certainly have alerted him to its scientific value. The capitalist in him knew that denying scientists a chance to describe the fossil would add to its mystery, keeping the fossil in the public's mind.

So anybody who wanted to work with the fossil would have to buy it and the rest of his collection. Häberlein's conditions were, in my opinion, a clever, if ruthless, exploitation of the scientific establishment's competitiveness and were tailored to obtain the highest possible price for the fossil of an animal about which practically nothing was known.

Feigning an interest in purchasing Häberlein's collection, Wagner dispatched a letter to him requesting that a representative of the museum be allowed to view his collection with a possible view to buying it. Much to Wagner's delight, the doctor agreed to the plan.

The Munich Bavarian State Collection was blessed with many great zoologists, palaeontologists and geologists any one of whom could have travelled to Pappenheim on Wagner's behalf. The man chosen for the job was Alfred Oppel, the curator of the Munich palaeontological collections. Wagner knew him to be an outstanding palaeontologist as well as being a good artist with a sound memory for detail. He was given strict instructions by Wagner to return with a detailed sketch of the *Archaeopteryx* and an accompanying full description.

Just over a week later Oppel returned to the university having made several visits to Häberlein's house. Although he had pretended to show an interest in the rest of Häberlein's collection, especially his pterosaurs, both he and the doctor knew that it was the *Archaeopteryx* that was the true centre of attention. Being devoid of both pen and paper during his visits, Oppel had been forced to commit details of the fossil to memory before scurrying back to his hotel room to sketch out what he had seen.

Over several visits he managed to make what is, in retrospect, a truly remarkable likeness of the fossil, exact in almost every detail. Wagner's trickery and Oppel's artistic skills and memory meant that the world outside Pappenheim was at last going to be allowed to see an image of the *Archaeopteryx*.

When viewed now, the only puzzling feature about the drawing is that despite its extraordinary accuracy on the position and detail of the fossil's features, it is a mirror image of the fossil. This mystery has never been adequately solved. It has been suggested that Oppel actually sketched the fossil's counterpart (that is the piece of rock containing the imprint of the fossil). However, the quality of Oppel's work shows that this was plainly not the case. Perhaps his photographic memory could only reproduce the image back to front in his mind, as has been seen with some autistic artists, or maybe he did manage to make some secret notes, which he interpreted the wrong way around. The truth will probably never be known but, even mirrored, his sketch was perfectly adequate for Wagner: he could use this as the basis of his prognosis as to the true nature of the *Archaeopteryx*.

Although not in the best of health, during October 1861 Wagner worked feverishly with Oppel's notes and drawings to compile a comprehensive description. Every bone and feather of Oppel's drawing was studied closely in an attempt to better understand the nature of the feathered animal. Wagner had to know whether it was bird or a reptile for he was convinced that it had to be one or the other and not a mixture. He knew that others would eventually get to hear of the *Archaeopteryx* and then perhaps see it or even buy it. It was vital that his first opinion on this fossil be the one that steered the direction of the inevitable debate that would follow.

Aside from Darwinism, Wagner was also battling against another enemy – his health. Although only sixty-four years old, not an advanced age by any means, his health had been failing

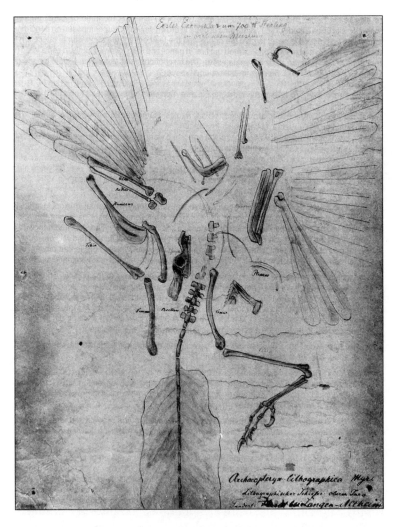

The first visual representation of Carl Häberlein's
Archaeopteryx made from memory by
Alfred Oppel in 1861. The drawing is a mirror
image of the specimen

for some time and had become progressively worse over the
spring and summer of that year. Although Wagner did not feel
as though the Grim Reaper was knocking at his door, he knew
that his time on Earth was more limited than most. Despite being
frequently bedridden during that autumn, Wagner worked furiously and managed to pull together a highly detailed description
of the *Archaeopteryx* in a matter of weeks. By the 9th of
November he felt confident enough to announce that he would
deliver an address on the specimen to the Bavarian Academy of
Sciences.

The title that Wagner chose for his talk was: 'Reports on a
New Reptile, supposedly Furnished with Feathers'.

In front of a select crowd at the Munich Bavarian State
Collection, a frail Wagner stood up and with some difficulty
addressed the assembled mass, choosing to read from a prepared
script. His text had been carefully written to ensure that he did
not stray or miss any of his central points. He began by outlining the history of the *Archaeopteryx*'s discovery and Mr Witte's
opinion that the animal could be part bird and part reptile. After
a brief description of the fossil, based solely on Oppel's drawing,
Wagner turned to his central thesis.

'Firstly,' he said, 'we must consider the features that connect
this fossil to the birds and then subsequently those that connect
it to the reptiles. The most evident similarity to the birds is in
the possession of feathers on the forelimbs and tail. A feather coat
is only known in birds.' After establishing the bird-like affinities
of the *Archaeopteryx* – really only its feathers and a bone in its
foot – Wagner went on to explain the reptile-like qualities of the
fossil:

> Its vertebral column is totally different from that of birds,
> but shows close similarity to that of the long-tailed flying
> saurians [i.e. the pterosaurs] such as *Ramphorhynchus*. Just as
> remarkable is the dissimilarity in construction of the tail
> which is extraordinarily long with over twenty vertebrae.
> A bird's tail will only have five to eight vertebrae. Again this

tail is more like that of a flying reptile than a bird. Other features of the skeleton, such as the ilium and pelvis are also reptilian.

'I have,' he continued, 'presented the information that has been made available to me, and will now attempt to answer the question: should this fossil specimen be placed in the class of the birds, or that of the reptiles? The certain answer to this question is greatly complicated by the fact that several important parts of the skeleton, most notably the skull and the hand, are missing; nonetheless, an attempt to clarify the situation should be made.'

Wagner had asked the $64,000 question: is the *Archaeopteryx* a bird or a reptile?

As far as he was concerned, he said, it could only belong to one animal group or the other. The third option, that the *Archaeopteryx* was the missing link between the birds and the reptiles, was, to Wagner, not an option at all.

His careful analysis of the fossil had, however, left him with a problem. In his talk he freely admitted that the skeleton was wholly reptilian in its form but that it also appeared to have feathers on its tail and arms. Feathers, as Wagner had stated, are known only from birds so wasn't he admitting that the *Archaeopteryx* was what Witte had initially thought it was – a reptile with bird's feathers and therefore a missing link? Wagner was about to explain all.

Because such an attachment of the feathers on the wing and tail is something quite peculiar for a bird, the question is raised whether these fossil feathers are really identical to real birds' feathers or merely have the same appearance. The identity of these epidermal structures as feathers has not been proven; they could also represent peculiar decorations. If special structures reminiscent of feathers are known from insects; then, why not, and in an advanced stage of development, in reptiles? And even though the latter class has thus far not known anything of this kind, palaeontology is used to finding previously unknown peculiarities in new discoveries.

In order to solve the missing link problem Wagner had displayed a masterful use of circular logic. Yes, he argued, the skeleton is that of a reptile but as reptiles are not known to have feathers then the fossil features on the *Archaeopteryx* that look like feathers cannot possibly be such. Because reptiles cannot have feathers, these must instead be physical features which when fossilized give the appearance of being like the feathers of a bird. Curiously, Wagner omitted to make any scientific comment on the single fossilized feather described by von Meyer which by now was actually housed in his own Natural History Museum and thus readily available for Wagner to study. This fossil was unquestionably that of a feather and one that is totally indistinguishable from those found on modern birds. To highlight the fact that other fossil feathers had been found in the Solnhofen limestone would, however, undercut Wagner's argument.

In fact, to ensure that the isolated feather fossil and Häberlein's fossil were not to be confused with each other, Wagner had one last trick up his sleeve:

> As long as I am not convinced of the contrary due to the discovery of the missing parts of the specimen under investigation, I have no hesitation in declaring it to be a reptile from the order of the saurians [dinosaurs, pterosaurs, etc.]. I therefore give it the name *Griphosaurus*, derived from *grifo*, enigma.[1]

In declaring that the *Archaeopteryx* did not have feathers, Wagner was also subtly saying that this fossil did not have anything to do with von Meyer's description of the single fossilized feather. As von Meyer had named the *Archaeopteryx* largely on the basis of this one feather, Wagner felt his new non-feathered reptile should have a different name. Although primarily intended to show that Häberlein's fossil was in no way related to

---

[1] Wagner tried to rename the *Archaeopteryx* as Griphosaurus (sometimes spelt Gryphosaurus) but this was illegal under the international rules governing the naming of new species. The correct name of *Archaeopteryx* will continue to be used here except in direct quotes.

the birds (as the name *Archaeopteryx* implies) but was a form of reptile (*saurus*, or 'lizard'), it was also a way for Wagner to stamp his personal mark on the fossil. It forced other scientists to consider his position before they could make any judgements of their own.

The fact that this one specimen had now been given two separate names was symbolic of the great Darwinian battle that was taking place. In the future months it would be possible to tell which side of the Darwinian debate individual scientists were on by the name that they chose to use for Häberlein's fossil. Those who called it *Archaeopteryx* were generally pro-Darwinian whilst those who chose to use Wagner's *Griphosaurus* were against. He had not yet clapped eyes on the real fossil, but Wagner had managed to create controversy and confusion that muddied the waters around the *Archaeopteryx*. But his circular reasoning was not the last word on the subject by any means. He chose to finish with a stark warning:

Finally, allow me to add a few words to ward off Darwinian misinterpretation of our new saurian. The first impression of *Griphosaurus* might well lead to the impression that we have before us an intermediate creature, engaged in the transition from the reptiles to the birds. Darwin and his followers will probably employ the new discovery as an extremely welcome occurrence for the justification of their adventurous opinions about the change of animals. However, they do not have any right to do so.

When I say of a frog that it was originally a fish, I can at least justify such an assertion by the factual demonstration of a row of intermediates from a fishlike tadpole to an amphibian. However, I can hardly demand that Darwin were to show me similar intermediate steps in the case of the *Griphosaurus*, because only one incomplete specimen is known from this species. Nonetheless, I am qualified to ask from the Darwinians, insofar as they wish to promulgate the *Griphosaurus* as a creature in transition, to show me the intermediate stages that mediated the transition of any living or fossil animal from one class to another. If they cannot, – and they can't – their views should be rejected as fantastic delusions, that have nothing to do with exact science.

Wagner's warning to Darwinians was a blunt one: steer well clear of the *Archaeopteryx*, it is not a missing link! The first shot in the battle had been fired. The war that it started was to last for over 140 years.

The speech delivered, Wagner returned home satisfied with the way the proceedings had gone. His wish to be the first to describe the *Archaeopteryx* had been achieved and his rhetoric against the missing link could not now be ignored. It was to be Wagner's parting shot in the battle over evolution. Only days later he became bedridden once more, too ill to continue with any further scientific research. Six weeks later he was dead.

In January of the following year Darwin wrote to a friend cryptically saying that the *Archaeopteryx* and evolution had 'killed poor Wagner but on his death-bed he took consolation in denouncing it as a phantasia'.

It is quite possible that the strain of composing and delivering his final talk had been too much for Wagner's already racked body, driving him into an early grave. The *Archaeopteryx* had claimed its first victim.

4

The Hard Bargain

IT WAS THE New Year of 1862 and news of Wagner's death had come as a shock to Dr Häberlein. Based on Wagner's interest, he had hoped he might be able to offload his entire Solnhofen collection to the Munich Bavarian State Collection and in double-quick time. The Bavarian science grapevine, of which Häberlein was a part, had informed him of Oppel's secretly made drawing and of how Wagner had used it to proclaim the fossil as an exotic reptile and not a missing link. All this was bad news to Häberlein. Such a frenzy of activity about the fossil might affect its perceived scientific importance and hence its eventual price.

All in all, Häberlein was not amused with the antics of the Munich Collection but he still hoped that they might buy the fossils. He had received a vaguely positive reply from Karl von Martius, the secretary of the Academy of Sciences at Munich, who had agreed to continue with the dialogue started by Wagner.

Elsewhere, other events were also not going well for Häberlein. Having been refused permission to see the original *Archaeopteryx* specimen, Hermann von Meyer managed to persuade Alfred Oppel to lend him his drawing so that he could make his own less biased pronunciations on the fossil. Wagner's death had also allowed Oppel to begin his own investigations. As he was the only qualified scientist to have viewed the *Archaeopteryx* in detail, Oppel was best placed to pass judgement on it. However, for some reason he chose not to comment on Häberlein's fossil, preferring to describe the single fossilized feather. Witte too was preparing his own study of the *Archaeopteryx* but had only his memory and a few scribbled notes to work from. Even at this early stage, the *Archaeopteryx* was already having a mesmeric effect on people.

The results of all these studies, including a transcript of Wagner's November speech, would trickle out over the next year or so. In the meantime, the original specimen remained in Häberlein's clutches awaiting sale to the highest bidder.

During the early weeks of 1862 news of the fuss taking place in Bavaria crossed the English Channel to London. Although we do not know how the news was delivered, it seems likely that a person who had attended Wagner's November talk sent a sketch of the *Archaeopteryx* to someone in the Natural History Department of the British Museum.

At this time the British Museum's Natural History Department (which included the Geology Department) was not housed in its current magnificent home in South Kensington, but was part of the greater British Museum complex in Bloomsbury, central London. The benefits of the gigantic British Empire had ensured that the Natural History Department was a treasure house of preserved animals and fossils from the four corners of the globe. Its size and success meant that the department was begging to be allowed to set up as a separate museum elsewhere in London so that its unparalleled collections could be housed and displayed more effectively. The British Museum's Board of Trustees, who controlled the museum's expenditure, reluctant to see one of their most successful departments devolve itself into a semi-autonomous body, regularly refused requests for the necessary funds to build a separate museum.

Leading the independence movement were the Natural History Department's two central characters: George Robert Waterhouse, Keeper of the Geological Department, and Sir Richard Owen, Superintendent of the Natural History Department. Between them, these two figures effectively controlled all the natural history affairs of the British Museum. Waterhouse ran the day to day business and Owen made the big decisions, taking them to the Board of Trustees for their approval. Whilst their ambitions for a separate museum would

Sir Richard Owen, the brilliant but objectionable palaeontologist who was desperate to study the first Archaeopteryx *specimen*

take another two decades to be realized, the matter of the *Archaeopteryx* presented a more immediate problem.

Owen and Waterhouse were very prominent figures in the European scientific community, and both had attracted more than their fair share of controversy. As we shall see in later chapters, this was especially true of Owen, who was viewed by many of his peers as Satan's representative on Earth. More importantly to our immediate story, both Owen and Waterhouse were firmly in the anti-Darwin camp and had managed to fall out with practically all of Darwin's supporters. Like Wagner, with whom Owen had periodically corresponded, the two shining stars of the British Museum's Natural History Department were fervently against the idea of a missing link and had fought many battles on just this principle. News of the *Archaeopteryx* did not go down at all well in the hallowed halls of Bloomsbury.

At this time Sir Richard Owen was often referred to as the greatest living naturalist (although not usually by his scientific peers). He had written hundreds of scientific papers on everything from amoebae to ammonites and was a confidant of the royal court. He was frequently asked to comment on the latest scientific discoveries to Queen Victoria herself. It was Owen who, in 1841, had coined the term 'dinosaur' and who had been responsible for first reconstructing these animals, albeit (with the aid of hindsight) wrongly. He had also discovered and named countless other living and fossilized animals and plants. Unfortunately, each new discovery seemed to swell his ego, turning him into an arrogant and deceitful man with megalomaniac tendencies. The *Archaeopteryx* was to drive all his worst features to the forefront and would ultimately break his reputation, isolating him from his peers.

Like Wagner, Owen greeted the discovery of the *Archaeopteryx* with mixed feelings. The anti-Darwinian in him feared the talk of it being a bona fide missing link but equally his ego relished the opportunity to study the fossil for himself: as soon as he heard of its existence, Owen knew that he had to have the *Archaeopteryx* in his possession. This was clearly a fossil that was in need of his expert opinion. The task could certainly not be left to the Germans to complete. After discussing the matter with Waterhouse, whose Geological Department included the palaeontology collections, the two men began to make plans to enable the British Museum to acquire Häberlein's increasingly problematic specimen.

On the 28th of February 1862, and without permission from the all-powerful Board of Trustees who held the purse strings, George Waterhouse penned a letter to Carl Häberlein in Pappenheim, asking about the *Archaeopteryx* and, more importantly, was it still for sale?

In Pappenheim Waterhouse's letter was received with some relief. Negotiations with the Munich collection were going badly and Häberlein welcomed a fall-back option should things go wrong. He might also be able to use the British interest to hasten along a decision from Munich: perhaps the thought of losing such a valuable fossil to the English might force Munich's hand. With this in mind Häberlein wrote a curt reply to Waterhouse:

Sir,
I am inclined to transmit the specimen desired to the collection of the British Museum. My collection contains numerous other fine fossils, of which you might select whatever you like. You could find a great difference between my specimens and between those from the collection of Count Munster.

Having promised to a palaeontologist not to give the specimen you wish away before he has inspected it in the course of next month, I must delay a more definite answer until then. The best would be if you or one of your colleagues could come and inspect it with my other collection.

Among the numerous visitors from all parts of Europe I will only mention Mr Agassiz, Lord Buckingham and Lord Enniskillen; the latter was here twice and I am sure he would repeat his visit, if he knew the extent of my fossil fishes. I will mention only the following fossils in my possession; four different pterodactyli, the width of the largest must have been five to six feet; it has a very long tail.

                    Carl Häberlein, 21st March 1862

Although Häberlein made no mention of the *Archaeopteryx* by name, it is clear that this is the specimen about which the negotiations would take place. It is also clear that he still had hopes of Munich purchasing the collection.

The letter was greeted in the British Museum with a mixture of hope and dismay. The *Archaeopteryx* was still for sale but another party had first bid for it. It did not take Owen long to find out that the other interested party was the Munich Bavarian State Collection. Being placed in a bidding war with the Germans only added to Owen's desire to own the *Archaeopteryx*. In a patriotic age, Owen and Waterhouse were nationalists and there had long been a rivalry between English and German scientists. The pair now immediately set about preparing a reply to Häberlein.

Communicating with Häberlein was a frustrating process. Neither Owen nor Waterhouse could read or write German and the Pappenheim doctor was unable to read or write English. This meant that that Häberlein's letters had to be translated by a third party in the museum. Likewise, Waterhouse's replies would have to be translated into German before they could be sent to Pappenheim. Turning a letter around could sometimes take days. Nonetheless, Waterhouse managed to get a reply written and translated for the 29th of March:

Sir,
In your letter of the 21st of March you allude to a considerable number of fossils from which you are so good as to offer to let us select such as we require – with regard to those particularly mentioned in your letter, I have little doubt that they would form desirable acquisitions for the Munich Museum and if you would set a price upon them, as well as upon any other objects which you will at the same time definitely name, steps would be immediately taken to carry out arrangements for reserving such as are desirable to us.

Probably it will be thought desirable that some person from the [British] Museum should, as you suggest, visit Pappenheim with the view of inspecting the specimens, but such a journey would only be reasonably undertaken upon said valuation of the objects having been previously made.

G. R. Waterhouse

The letter stated Owen and Waterhouse's position: it was subtly made clear that they would be prepared to enter into a bidding war with the Munich museum for the *Archaeopteryx*. Even the stubborn Häberlein could pick up the sense of urgency which the letter conveyed. The British Museum really, really wanted the *Archaeopteryx* and were quite happy to risk a spat with the Munich museum in the process.

In stressing their urgency Owen and Waterhouse had overplayed their hand. Häberlein was now alert to the fact that should Munich, still his preferred bidder, not come up with the goods then the British could be relied upon to pick up the pieces. Owen and Waterhouse had placed the ball firmly in Häberlein's court and it was at the doctor's discretion as to whether he need return it again. In fact, the doctor had already decided to use the British Museum's desperation to try and lever the sluggish von Martius in Munich, who had taken over negotiations after Andreas Wagner's death, into making a serious offer for the *Archaeopteryx* and his other Solnhofen fossils.

The ploy worked. After months of inaction following Wagner's death, a representative from Munich came to visit Häberlein in early April at his Pappenheim house. He was there to make an inventory of the doctor's main specimens, and more importantly, to try and get the doctor to name his price, something he had thus far been unwilling to do.

As he followed the Munich man about his house, Häberlein was careful not to let his visitor spend too much time studying the *Archaeopteryx* just in case, like Oppel, he had ambitions of making a covert scientific study of the beast. At every available opportunity Häberlein mentioned the British Museum's interest in his collection, showing off the second letter from Waterhouse and stressing the paragraph which hinted that they were prepared to outbid Munich for the privilege of owning the *Archaeopteryx*.

The inventory having been made, the man set off back to Munich, probably greatly relieved to be away from the eccentric doctor. The report of his visit and inventory of the Pappenheim specimens made their way to von Martius' desk where they were read with only mild interest. A botanist and not a palaeontologist, von Martius was advanced in his years and found it difficult to get excited about fossils at all.

A few days later a letter arrived from Häberlein stating that he wanted £750 (the equivalent of about £34,000/$55,000 today) for his entire collection of Solnhofen fossils. It was a considerable sum: the museum could probably just about afford it, but it would leave a dent in finances for a couple of years.

It was time for Munich to make up its mind. From the inventory, von Martius knew that Munich already had examples of many of the pterodactyl, reptile and fish species in the collection which had been purchased from Häberlein at vast expense only a few years previously. They did not, however, have an *Archaeopteryx* – but was this one specimen really worth £750, especially when Wagner had pronounced it to be nothing more than an exotic reptile vaguely related to the pterodactyls? Although von Martius suspected that Wagner's assessment was slightly wide of the mark and that the *Archaeopteryx* did indeed have feathers, his museum already had the single fossilized feather. Did it really need the entire animal to go with it? Not for £750, it didn't.

Over the next few weeks a series of letters passed between von Martius and Häberlein. The first was a polite refusal of Häberlein's offer but also requested whether the doctor would be prepared to sell the *Archaeopteryx* on its own. Häberlein would not budge. While he was prepared to discard some of the smaller specimens, the vertebrate fossils must be sold as a set. He would drop the price accordingly, but not by much. Von Martius was still not very interested but made a bid of £650 anyway. The final offer made by Häberlein was £708 for the whole collection but it fell on deaf ears.

At the beginning of June von Martius ended Munich's

involvement. He wrote to Häberlein stating that his collection contained too many duplicates of species they already had to make it worth their while purchasing it. Unless the doctor was prepared to sell the *Archaeopteryx* on its own, they could not possibly carry on negotiating with him. Häberlein's reaction was apoplectic. Having once owned Munich's other collection of Solnhofen fossils, in which the duplicates supposedly lay, he knew its contents well. He was convinced that the man who had visited him in April had misidentified many of his finest specimens and that Munich had few, if any, duplicates of his current fossils. He wrote to say as much and requested that they send somebody else to view his collection but his plea fell on deaf ears. Munich had never really been that keen in the first place, Wagner merely opening negotiations in order to get access to the *Archaeopteryx*. Von Martius had now shut down those negotiations. But at least Häberlein still had the British.

> Right Honourable Sir,
> It is only today that I am able for the first time to acknowledge your valuable communication of the 29th of March, as the preparation and completion of the catalogue has until now detained me from doing so. I have, during the preparation of this catalogue, caught cold since the 15th April, through the occurrence of very raw weather, which has unfortunately caused a recurrence of my rheumatic pains, so that I was forced to spend at least six weeks in bed and could do nothing. Now in my 75th year, I am becoming much more sensitive to changes of weather.
>
> I transmit herewith to you right honourables the catalogue of my collection of petrifications of fossils with regard to which I take the liberty of remarking that for the thorough inspection of the same, some days would be required in order to form a competent judgement thereon in case a competent man of science from the British Museum were inclined to view my collection – I much desire that the expert chosen for this journey should previously have a thorough knowledge of the fossils already to be found in the British Museum.

The price of the entire collection of fossils [is] £750 sterling. Should, however, a portion thereof not be desired, a proportionate deduction would be made . . . A personal inspection is for both parties indispensable.

I have no photographs or drawings of the principal specimens to give away although I have been frequently asked for them.

Requesting the favour of a reply.

Dr Carl Häberlein, 10th June 1862

Owen and Waterhouse received this letter with joy. It had been over two months since they had written to Häberlein confirming their desire to buy the *Archaeopteryx*. Through their European contacts they knew full well that the doctor had been conducting extensive negotiations with Munich but they did not yet know their outcome. Häberlein's letter, with the red herring of illness being the cause of his silence, confirmed that the negotiations with Munich had collapsed. The way was clear for the British Museum but they had to move fast lest anybody else decided to show an interest.

Four days later Mr Waterhouse was standing before the British Museum's Committee of Trustees recommending the purchase of Häberlein's fossils. The Trustees were an extremely eminent collection of the great and good of British society and they did not suffer fools gladly. That day Waterhouse had the pleasure of addressing Earl Stanhope, the Duke of Somerset, Lord Taunton, the Right Honourable Spencer Horatio Walpole and Sir Roderick Murchison. As neither he nor Owen had been given the authority to make the first contact with Häberlein, Waterhouse read an edited version of the letter of the 10th of June which made it appear as though the doctor had made the £750 offer out of the blue.

Trustees were receptive to Waterhouse's request that someone from the Geology Department be sent to Pappenheim to negotiate with Dr Häberlein. However, they also stipulated that in no circumstances should more than £500 be offered, even if this meant selecting a few fossils rather than buying the whole collection.

The committee's minutes record that 'Professor Owen concurred with this recommendation', making it sound as if Owen was somehow distant from Waterhouse's negotiations with Häberlein. The reality was somewhat different. Although he was letting Waterhouse handle the Trustees (and do the writing to Häberlein), it was Owen's manic obsession with the *Archaeopteryx* that was driving the entire process. The Trustees may have given them a ceiling of £500 but Owen had no intention of sticking to it. He was determined to pay the full £750 if necessary although he knew that persuading the British Museum to fork out this amount would be difficult.

It was probably Owen who decided that it should be Waterhouse who went to Pappenheim to check out the fossils and to negotiate with Häberlein in person. Waterhouse doubtless reluctantly agreed. The journey to Bavaria would take several days and time was certainly of the essence. Only a few days after being given permission by the Trustees, Waterhouse found himself leaving the English shores to travel across France and Germany. Owen's orders to get the *Archaeopteryx* 'at all costs' no doubt rang loudly in his ears.

The British Museum may have been quick off the mark, but interest in the *Archaeopteryx* was building elsewhere as well. By the time George Waterhouse had set off across Europe, there had been two further publications on the feathered fossil. The first was the transcript of Andreas Wagner's speech of the previous November, published verbatim in the Munich museum's journal *Sitzungsberichte der Akademie der Wissenschaften zu München*. This was followed closely by Hermann von Meyer's interpretation of the *Archaeopteryx* published in the widely read *Palaeontographica*. Comprehensive as they were, both works were based solely on Oppel's drawing. The only first-hand descriptions of any part of the *Archaeopteryx* to have yet appeared concerned the isolated feather, about which both von Meyer and Oppel had now written.

Wagner's paper in particular aroused interest. His virulent denial that the *Archaeopteryx* (or *Gryphosaurus* as he called it) was any form of missing link had served to draw attention to the issue. Few people outside Germany had yet heard of the fossil in any detail but news of its existence was spreading rapidly as were rumours that it was indeed the missing link. There was also speculation that it was a fraud manufactured by Darwin's supporters to shore up their ailing theory of evolution through natural selection.

As news of his find spread, Dr Häberlein began to receive letters from across Europe but, strangely enough, there were no further offers to buy the specimen. Most people were after further information about the find or wanted permission to come and view the fossil themselves. All such requests were turned down flat. Fortunately for Waterhouse and Owen, the world's scientific communities were spread apart and suffered from jealousy, poor communication and obsessive secrecy. For the time being there would be no co-ordinated support for or attack on the evolutionary potential of the *Archaeopteryx*.

As Waterhouse arrived in Pappenheim, news of the *Archaeopteryx* was only just reaching Darwin's supporters in Britain. The majority were far too busy on their own projects to take time to try and view it; most did not have the backing of a well-funded institution and made their living by charging students for attending their lectures. Some of Darwin's supporters barely had the means to feed themselves, let alone raise the capital to buy specimens. Even the wealthy Darwin, who at this time was still unaware of the existence of the *Archaeopteryx*, would have balked at paying such a high sum for a single fossil.

Owen and Waterhouse, on the other hand, did have the backing of a well-funded public institution and Owen in particular was determined to use it to secure the specimen.

Little is known about Waterhouse's journey to Pappenheim or of his time with Carl Häberlein. He did not lodge with the doctor but at a local hotel, an act that seems a little uncharitable on Häberlein's part but this could, of course, have been Waterhouse's choice. Which of us when travelling on business does not prefer to stay in a hotel at our company's expense?

He must have stayed in Pappenheim for a relatively long time as he was away from Britain for just over four weeks, only ten days or so of which would have been spent on the road. This was probably because after inspecting the fossils, Waterhouse stayed on to negotiate a price with Häberlein. Negotiations were a protracted process, for at every stage a letter outlining the latest deal had to be sent to Owen in London and his reply had to be received before Waterhouse could proceed.

Waterhouse was certainly resident there long enough to receive three letters from his wife and eldest son, one of which wished him well in the 'strange land'. We know that Waterhouse is unlikely to have seen very much of the doctor in person. Instead Häberlein's daughter was used to run letters between Waterhouse's hotel and Häberlein's suburban house. As Häberlein and Waterhouse had no common language, one can only guess at how the two managed to communicate at all; perhaps the daughter helped out there too. The negotiations must have tested the patience of both men.

Whichever way you look at it, this must have been a strange time for George Waterhouse as he sat in his hotel room waiting for written instructions from Owen which then had to be transcribed into German and sent on foot to Häberlein, whose eventual reply would in turn have to be translated and sent to Owen. Nowadays the process would take ten minutes to complete. In 1862 it took nearly a month.

Waterhouse's first communication back to Owen in early July revealed that Waterhouse had offered £600 for the entire collection, £100 more than the Trustees had allowed, but that he had got Häberlein to agree that the payment could be split across two years: £400 could therefore be taken out of that year's budget, with £200 from that of the next year. This was a compromise that the Trustees might go for. It appeared that a suitable deal had been struck. Owen ordered Waterhouse back to London.

On the 12th of July Owen went before the Board of Trustees, making it clear that he was acting on behalf of Waterhouse but proposing to go with Waterhouse's bid of £600 to be split unequally between the two years. Surprisingly, the Trustees agreed to the deal. The minutes record that 'the whole amount could be paid at once, £200 of it, however, to be appropriated from the grant for fossils for 1863–64'.

Owen must have been delighted. Not only did it mean that he had got his own way within the museum once again – an event that always pleased the power-broker in him – it also meant that he would at last be able to give the first 'professional' opinion of the *Archaeopteryx* which was based not on hearsay but on an actual study of the fossil.

Like the late Wagner, Owen did not want to see this fossil become a mascot for *The Origin of Species* and as he was arguably the greatest palaeontologist alive, his opinion would carry far more weight than that of the eccentric and embittered Wagner. Owen was not a man noted for his good humour but a small smile may have crept across his face as he walked away from the Trustees' committee meeting. Unfortunately, his jovial mood was to be short-lived. As soon as Waterhouse had left Pappenheim, Häberlein penned a letter to Owen which, although sent on the 10th of July, did not arrive in London until two days after the Board of Trustees' meeting. This letter was short and stark, stating bluntly that the doctor would not be prepared to part with the fossil for less than £700. He would, however, accept £650 for the few vertebrate fossils (including the *Archaeopteryx*) which Waterhouse had selected during his visit. The Pappenheim doctor had gone back on his word, waiting until Waterhouse was out of the way before reopening the negotiations.

The doctor had achieved what he wanted. He had persuaded the British Museum to send a representative to view his fossils and he felt sure that, having seen his collection, the museum would pay what he wanted. He did not, however, like having Waterhouse hanging around Pappenheim and so had provisionally agreed to his £600 bid in order to get rid of him. Like the stipulation that no drawings or notes could be made of the fossils, dealing with his bidders at a distance moved the odds in Häberlein's favour. In his mind, the museum's distance from his fossils would be bound to make their heart grow fonder of them.

Owen was in despair. He had been made to look a fool in front of the Trustees. Even so, his overwhelming desire for the

Archaeopteryx overrode his considerable pride. He would continue to negotiate with the doctor. Owen's diary for the 17th of July 1862 records his feelings:

> A visit from Mr Waterhouse just returned from Pappenheim where he has been in treaty for the collection of fossils, in which is the curious fossil with the alleged feathered vertebrate tail. The old German doctor is obstinate about his price and Mr W. has come away empty-handed. We ought not to lose the fossil!

On the 26th of July Owen was forced to go back to the Trustees, cap in hand, asking that they pay Häberlein's new price. To try and sweeten the pill he brought along a letter from one of the Trustees themselves, Sir Roderick Murchison, which heartily recommended the purchase of the Solnhofen collection. As before, Owen suggested splitting the cost across two years: £400 that year, £300 the next.

This time the Trustees were not so accommodating and felt that Häberlein was trying to take advantage of Owen and Waterhouse's desire for the fossils. After deliberating, the Trustees, 'having considered the expediency of admitting into their accounts so great a charge upon the next year's grant, declined the purchase of Dr Häberlein's fossils'. Owen was stuck. He knew that Häberlein was unlikely to change his price and that the Trustees were unlikely to change their minds and that while they fiddled news of the *Archaeopteryx* was travelling ever further afield. Owen and Waterhouse once again decided that the matter was urgent enough for them to work behind the Trustees' backs, risking the full wrath of the museum. They put their heads together to try and find a way around the directives they had been given. The plan they came up with is expressed in their letter to Häberlein of the 28th of July:

> Dear Sir,
> I have to inform you that your offer to part with your Solenhofen collection for £750 [*sic*] was laid before the Trustees on Saturday last, but as the money I have at my

command for this year falls far short of that sum, and as it is against the regulations of this establishment to dispose beforehand of any part of grants which may be made for the next year, the purchase of the collection was declined.

I consider, however, that by a former minute of the Trustees, I am still at liberty to spend a certain sum (as I informed you) in the purchase of a selection of specimens from your collection, and I am willing to do so. From what I have just said you will understand that I can make no promises for the future, but I may inform you that both Prof. Owen and myself think that the entire collection should be obtained for the British Museum and indeed recommend its purchase, and I do not think it at all probable that any circumstances will occur to cause us to change this opinion.

I shall be glad then, next year (our financial year commences in April) to have the offer (for £250) of those portions of your collection which for want of funds I am unable to purchase at present.

The sum I now have at my disposal is £450 and I wish to know whether you are willing for this sum to part with all the Solenhofen fossils belonging to the vertebrate classes – that is, the *Gryphosaurus*, and the reptilian, and fish remains.

George Waterhouse

Owen and Waterhouse had ignored the instructions given to them that negotiations with Häberlein should cease. Instead they looked back to the Trustees' minutes of the 14th of June when it had been agreed that Waterhouse had £500 to spend on the fossils. As far as they were concerned this offer still stood, although it had somehow been decreased to £450 (probably because of the £400 limit set at the 12th July meeting) and could thus be used as a down payment on Häberlein's collection.

This deal effectively meant Häberlein splitting his collection into two, selling the best specimens to the British Museum with no guarantee that they would come back to buy the remainder. To both sides the strategy was risky. Owen and Waterhouse were acting without any authority whatsoever, risking the wrath of the Trustees, while Häberlein could be left with a bunch of unwanted fossils, exactly the situation he had wished to avoid in the first place. However, the odds had at last shifted in favour of the British Museum.

Despite the increasing fame of the *Archaeopteryx* (or, as Owen and Waterhouse preferred, the *Gryphosaurus*), Häberlein had received no further offers and was beginning to wonder whether this animal was really the valuable specimen that he, Witte, von Meyer and Wagner had supposed it to be.

Worse still, there were now rumours that the *Archaeopteryx* was a clever fake and these had even reached the German press. His plan of denying scientists close scrutiny of the fossil was beginning to backfire. Häberlein worried that rumours of forgery might find their way back to England and jeopardize the deal with London. If he was forced to allow a proper scientific examination of the fossil in order to scotch the idea' that it was a fake it would dispel the air of mystery surrounding the fossil: an unfavourable report could ruin the chance of a sale altogether. For the first time, Häberlein was on the back foot and would have to consider a compromised deal with the British Museum. The prospect of splitting the collection still did not please him, so in his next letter to London, while effectively agreeing to the sale, he made one last attempt at an agreement:

Sir,
I can only enter into your proposal under the condition that you positively procure the remainder of my collection in the course of spring of the year 1863. I have made up my mind to deliver at once those portions which are asked for in your letter dated 28th of last month, for £450 sterling, if I have the certainty that the remainder will be taken at a later period for £250.

I have not put too high a price on my Solenhofen collection, which contains only the rarest and most interesting specimens – if you understood German the thing would have been settled in three or four days. I ask you

now for a final answer without intermediate interpreter or
agent.

Dr Carl Häberlein, 6th August 1862

Häberlein's blunt comment about the protracted translation
process showed that he was tiring of bargaining. Owen and
Waterhouse's patience was also wearing thin. They would dearly
have loved to give a favourable reply to Häberlein but already
their necks were stuck out further than they should have been.
To risk promising £250 of the museum's money for the next year
would definitely break the Trustees' instructions.

Waterhouse's reply was direct and to the point. It explained
once again that the museum could not promise money from the
following year's budget. He ended his communication with a
terse comment: 'You will perhaps reconsider my last letter and
hopefully will correctly interpret its contents.'

Owen and Waterhouse had let Häberlein know that this was
to be the last deal on the table. They could do nothing further
short of buying the fossils with their own private funds. If the
doctor was unwilling to sell on these terms, then that was that:
the *Archaeopteryx* would remain beyond the grasp of the British
Museum and also the ambitious plans of Owen. But Häberlein
too was up against a brick wall. He had found no other bidders
for his collection and rumours that the *Archaeopteryx* was a
forgery were still circulating freely. Much as it went against his
stubborn nature, he would have to surrender to the British
Museum's terms. After two weeks' deliberation, he wrote back
to London with a few terms of his own:

Sir,
In confidence in your good faith I will send the Solenhofen
fossils out of the class of vertebrata that is the *Gryphosaurus*,
the reptiles and three fish which were selected and marked
for your price of £450. I shall keep back only:
1) A *Pterodactylus longicauda* with counterpart, below
   which is an ammonite, there are two entirely similar
   specimens in the collections.
2) The so-called head of a crocodile in sandstone.

3) The chimera of which it is problematical whether it belongs to the vertebrata.

I doubt not that the Trustees will enter into your wishes in the next spring. If this will be the case you will receive those three specimens and the whole remainder just as you have left it for the price of £250.

If you will accept this fair proposal will you be pleased to send me the orders for packing and way of transmission by rail or by water and as to insurance, etc.

Dr Carl Häberlein, 26th August 1862

After six months of hard bargaining Owen and Waterhouse had won, but the canny Häberlein had not gone down without a fight! He had held on to three valuable specimens to ensure that the remainder of his collection was not totally redundant and that the museum would have a reason to purchase it next year. Not that Owen really cared – he had got precisely what he wanted: the '*Gryphosaurus*' aka *Archaeopteryx*. The urgency with which he wanted this fossil is revealed in the packing and transport details sent to Häberlein by return of post:

. . . I should like to have the *Gryphosaurus* sent *immediately* by Railway, and I think it desirable that the case should be enclosed in a second larger, strong, case, leaving room for some hay, or some other soft material, between the outer and inner box, to prevent any sudden jar in the journey. I should like it to be insured in any sum which would have the effect of making the railway people, etc., take extra care – say £20 . . .

George Waterhouse, 1st September 1862

The *Archaeopteryx* would shortly be winging its way across Europe to join the esteemed palaeontology collections of the British Museum's Natural History Department. Now Owen's problem was how to explain to the Trustees why he had made the deal without consulting them first. Tactfully he decided to wait for the fossil's arrival before making his actions known.

The *Archaeopteryx* arrived at the museum exactly one month

later on the 1st of October 1862. The excessive packing instructions had been followed to the letter and both the fossil and its counterpart were intact. A grateful note went back to Häberlein.

This was a particularly joyous time for Owen who had been impatiently expecting the *Archaeopteryx* for several days. Like a student awaiting exam results, he had been coming into the museum daily to check the post – only to leave again in a bad mood. When the wooden crate did arrive Owen set upon it, pulling apart the planking and straw until the two naked Solnhofen limestone slabs were freed.

Even on first sight the *Archaeopteryx* was everything he could have hoped for and was most certainly a fossil that was worthy of his immediate attention. He could at last give a first-hand opinion on this enigma before anybody else muddied the waters with talk of missing links. Like Wagner when he received Oppel's drawing, Owen was to devote his next six weeks to the *Archaeopteryx*. During the previous two years he had lost several key battles with Darwin's supporters. This was his chance to redress the balance in his favour.

The joy at the *Archaeopteryx's* arrival was short-lived. Owen and Waterhouse knew that they would have to account for their purchase of the Solnhofen fossils at the Board of Trustees' meeting on the 11th of October. Typically, and despite having been the driving force behind the negotiations, Owen largely left it to Waterhouse to explain their actions. Owen had been careful not to be seen to be directly involved in the negotiations with Häberlein: it was Waterhouse who had written all the letters and had gone to Pappenheim to make the selection of fossils. Owen gave the impression that he had merely agreed to represent Waterhouse to the Trustees during his absence in Germany.

When the time came to let the British Museum know that it had just spent £450 on fossils that it had previously refused to buy for £400, Owen gently told his old friend that because it was his Geology Department that was forking out for the fossils, it would have to be he who explained away the expenditure.

Fearing the worst, Waterhouse initially tried to hide the news of the purchase in the 'general business' section of his written report to the Trustees. This trick was spotted by the museum's gruff Principal Librarian A. Panizzi who wrote him a stinging memo:

> I must remind you of an order of the Trustees made so long ago as May 1778 that all reports on *extraordinary business* should be written on separate papers. Have the goodness to attend to this in future or I shall be obliged to trouble you to write your reports over again!

The purchase of the *Archaeopteryx* was clearly a matter of 'extraordinary business' and the next day Waterhouse stood before the Trustees explaining that he had just spent £450 of their money without permission. Owen supported the expenditure saying that the fossils selected 'were in every respect most desirable and the sum for which they had been obtained was reasonable and moderate'. Nonetheless the Trustees were not amused. Waterhouse's insistence that on the 12th of June the Trustees had allowed him to spend up to £500 on a selection of Häberlein's fossils did not wash with them. He was forced to read out the letters involved in the negotiations with Häberlein, which meant he had to reveal the provisional deal to pay a further £250 the next year. Owen's name was nowhere to be seen on these documents. Things looked bad for Waterhouse.

It was acknowledged by the Trustees that £450 had been promised to Häberlein on the museum's behalf and that this would therefore have to be paid from the Geology Department's budget. However, the Trustees saw no reason why they should pay another £250 the next year when they had the best specimens already. Waterhouse was instructed to write to Häberlein again stating that the museum did not pledge itself to buy his remaining fossils. Waterhouse's record in the museum was a good one and although the Trustees were most displeased, he escaped with an informal rebuke. Owen left the meeting room and went straight to his office to continue his study of the *Archaeopteryx*. He escaped the meeting without so much as a small blemish on his record.

In a further act of defiance, Waterhouse never did write to Häberlein as instructed and in the August of the next year he purchased the remainder of his collection as informally agreed.

In retrospect, despite the high cost, Häberlein's fossils were a bargain. Although nearly two years of the Geology Department's budget had been spent on obtaining the *Archaeopteryx*, the fossil's scientific value was beyond measure and in time it would become the Natural History Museum's most prized specimen. The *Archaeopteryx*'s later value was of course not known at the time, and even though a giant sloth fossil would have set them back £1,400 (about £64,000 or $103,000 today), this was over six metres in height. The *Archaeopteryx* was tiny and unlikely to draw the crowds in much the same way. It looked bad value for money. The social commentator John Ruskin disagreed when he wrote of the *Archaeopteryx*'s purchase a couple of years later. He believed the British Museum to have been stubborn in their negotiations and praised Owen.

'Suppose,' wrote Ruskin, 'a gentleman of unknown income, but whose wealth was to be conjectured from the fact that he spent two thousand a year on his park-walls and footmen only, professes himself fond of science; and that one of his servants comes eagerly to tell him that an unique collection of fossils, giving clue to a new era of creation, is to be had for seven pounds sterling; and that the gentleman who is fond of science, and spends two thousand a year on his park, answers, after keeping his servant waiting for several months, "Well! I'll give you four-pence for them, if you will be answerable for the extra three-pence yourself, till next year!" '

The analogy was a none too subtle one. The 'gentleman of unknown income' was the British Museum, the 'eager servant' Owen. The implication was that Owen funded the remaining purchase from Häberlein himself, something that simply did not occur. Poor old Waterhouse's role seems to have got lost altogether. In matters where Owen became concerned it was not unusual for his co-workers mysteriously to be forgotten at a later date.

Whether the *Archaeopteryx* was a bargain or not, the Germans had been deprived of yet another valuable Solnhofen fossil. The Munich museum, on hearing of the British Museum's interest, tried to make a last-minute bid, offering Häberlein the previously agreed £708.

One can imagine the foul atmosphere inside Häberlein's Pappenheim house as he wrote to inform von Martius that the central fossils in the collection were already packed and in transit to London. Nonetheless, he seems to have claimed back more than the £8 difference between the London and Munich bids by charging the British Museum £16 for the postage and packing of his specimens. This extortionate amount caused Mr Panizzi to fire off yet another memo to Waterhouse, asking whether it was reasonable. Waterhouse, tired of being a pawn in a game of Owen's making, instructed it to be paid. He had barely seen the *Archaeopteryx* since its arrival in his department. He had not seen much of Owen either. Both were locked away in Owen's office where the Professor slaved away furiously, preparing to deliver his judgement on what was to become the fossil find of the century.

5

Evolutionary Rivals

THE SCIENTIFIC WORLD in which the *Archaeopteryx* had arrived was in turmoil. Only one issue was the talk of the day – evolution.

It is a common error to say that Charles Darwin 'discovered' or 'invented' the notion of evolution. He did not. The idea that there was evolution in the fossil record had been around since the late eighteenth century: it was just that nobody could offer any proof of its existence or of how it might work. *The Origin of Species* and its theory of natural selection put forward an explanation as to how evolution could work on its own but could still offer no proof that one animal could gradually evolve into another totally separate species. This is why the *Archaeopteryx*, as a potential missing link, was so important and why Owen had been so keen to get his hands on it.

In modern terms it is difficult to understand quite how powerful a figure Richard Owen was in the mid-Victorian era. Born to a well-off Lancaster family in 1804, he was assured the best education that money could buy and by 1824 had entered the famous medical school at Edinburgh. Although it was family money that enabled him to attend college, it was Owen's undoubted talent for anatomy that took him to London's St Bartholomew's Hospital to study surgery. It was here, in 1828, that he was appointed as a lecturer in comparative anatomy.

By this time his interest in the natural world, and in fossils in particular, had already been sparked. At the age of just twenty-two, he had been one of the founding members of the London Zoological Society and eventually he abandoned his surgical career altogether in favour of a shakier profession as a naturalist. Right from the outset Owen was noted for his brilliance in identifying and reconstructing entire animal from just a few bones (or sometimes even just a single one).

Unfortunately he also gained another reputation, as arrogant, rude and dismissive. He also appears to have been a plagiarist, that worst of scientific habits, sometimes even republishing other people's manuscripts with his own name at the top. The pioneering geologist Gideon Mantell spoke for many when he wrote of Owen that 'it is deeply to be deplored that this highly eminent and gifted man can never act with candour and liberality'. This statement sums up the general academic opinion of Owen. Yes he was gifted, but he also had an attitude problem to go with it.

The British public, however, thought differently. From the 1820s onwards Owen had become an increasingly public figure after being associated with several wondrous natural history discoveries, such as a whole group of extinct and gigantic South American mammals and the even more impressive group of immense fossilized reptiles which Owen named 'dinosaurs'.

He may have lacked friends in the everyday scientific world, but Owen made up for this with his contacts in the upper ranks of society and over time gathered around himself a set of acquaintances that reads like an extract from *Who's Who*. Members of Parliament, bishops, earls, the Prince Consort and even the newly crowned Queen Victoria were all in Owen's entourage. Having well-placed contacts ensured that Owen's coverage by the press was favourable.

Much as he was disliked by many scientists, few had the nerve to tackle Owen head on and preferred to curse him behind his back. This was to change in 1850 when a twenty-five-year-old ship's surgeon stepped off a ship in Portsmouth after serving over five years in the Queen's Navy. The young man was Thomas Henry Huxley, who ten years later would be slandered by Bishop Wilberforce during the Oxford debate.

Huxley was to be the exception to the unwritten rule that Owen was untouchable. Where others shied away, Huxley later dared to tackle the master naturalist in a series of frontal assaults that would leave many in the scientific establishment reeling.

Huxley was to become a central character in the story of the *Archaeopteryx* and he was to do so chiefly because of his dislike of Richard Owen. The two would do battle over the fossil until the reputation of one of them was in tatters.

In the nineteenth century being a ship's surgeon was a most unpleasant job, but Huxley had come from a poor middle-class background and the debts he had incurred from studying at medical school had forced him into the Navy. One benefit from his time aboard ship was a new-found love of natural history, a field in which he apparently had quite considerable talent. Even before his return to England Huxley's work on various sea animals had gained him high praise. Consequently, he left the Navy not in search of a medical post but, like Owen in his medical days, in pursuit of an academic career as a naturalist. Unlike Owen, he was to find entry into academia very trouble-some indeed.

In the mid-Victorian era money and status spoke louder than talent. Huxley discovered that his abundance of the last attribute could not make up for his lack of either of the first two. Where the privileged Owen had sailed into the lectureships and museum posts of his choosing, in the months after his return Huxley applied for one menial museum post after another, all without success. In the meantime, and ironically, his scientific work was earning him awards and praise from every quarter.

It was in this trying time that Huxley and Owen first came into contact. Like many eventual enemies, the two gentleman first met on friendly terms when Huxley asked Owen to be his referee for a for a job application. Over the coming months Huxley was to ask this favour of Owen several more times, sometimes only a week or so apart, and Owen was obliging, if in a condescending manner.

It was Huxley who started the feud. His inability to land himself a job had made him increasingly desperate and irrational and he eventually formulated the idea that instead of helping him, Owen was writing bad references that ensured that he did not get a job. Huxley too could be arrogant and it looks remark-ably as though he thought that Owen, then considered the nation's greatest naturalist, felt threatened by him – something which is unlikely in the extreme and for which there is no evidence. And to the struggling Huxley, Owen must surely have been the embodiment of the system of wealth and patronage which was keeping him from his chosen career.

An insight into Huxley's thinking can be gained from his description of a chance meeting with Owen just after one of his many requests for a job reference:

> [Owen] stopped me, and in the blandest and most gracious manner said, 'I have received your note, I shall *grant* it.' The phrase and the implied condescension were quite 'touching' – so much that if I had stopped a moment longer I must knock him into the gutter. I therefore bowed and walked off.

Whoever was at fault, it was the young and fiery Huxley, ever the iconoclast, who determined to knock Owen from his pedestal. This was quite an ambition from someone so young and so powerless.

During the 1850s, while Huxley was struggling to make ends meet, the issue of evolution had become an important scientific topic for the first time in several decades. The last time the spectre of evolution had raised its head was during the 1820s when the possibility that there was any form of progression of fossil life from simple to complex organisms was still considered heretical. Fossils, it was widely believed, were probably the result of animals that had been buried during the great flood of Noah. All these different animals died together at the same time and thus could not have 'evolved' in the way that some French scientists were then suggesting.

However, as time had passed so wonderful new fossils were discovered in all parts of the world, many of them ending up in the powerful European museums. It became obvious to even the most stubborn scientist that at the very least the Earth was considerably older than the 6,000 years that was traditionally given by the Christian Church.

Many scientists, including Owen, saw that there was a structure to the fossil record. The older the rock, the more 'primitive' the fossils would be. When put in order of age it could be seen that the earliest rocks contained only fossil seashells while younger ones contained fish, then amphibians, then reptiles, then mammals and eventually the birds. By the 1850s the evidence in favour of evolution was so strong that it couldn't all be ignored.

In a world which viewed evolution and religion as mutually exclusive, Owen managed to pull off a great triumph when, in the mid-1850s, he put forward his 'theory of the archetype'. This theory not only accepted the doctrine of evolution, but offered an explanation for it. Animals progressed from one form to another, said Owen, only by the will of God. This was achieved by God having laid out an archetypal body plan for every animal and plant group on Earth so that when He wanted to create a new species, he simply tweaked this archetype to produce it.

The vertebrate archetype, for example, is a backbone, ribs, four limbs and a skull. Every vertebrate from a digging mole to a flying pterodactyl had an almost identical body plan and even many of the same bones, but it was God who decided how the final body should look and what the various limbs, etc., were used for. It is a bit like a car manufacturer putting different pieces of bodywork on to the same basic chassis and four wheels – some cars end up being Porsches whilst others are delivery vans. They still share the same basic design underneath despite their different end uses. Most crucial to our story is that, because each species was individually created by God, there could be no room for intermediates. Missing links were definitely out!

Owen's theory (which is now thought to have been plagiarized from an obscure piece of work published by Karl Gustav Carus in 1828) was greeted with relief by a scientific and religious world which was growing nervous at the atheistic undertones that were becoming associated with discussions of evolution and the fossil record. Owen was already famous but the theory of archetypes propelled him to superstar status. This doubtless fuelled Huxley's dislike of him further. Huxley saw that if he was to hit Owen where it really hurt then he would have to attack his theory of the archetype, but this presented a problem. Brilliant as he was, Huxley had no theory of his own with which he could explain how evolution worked. Instead of finding such a theory, he decided simply to take the diametrically opposite position to Owen.

Where Owen saw a God-inspired progression of life through the fossil record, Huxley the agnostic (a term he actually coined) saw no progression at all. He refused to believe that life had changed through time. Instead of a lineage whereby a fish becomes an amphibian which becomes a reptile which becomes a mammal, Huxley believed that all these animal types must have coexisted throughout time. Where most believed that the ancient 400-million-year-old Silurian rocks of the British midlands to contain no more than a few shelled fossils and primitive fish, Huxley stated that there must also have been reptiles, mammals, dinosaurs and even birds present on land. It was just that their fossils had not yet been found. Nowadays Huxley's position looks ridiculous but in the 1850s palaeontology was still an infant science where a single fossil was capable of changing an entire world view, as the *Archaeopteryx* would soon demonstrate.

In 1855 Huxley, now with an academic position and a meagre salary, used his view of evolution deliberately to start what would become a long and grinding war of words with Owen. Like many of his day, he chose not to criticize his nemesis face to face, but to do it in print. Huxley had been asked to review a much-hated book entitled *Vestiges of the Natural History of Creation* published anonymously by Robert Chambers.

Owen had previously panned the book because of its unashamedly populist look at evolution (it drew on every crackpot theory then in existence) and for its daring to suggest that his theory of archetypes was wrong. Huxley too hated the book but when asked to review it he used the opportunity to take Owen down a peg or two. In fact, his review was so cutting that Darwin remarked of it: 'By Heavens, how the blood must have gushed into the capillaries when a certain great man (whom with all his faults I cannot help liking) read it!'

Thanks to Huxley, a feud between himself and Owen had begun. Over the coming weeks the two men publicly argued about any and every topic that could be used to beat the other one down. Seashells, fish, fossils and living animals were all fought over but the big prize was evolution (or the lack of it, according to Huxley) in the fossil record, with Huxley constantly trying to find older and older fossilized examples of certain animals in order to disprove Owen's progressive idea of archetypes.

They were never the best of friends, but the scientific establishment was by now very aware that Owen and Huxley were the bitterest of enemies and woe betide anybody who dared to favour either one of them. To do so meant instant excommunication by their opponent.

The public brawling between Owen and Huxley was, to most people, a great entertainment. To one person, however, it was the cause of great sadness.

Charles Darwin had no great love of Richard Owen but he did not detest him either. However, Darwin had grown increasingly fond of the young Huxley whose kind nature, talent for science and extrovert ability to promote natural history to the general public had greatly pleased the middle-aged man.

Darwin was able to watch Owen and Huxley fight over evolution from a unique standpoint. He knew that both their points of view were wrong and that he alone had the solution to the problem of evolution. Darwin also knew that Owen was far too arrogant and self-important ever to be converted to his idea of natural selection but he had hoped that the more pliable Huxley might be persuaded by his way of thinking. When it came to publishing his theory of natural selection Darwin was aware that Owen would automatically oppose him, which he could handle; but to have the vocal and vociferous Huxley as an enemy as well would be a disaster.

During 1855 and 1856 Darwin watched Huxley become more and more of a loose cannon as he started to target not just Owen, but many others besides. Enough was enough. Darwin decided it was time to take a great risk and over a weekend in April 1856, he invited a small circle of friends and scientific acquaintances to his Kent house. To the illness-racked and hermit-like Darwin this was a major concession and it was certainly not done for social reasons. Instead he wished to gather those people whom he thought could be turned from their current viewpoints on evolution towards his own theory of natural selection. Although they had been friends for just a short while, Huxley was the first to be invited. He accepted willingly, no doubt aware how highly regarded Darwin was by almost everybody in the scientific community, including Owen.

The weekend was a strange one. Darwin's large house was also his laboratory and although he was a lover of wildlife, the scene which confronted his guests on the Saturday of their arrival was horrific.

Darwin's theory of natural selection relies fundamentally on the ability of one species to transform gradually into another entirely separate species over time. For years Darwin had been trying to see whether it was possible to breed certain characteristics in and out of various types of plants and animals. Using pigeons, Darwin adopted the same techniques as pigeon-fanciers, choosing birds with a particular characteristic, such as strong flight or colour, and then trying to exaggerate that characteristic by carefully choosing which birds bred with each other. If the same experiment could be done over several dozen generations, theorized Darwin, that characteristic would become so strong as to create a bird of a separate species from that of its ancestors. Thus a new species could be created, not by God as Owen believed, but by simple selective breeding.

In order to achieve this Darwin had devoted a large part of his garden to breeding pigeons which would be selectively bred and then killed, hung and de-fleshed so that the skeleton could be examined properly. At any one time there would be dozens of killed and rotting birds hanging about the sheds and cellar. The stench was appalling and the sight a grisly one that did not befit Darwin's pacifist image. Needs must, he explained to his weekend guests, while at the same time gently prodding them into thinking about the possibility of how species could vary through time.

It was on the Sunday that the real examination began. One by one each guest was invited into Darwin's study for a chat about their views on evolution. Huxley received a grilling about his refusal to believe in the progression of life through time but the young man was obstinate and refused to budge an inch. Darwin abandoned any hope that he could turn Huxley that day and moved on to his other guests, most of whom believed that life could evolve but were equally stubborn about the idea of natural selection, preferring other theories instead. The stress of the weekend caused Darwin to be ill for several days afterwards and yet he had little to show for his trouble. With no new converts to his way of thinking, his efforts seemed to have been in vain and served only to convince him that the world was not yet ready for his theory of natural selection.

Not all of Darwin's seeds of wisdom had fallen on barren ground. His talk of the variation of physical characteristics within a single species had rattled about inside Huxley's brain. The more he thought about it, the more sense it made. After all, he had seen enormous variation in nearly every species he had studied.

Furthermore, Darwin's ideas sat very badly with Owen's God-created archetypes and it was probably this above all others that caused Huxley to start exploring Darwin's work. If Huxley could prove that there was a certain amount of variation within an individual species then Owen would be in trouble. Owen's theory of archetypes did not allow for variation within a single species: it would be too close to suggesting the existence of a missing link. Over the coming weeks little hints started to appear in Huxley's newspaper and magazine columns that he had taken on board some of Darwin's ideas. However, he merely seemed to have incorporated them into his own theory of fossil persistence and still he continued to act like a bull in a china shop, especially where Owen was concerned. Darwin despaired but kept in contact with Huxley, the two gradually becoming firm friends.

The crisis point arrived in 1857 when news reached Darwin of a new theory developed by Alfred Russell Wallace, a professional animal capturer working in the Far East. Although Wallace's theory had only been scribbled across a few loose pages, it perfectly summarized everything that Darwin had been working towards since his journey on the *Beagle* two decades previously. Having been putting the moment off, Darwin began to work on his book about natural selection in earnest, expressing a wish that he would yet be able to turn Huxley before its publication.

While Darwin battled with ill health and his manuscript, Huxley's feud with Owen deepened. Having argued over everything from aphids to embryos Huxley was slowly moving into the field of palaeontology, Owen's sacred territory. For the first time Owen was actually beginning to feel threatened by Huxley. The young upstart was no longer so naïve nor lacking in credibility as he once had been. He was science's rising star and, like Owen before him, was becoming a public personality chiefly because of his free lectures in London which were aimed at giving 'working people' an understanding of science. In return the working people had taken Huxley to their heart, turning him into a popular science hero.

On the eve of the publication of *The Origin of Species* Huxley had still to be convinced of Darwin's full argument. Variation within a species was fine but evolution of one species to another through natural selection was still out of the question. 'If I can convert Huxley I shall be content,' wrote Darwin. *The Origin of Species* was finally published in November 1859.

The turmoil caused by the publication of *The Origin of Species* is legendary. Darwin's hermitic habits meant that few people knew that this tome was going to hit the shops and when it became a bestseller the conservative scientific community had little time in which to organize a campaign against it.

Although Darwin's supporters had the element of surprise on their side, they rapidly found that they had a noticeable and very big problem with their campaign to defend the book. There was nobody who wanted to lead it.

In contrast, the anti-Darwinians seemed to have more generals than foot-soldiers. Richard Owen and Bishop Wilberforce were just a few of the dozens of notable scientists, politicians, clergy, landed gentry and others who were willing to stand up and attack the ideas put forward by *The Origin of Species*. If only the Darwinians could have half as many vocal supporters, then perhaps their case could make some headway.

The natural leader would of course have been Darwin himself. After all, it was his theory on trial and he was the one who had spent decades gathering the evidence in favour of it. Unfortunately, although Darwin may have been a great thinker, he was not one for a fight. In the months after publication Darwin again suffered from ill health, and had guilty feelings about the effect his book was having on his devoutly religious wife. He rarely ventured outside his country home and when he did it was not to defend himself in public but to visit a friend or see some quack doctor about the latest fashionable cure for his vomiting fits.

In the few weeks following the publication of *The Origin of Species* there was a remarkable silence even from Darwin's more vocal supporters. In an era when one's reputation was everything, few scientists wanted to associate themselves with the drubbing that Darwin's book was receiving from the scientific and popular press.

Hostile review after hostile review tumbled out of the broadsheets, periodicals and scientific journals. Richard Owen's, which was typically anonymous, described *The Origin of Species* as 'purely conjectural'. Again the idea of a missing link was the sticking point. 'We have searched in vain,' wrote Owen, 'for the evidence or the proof, that it is only necessary for one individual [species] to vary, be it ever so little to validate the conclusion that the variability is progressive and unlimited, so as, in the course of generations, to change the species, the genus, the order, or the class.'

Bishop Wilberforce (Soapy Sam), who had been shown *Origin*'s weak points by his friend Owen, was more insidious, portraying the book as some kind of misguided atheist's Bible. Many others were more tactful but no less damning in their views. Darwin's worst fears had come true. His theory of evolution through natural selection had caused a religious and scientific outcry. Worse still, few people were bothering to take in the evidence and arguments he had carefully and exhaustingly collated. The few converts that Darwin had made seemed to come mostly from the socialist, occultist, anarchist and atheistic wings of society, all of whom were considered to be fringe lunatics by mainstream Victorians. Things were looking bleak.

Then, during the Christmas of 1859, came a small ray of hope. An anonymous and eloquent review in *The Times*, no less, could not praise *The Origin of Species* highly enough. Stretching over several pages, the review carefully stated Darwin's case while also taking a swipe at the views of Owen and other detractors. The analogies used by the reviewer were brilliant and designed to make Darwin's ideas understandable in laymen's terms. The notion of natural selection, for example, was given thus: 'The individuals of a species are like the crew of a foundered ship, and none but good swimmers have a chance of reaching the land.' But it was the closing paragraph which delighted Darwin the most.

> Mr. Darwin abhors mere speculation as nature abhors a vacuum. He is as greedy of cases and precedents as any constitutional lawyer, and all the principles he lays down are capable of being brought to the test of observation and experiment. The path he bids us follow professes to be, not a mere airy track, fabricated of ideal cobwebs, but a solid and broad bridge of facts. If it be so, it will carry us safely over many a chasm in our knowledge, and lead us to a region free from the snares of those fascinating but barren virgins, the Final Causes, against whom a high authority has so justly warned us. 'My sons, dig in the vineyard,' were the last words of the old man in the fable: and, though the sons found no treasure, they made their fortunes by the grapes.

No higher praise could have been lavished upon *The Origin of Species* – but who could Darwin's saviour be? People did not have far to look. It was an open secret that the reviewer was none other than Thomas Huxley, that young up-and-coming zoologist noted for his intellect, cutting wit and love of a fight.

Darwin too recognized Huxley's hand and wrote to him saying, 'I should have said that there was only one man in England who could have written this essay and you were the man.' Flattered by the praise, Huxley determined that his defence of Darwin should not be a one-off. Shortly afterwards, in February 1860, Huxley publicly defended *The Origin of Species* in a debate organized by London's Royal Institution. This was the first public test of Darwin's book but it did not go entirely to plan. Huxley couldn't find his form and seemed less interested in defending Darwin than in antagonizing the churchmen present by talking of humans and apes having originated from a common ancestor.

Darwin was deeply disappointed and believed that Huxley had done his book more harm than good. Nonetheless, Huxley had had the courage to stand up and defend *The Origin of Species* which was more than most of Darwin's other so-called supporters had done.

Then, a few months later, came what has been described as Darwin's first rally call in an article written by Huxley for the *Westminster Review*. Shortly afterwards came the infamous Oxford debate with Bishop 'Soapy Sam' Wilberforce in which, as we have seen already, Huxley's quick temper, rather than his intellectual defence of Darwin, won him the day and really got him noticed by the public at large.

Darwin may have started the war of words but he very soon absented himself from the ensuing battles. His troops would need to look elsewhere for leadership and when all options were considered there was really only one possible candidate.

Huxley built on the public reputation that he gained from the Oxford debate and appears to have become a born-again Darwinian, defending the ideal of natural selection in both private and public. Within a short time the Darwinian community realized that Huxley had everything that they could wish for. He was young, handsome, quick-witted, outspoken and did not suffer fools gladly, if at all. Best of all, he appeared to truly understand the ins and outs of the theory of natural selection and was able to defend himself against even the heaviest of guns.

Once Huxley even called himself 'Darwin's bulldog'; others

named him 'evolution's high priest' in honour of his services to the Darwinian cause. Darwin himself considered Huxley his 'warmest and most important supporter.' After some years in the wilderness, it looked as though Huxley had found not only the fame he had sought, but also his niche as Darwin's most vocal and keen supporter.

The arrival of the *Archaeopteryx* so soon after the publication of *The Origin of Species* should have been a God-given opportunity for Huxley once again to seize the moment and use this magnificent fossil to his best advantage. If the fossil *was* a missing link then Darwin's case was proven. Best of all, the fossil was in the hands of Richard Owen, Huxley's avowed enemy. The two gentlemen were bound to have differing opinions on the fossil and the stage seemed to be set for the ultimate showdown.

6

The Eagle has Landed

IN OCTOBER 1862 the *Archaeopteryx* was safely housed in its new home at the British Museum, jealously guarded by Richard Owen, the man whose scheming had brought it to England in the first place.

For the next few weeks the normally omnipresent figure of Owen would be rarely glimpsed about the British Museum. Like the unfortunate Andreas Wagner before him, Owen was determined that his opinion of the *Archaeopteryx* should be the defining one and that it would quash any loose talk of missing links. This was his golden opportunity to hit back at Darwin's supporters, especially Thomas Huxley.

As an acknowledged world expert on fossil animals, Owen knew that his opinion on the *Archaeopteryx* would be listened to closely and he was determined to take advantage of his head start over the rest of the scientific community. He spent long hours poring over the fossil, occasionally emerging from his office to order the curators to clean or prepare sections of the fossil. All but the most essential of his official duties were ignored. Grudgingly he would attend committee meetings, sometimes making his excuses and leaving early.

George Waterhouse could only observe Owen's behaviour in amazement while he began the long and tedious task of cataloguing Häberlein's other fossils which the museum had been forced to purchase, a task which Owen had adamantly refused to assist in. The *Archaeopteryx* was his obsession. But Owen was not to have things entirely his own way.

The *Archaeopteryx* was not Owen's personal property although he often acted as though it were. It had been purchased by a publicly funded institution and any member of the public was allowed reasonable access to it. This meant that although Owen was the scientist best placed to gain access to the fossil, others with an equally vested interest in the debate about evolution would soon learn of its existence and ask to view it.

Like a politician with a guilty secret, Owen was trying hard to keep news of the *Archaeopteryx* away from the public domain, and especially the scientific community at large, until he was ready to announce his findings. Although he had been working on the fossil for only a few weeks, by the beginning of November he felt confident enough to announce that he would give a talk on his findings at the next Royal Society of London meeting, scheduled for the 20th of the month. Surely he could keep news of the *Archaeopteryx* quiet until then. However, Owen, like many control freaks, was finding that the harder he tried to stop the sand from running through his fingers, the quicker it would flow.

On the morning of the 12th of November 1862 Owen opened his copy of the London *Times* to find a lengthy letter on page 9 entitled 'A Feathered Enigma' written by the anonymous 'Y' of London. His heart sank, and continued to drop as he read on:

> Sir,
> We live in an age of marvels, and it may surprise your readers to be informed that a bird can no longer be known by its feathers. A discovery has recently been made which has thrown the geological world into convulsions . . .

There then followed a detailed account of the entire history of the discovery of Häberlein's *Archaeopteryx* fossil and of the isolated fossil feather described by von Meyer. The letter was careful to name each person's involvement and most especially to highlight the names of the journals in which the von Meyer and

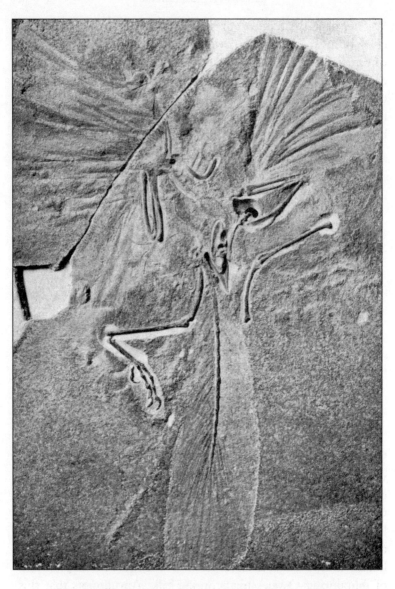

The London Archaeopteryx *specimen. It was bought by the London Natural History Museum and is now its most prized specimen*

Wagner papers had been published. The British Museum's purchase of the fossil was also covered, including the price and terms of purchase. Somebody was determined to let the world know of the *Archaeopteryx*'s existence but as he read on, Owen realized that the intent behind the letter was far worse than this. It was no less than a direct attempt by one of Darwin's supporters to blow the lid off his carefully planned study of the *Archaeopteryx*.

The letter gave a detailed description of the fossil itself:

> What remains of this creature is admirably preserved; but, unfortunately the head, neck, breastbone, and vertebral column of the body are absent. The fore and hind extremities, the pelvis, and several of the ribs, and the long slender tail – which is perfect to the tip, are distinctly visible. The foot is formed precisely like that of a bird; the fore limbs are feathered at their extremities, but the mode of insertion of the feathers differs from that of birds. The tail, a bony structure, resembles that of a lizard, and consists of about 20 slender, elongated vertebrae, to each side of which severally a feather is attached. The absence of a head and other important parts of the skeleton is much to be regretted, as without these it is impossible to pronounce with certainty on the affinities of the creature.

This was a near-perfect description of the *Archaeopteryx*, and it was careful to make reference to the foot and feathers being 'precisely like that of a bird' whilst the tail 'resembles that of a lizard'. Only someone who believed the *Archaeopteryx* to be a missing link between the birds and reptiles would describe the fossil in this way, highlighting the apparent mixture of features. The letter's author seems to have been writing with the express aim of scuppering Owen's forthcoming talk. Any doubts that this letter was not written by one of Darwin's supporters were dispelled in the last few paragraphs:

> We must rest contented with the deduction of von Meyer; and all that we can say is that it was a feathered animal intermediate between birds and reptiles, wholly different from

any creature previously known. It is probable that the followers of Darwin will not be slow to avail themselves of this new discovery, and adduce it in support of the transitional hypothesis respecting the origin of animals.

It is announced that Professor Owen will read a paper on this fossil at an early meeting of the Royal Society, and it is to be hoped that much additional light will then be shed on the subject.

The German philosophers will probably display magnanimity, and not complain that British gold should have deprived them of the means of completing the investigation which they had so successfully commenced.

I remain, Sir, yours faithfully,

Y.   London, Nov. 11

Any knowledgeable scientist reading the letter could not mistake its true intent. It was nothing less than a call to arms for Darwin's supporters. The anonymous 'Y' had provided all the information that anybody could need in order to read up about the *Archaeopteryx* presumably so that when Owen delivered his talk, which the letter is also careful to mention, the Darwinians could be prepared with evidence to counter his arguments.

The *Times* letter named the people who had studied the *Archaeopteryx* (noting that the anti-Darwinian Wagner had never actually viewed the fossil himself), the places where it had resided and, most importantly, the journals in which scientific papers could be found. Just for good measure a description of the *Archaeopteryx* was thrown in with a pro-Darwinian conclusion. Effectively it was saying of Owen's work on the *Archaeopteryx*, 'Come on boys, let's nail this bastard!'

The real identity of 'Y' remains a mystery but he was obviously a man of some cunning. Owen was notorious for his habit of vetoing letters and papers from scientific journals which did not agree with his viewpoint. This meant that letters concerning the *Archaeopteryx* were unlikely to make it into print until after he had given his pronouncement. He did not, however, have any control over the editorial content of *The Times*. 'Y' had until Owen had announced the date of his talk at the Royal

Society, due only days later, before going to the press. Darwin's supporters may have been few in number, but they were for the most part very well placed to cause trouble when the need arose.

As regards the identity of 'Y', I suspect him to have been somebody working within the British Museum, as the letter provides detailed information about the history and purchase of the *Archaeopteryx* which could only have come from an insider. He also gives a very precise description of the fossil, suggesting palaeontological training and access to the fossil itself.

To my mind there are two probable candidates. The first is John Evans, a noted museum palaeontologist and Darwin supporter who had performed much of the preparation work on the *Archaeopteryx* fossil after its arrival in London. His closeness to Owen may explain the desire for anonymity. The other likely candidate is Hugh Falconer the Scottish botanist and palaeontologist, who was also a close friend to Darwin and who became obsessed with the *Archaeopteryx* in the months after its purchase, viewing it several times.

Based on his previous form, it might be suspected that Thomas Huxley could also be a candidate but his hatred of Owen was such that he rarely stepped inside the British Museum at all and would have no qualms in signing his own name on a letter against Owen. He had done so on many occasions already. We may never know the real identity of 'Y' but his motives remain clear to see.

The 20th of November 1862, the day of Owen's *Archaeopteryx* talk, provided few surprises. It had been a grey and unremarkable London autumn day and in the early evening the great and good of the British scientific community began to leave their houses and clubs and head towards the Royal Society's headquarters near Piccadilly.

The attendance was notably larger than usual but nothing like that of the Oxford debate of two years previously. The affinity of the *Archaeopteryx* may have been an important issue but it was also one that largely concerned the academic community.

Nonetheless, the evening still held the promise of a clash of raw egos for it was well known that Owen's arch-enemy Thomas Huxley was to be in the audience. The two men could no longer be in the same room as each other without starting an argument and the *Archaeopteryx* was an issue worth fighting over.

Shortly after seven o'clock the middle-aged figure of Richard Owen took to the low podium at the front of the hall. Next to him was a sketched drawing of the *Archaeopteryx* hastily made during the previous few weeks. Looking down on the audience he must nervously have eyed several of Darwin's other key supporters such as the botanist Joseph Hooker and palaeontologist Hugh Falconer. Worst of all, there, a few rows from the front, was the steely-eyed and silent figure of Thomas Huxley who looked like he meant business. During their last few public encounters, which had mostly been about the differences between the gorilla and the human brain, it had been Huxley that had come away the victor. Indeed, Huxley was beginning to make a habit of pulling apart Owen's work, somehow finding obvious faults with everything he did. Now Owen was faced with delivering a lecture on what was already a highly controversial fossil. Would Huxley be the victor once again?

If Owen had decided to adopt a tactic for that night, then it seems to have been to bore his audience to death. Later accounts speak of his talk being 'verbose and minute'. But most people knew that this talk was not really about accurately describing the fossil. Far from it. It was Owen's opportunity to scotch the fast-spreading rumour that the *Archaeopteryx* was Darwin's hypothetical missing link. His measurements may have been precise, but his overall description of the *Archaeopteryx* seems to have been selective, ignoring several vital parts such as the distinctly reptilian clawed fingers. As Owen read out his list of tedious bone measurements he occasionally pointed towards the sketch of the fossil. And as he droned on more than one yawn had to be stifled.

Forty-five minutes later and the minutiae were finished with. Owen at last moved on to the subject that most people were there to hear about – was the *Archaeopteryx* a missing link or not?

'This animal is not an intermediate between the reptiles and the birds,' said Owen, 'but in fact simply the earliest known example of a fully-formed bird not dissimilar to several types of modern raptors and other birds. Furthermore, I can with confidence say that this bird would in life have been a powerful bird of flight.'

After nearly an hour's waffling on the size of toe bones, Owen had managed to summarize the evolutionary affinity of the *Archaeopteryx* in only a couple of sentences. In calling *Archaeopteryx* a bird Owen had taken the opposing view to that of Wagner a year earlier who had, with just as much confidence, pronounced the *Archaeopteryx* to be a reptile with no bird affinities whatsoever.

Owen had little more to say on the fossil origins of *Archaeopteryx*. 'The *Archaeopteryx*,' he declared, 'could only have transmuted [evolved] from a long-tailed pterodactyl such as are also found in the lithographic limestone of the Solenhofen region.'

And that was it. The performance had been an uncharacteristic one, with none of the bumptiousness and certainty for which Owen was known. Where was the arrogance and the spurious claims that were Owen's trademark?

Given his recent lack of success when presenting papers to a scientific audience, thanks largely to Huxley's aggression, it seems likely that Owen had been keen to give his audience as little ammunition as possible with which they could attack him. His talk had promised to be a description of the *Archaeopteryx*, and this it certainly was – millimetre by millimetre. His only other message was simple: there really was nothing for Darwin's supporters to get excited about. Many in the audience were left grasping for a means of criticizing Owen for what had been a remarkably uncontroversial talk.

The Duke of Argyll, a noted ornithologist, tried to argue that with its wings, the *Archaeopteryx* was unlikely to have ever taken to the air. But it was a minor point and one that was ultimately difficult to prove either way. Hugh Falconer was on stronger ground when he voiced his opinion that the fossil had not yet received enough study for anyone to say one way or the other whether it was reptile, bird or something in between. He felt that further bones and organs might yet lie in the slab.

Darwin's best friend, the botanist Joseph Hooker pointed out that whilst the affinity of the *Archaeopteryx* could be said to be in doubt, the animal did prove another of Darwin's theories – namely that the geological record is imperfect. He said, 'This animal is only now found in the identical quarries that have been worked for all the lithographic stones used all over Europe, ever since lithography was an art!'

After each time that Owen answered a question successfully, the hall would fall silent in anticipation. All eyes would dart towards Huxley, as everyone waited for him to motion his desire to speak but the man simply sat there in silence, his arms folded across his chest. Darwin's 'bulldog' had withdrawn his teeth and as the audience dispersed into the cool night air there was a sense of anger amongst Darwin's supporters that Huxley had let them down badly. Why, when Huxley was prepared to stand up and declare that humans and apes are related, was he so scared of what looked like a clear-cut example of a 'missing link', the one piece of proof that could immeasurably advance Darwin's cause?

While Huxley brooded, Owen's carefully chosen words and a lack of confrontation meant that most people present accepted his idea that the *Archaeopteryx* was closely related to the birds and probably 'transmuted', assumedly with divine help, from a pterodactyl. Not everybody was so convinced. In a letter to Darwin, Hugh Falconer described the evening thus:

> You are not to put your faith in the slip-shod and hasty account of it [the *Archaeopteryx*] given to the Royal Society. It is a much more astonishing creature than has entered into the conception of the describer [Owen], who compares it with a round winged bird of flight. It actually had at least two long free digits to the fore limb and those depth bearing claws as long and strong as those on the hind legs! Complete with a long tail and other odd things – which I took for a jaw – and you have in the sort of mix-begotten bird-creature the dawn of an oncoming conception *a la* Darwin.

The anonymous 'Y' was more congenial in a further letter to *The Times* published on the 23rd of December. In it he describes Owen's talk but concludes that the *Archaeopteryx* remains 'an enigma, for a bird with a bony tail about twice the length of its body would be scarcely, if at all, less remarkable than a reptile with the feathers and feet of a bird . . . "Let not fools rush in where angels fear to tread!"'

'Y' again states the price paid for the Solnhofen fossils, adding that 'the publication of these high prices in *The Times* will surely operate as a stimulus to further research in the Solenhofen quarries, and may lead to the speedy recovery of the head as well as other missing parts of the "feathered enigma"'.

Now that Owen's pronouncement on the *Archaeopteryx* had been made, news of the fossil began to spread to all sections of the scientific community both in Europe and abroad. The reclusive Charles Darwin, who rarely ventured from his grand house in the Kentish village of Downe, relied on others to bring him the latest news from the outside world of science. At the beginning of January 1863, perhaps prompted by the letters in *The Times*, Darwin wrote to Hugh Falconer, requesting more information on the fossil:

> I particularly wish to hear about the wondrous bird: the case has delighted me, because no group is so isolated as Birds. I much wish to hear when we meet which digits are developed; when examining birds two or three years ago, I distinctly remember writing to [Charles] Lyell that some day a fossil bird would be found with the end of wing cloven, i.e. the bastard-wing and other part, both well developed.

Darwin developed a minor fascination with the *Archaeopteryx* and for several weeks letters batted backwards and forwards between himself and Hugh Falconer as Darwin asked for clarification on certain points. It seems that he was fairly quickly convinced of the potential usefulness of the *Archaeopteryx* to his cause as he went on to describe the fossil as being variously, 'a grand case for me', 'a splendid case' and 'some great peculiarity' in various letters over the coming months.

Darwin was especially delighted because he had long been puzzled about where the birds lay in his new order of evolution. The fossil record of the birds was patchy in the extreme (the discovery of the *Archaeopteryx* doubled their known time on Earth) and it was difficult to see from which animal group they could have evolved. The suggestion that they were in fact descended from the reptiles seemed, to Darwin, a logical one.

When the sixth and final revision of *The Origin of Species* was published in 1872, Darwin had added a small piece on the fossil:

> . . . that strange bird, the Archeopteryx [*sic*], with a long lizard-like tail, bearing a pair of feathers on each joint, and with its wings each furnished with two free claws, has been discovered in the oolitic slates of Solenhofen. Hardly any recent discovery shows more forcibly than this, how little we as yet know of the former inhabitants of the world.

Darwin's comments were typically conservative and do not mention the fossil's controversial transitional nature at all. Even though this was written over a decade after the *Archaeopteryx*'s discovery, Darwin was still keen on avoiding confrontation at all costs.

This was not true of others who chose to write about this fossil. In the months after Owen's talk a number of popular articles dealt with the issue of the *Archaeopteryx*. Most agreed that the animal was a marvel but nonetheless took the anti-Darwinian line, as was the mood of the day. For example, Louis Agassiz, a vociferous opponent of Darwin, claimed that the *Archaeopteryx* was a reptile 'with certain bird-like features'. John Evans, a supporter of Darwin's, was more optimistic, claiming that it linked 'the two great classes of birds and reptile. Its extreme importance as bearing upon *The Origin of Species* must be evident to all.'

The discussion of *Archaeopteryx*'s merits in newspapers and journals did little to change the general view that Owen had got the measure of this fossil. The *Archaeopteryx* and the Darwinians were still missing their champion. Somebody who could stand up and defend their honour. What on earth had happened to silence Huxley?

7

Making Sense of it All

THE BOTANIST JOSEPH Hooker explained Huxley's behaviour to Darwin. According to him, the 'polemical Philosopher is resting on his spear at present, and giving Owen a little more time to commit himself again'. Hugh Falconer was less subtle, almost accusing Huxley of treason against the Darwinian cause. Worst of all was an article by S. J. Mackie in the *Geologist* which interpreted Huxley's silence as a seal of approval for Owen's work on the *Archaeopteryx*:

> Those palaeontologists who were silently present at the Royal Society's meeting, or who were 'conspicuous by their absence,' whose opinions we should have been glad to know, have maintained a significant silence. And the practice of naturalists in this respect seems nowadays like the practice of superior officers in Government establishments, – to find fault whenever they can, but never to give any praise.

Huxley had received letters from Darwin's supporters begging him to examine the *Archaeopteryx* fossil himself and to correct Owen's undoubted errors but all in vain. Huxley's problem with the *Archaeopteryx* was a big one. He had been happy to use the controversy over *The Origin of Species* both to get back at Owen and to enhance his own personal notoriety. However, deep down he still believed in his old theory concerning the continuity of all life throughout the whole fossil record. Huxley's chief problem boiled down to a matter of geological timing.

Whilst he fully accepted that there could be a link between the birds and the reptiles, he could not accept that this change had occurred 150 million years ago during the late Jurassic, as the *Archaeopteryx* implied. He believed that the birds as a group were much older than the *Archaeopteryx*, possibly as many as 200 million years older. Furthermore, Huxley felt that he had some proof that the ancestor to the birds was not a demure form like the *Archaeopteryx* but a much bigger beast not unlike modern flightless birds such as ostriches, emus and rheas. This evidence was in the form of gigantic footprints from Connecticut described by Edward Hitchcock, which looked identical to those of modern flightless birds. To Huxley it was obvious that the ancestors to the birds were gigantic striding, flightless birds, and not a scrawny clawed animal like *Archaeopteryx*.

Most importantly, Hitchcock's Connecticut fossil footprints were Triassic in age and thus over 70 million years older than the *Archaeopteryx*. This large gap seemed to disqualify it from being an ancestor to the birds. It must – it was thought – instead have been a weird type of bird, part of a long-vanished group of clawed avians, and certainly not a missing link. (In fact, as it turned out, Hitchcock's fossil footprints were produced by dinosaurs.)

For these reasons Huxley was inclined to agree with the belief that the *Archaeopteryx* was simply an anomalous type of bird, rather than a missing link, but his pride could not allow him to be seen to be in agreement with Owen. For the time being Huxley would have to ignore the *Archaeopteryx*.

While Huxley brooded, other more unexpected things were happening to the *Archaeopteryx* fossil itself.

Early in 1863 the proceedings of Owen's November talk were published by the Royal Society. The paper stuck to the detail of the original talk but, in a move typical of Owen, he renamed the fossil, replacing the second name, *lithographica*, with his new invention of *macrura*. His excuse was that the original name referred only to von Meyer's fossilized feather and that there was no way of telling whether or not that feather belonged to the

Archaeopteryx specimen now in the British Museum. In reality, Owen simply wanted to get his own name associated with what was rapidly becoming the most famous fossil in the world.

It appears that Owen wanted to go further than this. A foot-note in a magazine article by Henry Woodward notes that Owen was initially going to call the *Archaeopteryx* by its old name of *Gryphosaurus*. Unfortunately for Owen, Hugh Falconer (that strong Darwinian) had been given a copy of Owen's paper to referee by the Royal Society. Falconer was apoplectic at Owen's attempt first to change the main name of *Archaeopteryx* to Griphosaurus and then to give it a new second name. He knew that the change was not for scientific reasons but was meant to boost Owen's already considerable ego. A series of terse letters were exchanged between Falconer and the Royal Society. In the end Falconer made such a fuss about his wanting to use the invalid name of *Gryphosaurus longicaudatus* that Owen was forced to back down at the last minute.

Owen's other reviewer, Philip Egerton, was an old friend of his and was happy to let the name changes go through. Egerton wrote, 'I am of the opinion that the interest and novelty of the subject as well as the intrinsic merit of [Owen's paper] eminently qualify it for publication.' A balance between Falconer and Egerton was reached and in Owen's paper *Gryphosaurus longicaudatus* became *Archaeopteryx macrura,* keeping the important first name but allowing Owen to attach a species name of his own invention to the fossil. Owen's initial desire to use Wagner's anti-Darwinian *Gryphosaurus* again shows exactly where his sympathies lie in the debate regarding 'missing links'.

In the long run Owen was wrong on all counts. A rereading of von Meyer's text reveals that the German palaeontologist did actually name both the London specimen and the feather *Archaeopteryx lithographica.* This is the name that is still in use today, Owen's having long since been consigned to history.

Soon after Owen had finished studying the London specimen, another of the museum's semi-professional curators, John Evans (later Sir John), started to explore a region just above the main body of the *Archaeopteryx* in the hope that there might be some vague remnants of a skull there. In the closing months of 1862 a rumour started to circulate that Evans had found the animal's jaw-bone and that it had teeth. This seemed to be confirmed when, on the 1st of January 1863, the *Geologist* published a brief note saying as much. This prompted an over-enthusiastic Hugh Falconer to write to Evans exclaiming:

> Hail Prince of Audacious Palaeontologists! Tell me all about it. I hear that you have to-day discovered the teeth and jaw of *Archaeopteryx*. To-morrow I expect to hear of your having found the liver and lights! And who knows, but that in the long run you may get hold of the fossil song of the same creature, impressed by harmonic variation on the matrix.

To Darwin, who still mused about the *Archaeopteryx*, news of the skull gave him hope that the fossil might yet be claimed by his supporters. He wrote to Falconer exclaiming, 'Has God demented Owen as a punishment for his crimes that he should overlook such a point?'

The discovery of teeth in the *Archaeopteryx* should indeed have been a major breakthrough for the Darwinians. Teeth are a characteristic of reptiles but not of modern-day birds. It all seemed so straightforward and simple. If the toothed skull were genuine, the *Archaeopteryx* could truly be said to be a mascot for *The Origin of Species*. Needless to say, a problem arose.

Evans had found a jaw complete with four minute teeth – but it was on the *Archaeopteryx*'s counterpart (the bit of rock over-lying the fossil) which made it difficult to be certain that this bone did actually belong to that fossil and not some other one. This uncertainty was exploited by Owen's trusted British Museum ally George Waterhouse, who told anybody who would listen that Evans' discovery was in fact the jaw of a fish and thus could not belong to the *Archaeopteryx* fossil. This caused Hugh Falconer, who had by now become a behind-the-scenes promoter of the *Archaeopteryx*, to remark that it was the first 'feathered fish' that he had ever seen.

Evans went further and claimed to have found traces of the animal's braincase, which he compared to that of a magpie. But all to no avail. The world was happy with Owen's explanation of the *Archaeopteryx* and did not need to hear about Evans' contradictory evidence. Even Huxley did not want believe in Evans' toothed-jaw, which would have upset his belief in the *Archaeopteryx* as a true bird and not some reptilian half-caste. Several years later Huxley was still insisting that the *Archaeopteryx* had no skull.

Hermann von Meyer, who had largely remained quiet since he had coined the name *Archaeopteryx* and who was once assumed to be neutral on the issue of it being a missing link, put in his oar on the side of the anti-Darwinians:

It would appear that the jaw really belongs to the *Archaeopteryx* and arming the jaw with teeth would contradict the view of the *Archaeopteryx* being a bird or embryonic form of bird. But after all, I do not believe that God formed His creatures after the system devised by our philosophical wisdom. Of the classes of birds and modern reptiles as we define them, the Creator knows nothing, and just as little of a prototype, or of a constant embryonic condition of the bird, which might be recognised in the *Archaeopteryx*. The *Archaeopteryx* is of its kind just as perfect a creature as other creatures, and if we are not able to include this fossil in our system, our short-sightedness is alone to blame.

Logic based on supernatural supposition, such as this, is hard to argue against and so, with the weight of the scientific community and the academic press against them, the momentum behind the *Archaeopteryx* as a symbol of Darwin's transmutation of species began to dissipate. The battle for the *Archaeopteryx* had been a badly planned campaign by Darwin's supporters, made worse by the refusal of the movement's two big guns, Huxley and Darwin, to become drawn into the war of words. A golden opportunity had been allowed to slip through their fingers and Darwin's war would have to be fought on other fronts, without the benefit of the *Archaeopteryx* as an accepted and bona fide 'missing link'. How frustrating it must have been.

There is an irony in the way that the story of the *Archaeopteryx* pans out during the remainder of the 1860s, for while the rest of the scientific world began to move on from the discovery, Huxley, contradictory as ever, began to develop an interest in it.

The *Archaeopteryx* issue must have seriously vexed Huxley. Not just scientifically, but also because of his inability to strike at Owen without exposing his belief in the 'persistence' of animals throughout the entire fossil record which in turn would have reflected badly on Darwin. The *Archaeopteryx* had messed up Huxley's neat plans. Prior to its discovery Huxley had outlined a vision of a Triassic period (70 million years before the time of the *Archaeopteryx*) filled with giant ostrich-like birds streaking across the dusty plains, leaving their giant footprints behind for later geologists to marvel at. Now the *Archaeopteryx* had allowed Owen to get the upper hand.

It was probably in response to this problem that, as the debate surrounding the *Archaeopteryx* began to die down, Huxley started to examine the whole area of living birds and their fossil relatives. It was a study begun out of despair for the *Archaeopteryx* but it was eventually to be his greatest triumph. He did not know it at the time, but Huxley was to be drawn deeper into Owen's territory until their feuding would at last be ended once and for all.

The feud between Huxley and Owen was so great that for most of his early scientific career Huxley had refused to take an interest in fossilized plants and animals. He considered these to be Owen's preserve and by trying to contradict the acknowl-edged master of palaeontology Huxley would probably have only shown up his lack of experience in this field. However, as Huxley's fame and power increased he felt better able to tackle the issue of fossils head on. Besides which, Huxley was ever the populist and hungry for media coverage and in mid-Victorian society fossils had captured the public's imagination, with prized specimens being bought and sold for vast sums of money.

Huxley's first dabbling with palaeontology was successful and, like many anatomists before him, he soon became hooked on the seemingly limitless potential offered by the Earth's fossil record.

Over the years Huxley had discovered that one of the best means of attacking Owen was to examine his published work, much of which was either plagiarized or quickly put together and consequently full of holes. The unmasking of these errors was, to Huxley, easy and gained him much publicity.

As he sat in the audience of Owen's talk on the *Archaeopteryx* and its hastily drawn conclusions, Huxley must have instinctively known that there were big problems with the presentation. Although he could say nothing at the time without exposing himself to criticism, he must have determined not to let the matter rest there. But to Huxley the *Archaeopteryx* was not just a problem involving the 'missing link', as it was to his Darwinian colleagues: it undermined his belief in the persistence of animal groups through the fossil record. To understand where the *Archaeopteryx* fitted into this scheme of things would mean systematically taking apart all the known studies on both living and fossilized birds. It was a task that Huxley began shortly after the *Archaeopteryx* debate and within a very short while it pushed him straight on to one of Owen's greatest and most public triumphs – his work on dinosaurs. A clash was now inevitable.

Although the bones and teeth of dinosaurs had first been brought to the attention of science in the 1820s, they were very fragmentary and difficult to interpret. The few known specimens all came from southern England and after much prevaricating it was agreed that at least two types of giant reptile had lived during the Mesozoic era. One of these was a vegetarian beast, named *Iguanodon* because its teeth were shaped like those of an iguana; the other was carnivorous, and was named *Megalosaurus* because of its size. It had sharpened teeth. Very little was known about these animals other than their teeth plus a few leg bones.

Owen's interest in these giant reptiles started early in his career and it is probable that it was he who started the first wave of dino-

saur mania amongst the public during the 1850s. Owen's mete-
oric rise during the 1830s was capped by his 1842 *Report on British
Fossil Reptiles* in which he not only reviewed the giant reptiles
then known, but also coined the term 'dinosaur' (based on his
new Suborder *Dinosauria*) to collectively describe them. As with
most aspects of Owen's work, this report was not free from controversy and it has reasonably been suggested that his work on
fossil reptiles was designed solely to eclipse the work of Gideon
Mantell, a medical doctor and amateur fossil hunter whose work
on fossil reptiles had received much praise and thus threatened to
eclipse Owen's growing reputation. It is certainly true that in his
report Owen had changed many of Mantell's valid scientific
names and claimed some of Mantell's discoveries for himself.

Like Huxley, Gideon Mantell had also found himself locked
in a bitter feud with Owen, this time over the dinosaurs. Even
the young Huxley picked up on this in 1851, observing that 'it
is astonishing with what an intense feeling of hatred Owen is
regarded by the majority of his contemporaries, with Mantell as
arch-hater'.

In 1852 the terminally ill Mantell took an overdose of barbit-
urates. The timing of both Mantell's illness and death were most
unfortunate for the palaeontology world and for the dinosaurs.
Only a few months earlier he had received an invitation from the
Crystal Palace Company to supervise the building of 'full sized
models of the animals and plants of certain geological periods',
which included the dinosaurs. His death meant that the job fell
instead to Richard Owen, whose opinions about how the dinosaurs would have looked in life were greatly different.

Owen's belief in a religious, Creation-led fossil record of
'archetypes' prevented him from having an objective opinion.
The dinosaurs were still known from just a handful of disarticu-
lated remains, and how they would have looked during life was
very much open to question. Mantell's opinion had been that
these beasts were gigantic, reptile-like and truly unlike anything
else that the world had ever seen. Owen, on the other hand, had
to try and fit them into his predetermined view of the evolution
of life, and this did not allow for great differences between living
and fossil animals, all life simply being a variation on the same

basic blueprint. So it was that during 1853 Owen and the mod-
eller Benjamin Waterhouse Hawkins conspired to produce the
first ever life-sized reconstructions of prehistoric creatures for
the London Crystal Palace exhibition. A brace of metal moulded
models were created most of which were, for their time, reasonably accurate reconstructions based on the near-complete skeletons of animals such as the pterodactyls (known from the
Solnhofen) and the 'sea reptiles' *Ichthyosaurus* and *Plesiosaurus*,
recovered from the Jurassic rocks of England, France and
Germany. However, it was the three dinosaurs chosen to be portrayed that were to cause trouble. They were *Iguanodon*,
Megalosaurus and *Hylaeosaurus*, animals which few had hitherto
tried to recreate as they would have looked when alive. With
Mantell dead, Owen's hand was free to do as he pleased and he
certainly took advantage of it.

As one by one the covers were removed from the life-size
dinosaur models, many palaeontologists saw a very strange sight
indeed. Instead of the giant reptiles of the Mesozoic era Owen
seemed to have created a strange race of hybrid animals, part
reptile, part mammal.

Instead of being sleek and graceful, Owen's dinosaurs were all
fat, wallowing animals which prowled about on four thick ele-
phantine legs. In fact, they all resembled some kind of mutated
and heavily overweight rhinoceros, with the only real concession
to the reptiles being their scaly skin and the occasional bit of
ornamentation such as the line of spiky plates running down the
back of *Hylaeosaurus* and the spiked horn on the nose of
Iguanodon which, as later palaeontologists have often observed, he
presented as in reality its thumb. Owen had achieved his aim. By
sleight of hand all his models conformed to his archetypal view
of evolution, looking more like giant mammals than reptiles.

These models are still on show in the new Crystal Palace site
on Sydenham hill in south London and to a modern audience,
to whom dinosaur reconstructions are an everyday sight, they
look unfamiliar. But to a Victorian audience hungry for information about the newly discovered fossil history of their planet,
Owen's and Waterhouse Hawkins' dinosaurs were a marvel: at
last the prehistoric world had been brought to life.

*Designed by Sir Richard Owen to look more like a mammal
than a reptile, this model of* Iguanodon *was used to seat
22 diners in 1853*

Even though Owen had scaled down Mantell's original sizes,
the models were still enormous. The *Iguanodon* alone was 12
metres long and had been built using some 600 bricks, 38 casks
of cement, several tons of iron and thousands of miniature tiles
for its scaly skin. In 1853 this beast famously held a New Year's
Eve dinner party, with twenty-two people (including Owen)
inside it, a publicity stunt which helped announce the arrival of
the models at the Crystal Palace.

The stunt worked and thanks to the Crystal Palace models the
world underwent the first of many bouts of what is now termed
'dinomania'. Mantell's untimely death ensured that in the public's
mind Owen was now largely credited with the discovery and study
of these extinct reptiles and remained so up to and for some time
after his study of the *Archaeopteryx* fossil in 1862. But as Owen
basked in the reflected glory of his purchase and his unhindered
description of the *Archaeopteryx*, behind the scenes Huxley was
beavering away, determined to bring down Owen once and for all.

★

Through the middle part of the 1860s Huxley must have devoted a great deal of work to the study of living and fossilized birds and reptiles. This was no mean feat for Huxley, who was consistently over-committed and overworked, having subscribed himself to so many committees, scientific journals and lectures that he suffered at least two nervous breakdowns during his life.

His study of birds would have taken him right into the lion's den as most of the decent reptile and bird specimens were housed in the British Museum collection which was then under the control of Owen himself. Huxley must have swallowed his pride (and anger), for he would have had to visit the museum on several occasions during the course of his study. No doubt Owen would have kept a keen eye on the types of specimens which Huxley was asking to see. He must have been pleased to note that Huxley was focusing on the Zoology Department's collection of stuffed birds and not the petrified collections in Palaeontology.

By the end of 1866 the world began to get glimpses of the way in which Huxley's mind was turning. At one of his lectures to the 'common people' he commented that the stork and the snake which it swallows were in fact relatives. So he was in effect saying that the birds and reptiles are indeed related, a point that he continued to make during several other lectures in the coming months, but without clearly stating the nature of this link. In April 1867 Huxley produced a staggering and monumental piece of work which completely reclassified all living birds. But it was still not specific on their evolutionary affinity, save for again stating that there was an undoubted link between the reptiles and the birds.

It seems probable that much of Huxley's secretive behaviour regarding the origins of birds probably stems from the fact that he had not made his own mind up about the nature of their relationship to the reptiles. Even though he still outwardly defended *The Origin of Species*, Huxley was still not sure how to reconcile Darwin's natural selection with his own view of evolution. As with much of Huxley's success, fate was to play a big hand in what happened next.

★

In late October 1867 Huxley was making his way north from London to the city of Birmingham when he decided to call in at the Oxford Museum, scene of his triumph over Owen in 1860. Huxley did not make many visits to Oxford as it was still a major centre of anti-Darwinian sentiment and also because he had once been terribly rude about the museum's aged curator, John Phillips, of whom Huxley had once said that in regard to his position on *The Origin of Species* he was neither 'on God's side nor on that of the Devil'.

It seems that Huxley wanted to stop at Oxford in order to look at the museum's exquisite collection of marine reptiles whose ancient skeletons were occasionally pulled from the nearby Jurassic marls. Huxley was cordially greeted by John Phillips and the two set off towards the cases at the rear of the museum where the marine reptile specimens were housed. On the way Phillips made Huxley stop at a case which contained the remains of the carnivorous dinosaur *Megalosaurus*, bits of which had also been recovered from the local region.

Megalosaurus was the first dinosaur to receive a proper scientific description (apart from the now lost bone of *Scrotum humanum* which was erroneously described as a giant fossilized testicle in 1763) and had been described by the eccentric palae-ontologist William Buckland, a man noted for his ambitious attempt to eat one of every animal species on Earth. (The mole was apparently the most repellent.)

Buckland had been the museum's curator prior to Phillips but his successor had also developed a penchant for the dinosaurs in his charge and had delayed Huxley at the *Megalosaurus* display in order to point out the various bones and their function. As Phillips continued to ramble, Huxley's eye began to wander across the exhibit, his mind racing away at its usual unstoppable pace. His eye came to rest on an unusual bone, one that seemed totally out of place among the remains of the giant Jurassic reptile. The bone itself was labelled as part of the animal's shoul-der but the more he looked at it, the odder it seemed.

Suddenly the penny dropped. The bone was in totally the wrong place. Huxley had examined dozens of bird specimens during the previous few years and he realized that the misplaced

Megalosaurus bone was nearly identical to a bone called the ilium, found in the pelvic region of living birds. An almost identical bone in the skeletons of both birds and dinosaurs suggested that these two fossil groups might in fact be related, and might once have shared a common ancestor.

Huxley stopped Phillips in mid-sentence and drew his attention to the bone. The two ruminated for several minutes, Huxley characteristically sure of his new find, Phillips as ever more cautious. In the end they did at least agree that the strange bone was definitely part of the *Megalosaurus'* skeleton and that no other scientist, as far as they knew, had noticed this unusual similarity between the birds and the dinosaurs.

All thoughts of marine reptiles were dismissed. Huxley spent the remainder of his Oxford visit examining the few dinosaur bones in the museum's collection and quizzing Phillips closely about the skeletons of the known types of dinosaur. As the Oxford Museum's ornate Gothic architecture faded into the distance, Huxley became certain that he was on the verge of a major discovery.

As far as Huxley was concerned, his conjectured link between the birds and the reptiles was no longer just a theory. His chance visit to Oxford had furnished him with undeniable proof that the dinosaurs and birds had similar skeletons and were directly related. But if Huxley was to unleash his theory on to the scientific establishment then he would need to make sure that all his bases were covered. This meant looking at as many fossil birds as he could find. He could no longer afford to ignore the *Archaeopteryx*.

The discovery of a possible link between the birds and the dinosaurs left Huxley with a tricky problem. For years his bitter feud with Owen meant that he had shunned the British Museum's palaeontological collections, only going into the Geology Department for social functions or lectures. Since Owen ran his department with half an eye on his own needs, the spectre of Huxley pawing over what Owen considered to be 'his fossils' was something that neither scientist could comfortably entertain.

Unfortunately for Huxley, the British Museum held the greatest collection of fossil material in Britain. It certainly had the majority of the country's dinosaur fossils (the ones which had made Owen a household name in the 1850s) and it had the world's only known *Archaeopteryx* specimen, which was also the oldest known fossilized bird (or bird-reptile 'missing link', depending on your point of view). If he was to really make an impact with his announcement, Huxley had no choice but to visit the British Museum.

Ever the strategist, Huxley chose to do his work at the British Museum during the Christmas period of 1867 when the halls and collection rooms were largely empty of both visitors and staff, leaving him largely free to carry on his work without inter-ruption. Spending Christmas surrounded by the remains of giant reptiles from the Jurassic and Cretaceous periods may not be everybody's idea of a happy yuletide but to Huxley his explora-tions were giving him the best present he could wish for. Delicately handling the gigantic fossilized bones of *Iguanodon*, *Megalosaurus* and others he began to realize that not only did these creatures conform to his bird–dinosaur theory, but that Owen's study of them had been very wide of the mark.

As Huxley fiddled with the dinosaur bones, he sketched them and tried to make them fit into place. Try as he might, he could not get the bones of these great beasts into the rhinocerotic poses given to them by Owen for the Crystal Palace models. In fact, given the bird-like pelvic bone that he had discovered in the Oxford Museum *Megalosaurus*, the only way that the British Museum dinosaurs could be made to walk comfortably was if they had stood on two legs, not four.

In a letter to Phillips, Huxley described his new reconstruc-tion of the massive *Iguanodon* as being 'a sort of cross between a crocodile and a kangaroo with a considerable touch of a bird about the pelvis and legs!' In return Phillips wrote to Huxley to say that his doubts about Huxley's bird–dinosaur affinity had now been replaced by 'a decision' and that he believed Huxley to be correct.

With Phillips as an influential backer, Huxley was now sure that not only were the dinosaurs and birds closely related to one another but that Owen had made a total mess of reconstructing these animals. But the best was yet to come.

Huxley's final action was to tackle his long-standing problem with *Archaeopteryx*, the fossil which itself appeared to be halfway between a reptile and a bird. If his theory was to stand then he would have to take this strange creature into account. He must have approached this fossil with some trepidation after the personal trouble it had caused him and the Darwinian cause in general. Yet, within a few minutes of looking at the delicate fossil skeleton and feathered impressions on the buff Solnhofen limestone, Huxley knew that he was safe. He noticed something about the fossil that every other person to view it had totally missed. It was the beginning of the end for his feud with Owen.

While Owen was always keen to take credit for other people's work, it was more difficult for him to divorce himself from his mistakes which, by the late 1860s, were beginning to turn up regularly.

Even while Huxley was examining dinosaur bones at his museum Owen was getting himself into trouble. His arrogance had landed him in hot water over a debate about the cause of a small hole in the keel of a ship called the *Dreadnought*. The owners claimed that the hole, which had caused the ship to flood, was made by a swordfish striking the boat. However, their insurance company considered it man-made damage and thus not covered under their policy. The British Museum had a swordfish specimen and was duly called in as an expert witness. The museum's senior officers John Gray and Albert Günther prepared a statement saying that a swordfish could in no way have been responsible, it being impossible for it to remove its 'sword' from wood once it had been embedded. The statement was given to Owen to read out in court but when he stood up to do so he decided to give his own opinion, which was in favour of the swordfish theory and disregarded the museum's official policy. Owen's evidence led the court to find in favour of the ship's owners, costing the insurance company £500.

To the outraged John Gray, whose advice had been ignored,

Owen had gone too far and Gray unmasked his error in a series of letters to respected journals whilst at the same time proving that the hole in the ship was the result of a careless repair to the hull. Others joined in the fun, supporting Gray's conclusions and making Owen look thoroughly dishonest and ill-informed. Owen's past behaviour was now gradually catching up on him but he could hardly have expected what was to be delivered to him on the evening of 7th February 1868, the date that Huxley had chosen to reveal his bird–dinosaur link to the world in a talk at the Royal Institution.

It was to be Huxley's belated reply to Owen's *Archaeopteryx* talk of 1862. The five years of deliberation may have been uncharacteristically considered for the normally hot-headed and impulsive Huxley, but the reply was to be decisive and to settle their old feud once and for all.

Huxley was confident as always. This time he could afford to be, for this time he was sitting on the discovery that would make his career. He believed that he could solve the long-standing debate regarding that great question – what are the origins of birds? A hint of what was to come could be gathered from the title of his talk: 'On the animals which are most nearly intermediate between Birds and Reptiles'.

On the podium Huxley began his talk in a sombre tone. 'We who believe in evolution are often asked to produce solid evidence to prove our theories. If one animal group can evolve into another then why do we have so many gaps in the fossil record? Where, ask our critics, are the missing links? Tonight I believe that this question can at last be answered by looking at that most isolated group of living animals, the birds.'

He continued by explaining that whilst many evolutionists had long believed the birds to have been descended from the reptiles, the proof had yet to be forthcoming. In searching for this proof it was necessary to ask two simple questions:

– Are there any fossil birds which show greater reptilian characteristics than any living bird?
– Are there any fossil reptiles which are more bird-like than any living reptile?

'I believe,' said the serious-looking Huxley, 'that I can answer both questions in the affirmative.' With no further ado he introduced his audience to the *Archaeopteryx* and to a small meat-eating (theropod) dinosaur called *Compsognathus*, also from the Solnhofen limestone.

As he stood before them, Huxley patiently pointed out the numerous similarities between the skeleton of *Archaeopteryx* and that of the dinosaur *Compsognathus*. The similarities were indeed obvious for all to see. To all intents and purposes *Compsognathus* was identical to *Archaeopteryx*, except for the feathers. The similarities between the tail, arms, claws, legs, feet and pelvis of both animals were so close as to be outstanding. Effectively Huxley was saying that *Archaeopteryx* had been a dinosaur with feathers.

'Birds,' he confidently stated, 'are evolved from dinosaurs and the proof is here in these fossils. These are your missing links.'

It may have been a long time coming but Huxley's pronouncement on the *Archaeopteryx* was a masterpiece. Of the hundreds of talks that Huxley delivered during his lifetime, this is the one for which he is best remembered. His suggestion that birds had evolved from the dinosaurs was cutting edge but his ability to point to an actual missing link in defence of Darwin was better still. No longer would Darwinians have to mumble about imperfections in the fossil record covering up the missing links. Now they had *Archaeopteryx*. But Huxley hadn't finished. He had one further score to settle.

Almost as an afterthought, he mentioned an interesting feature of the *Archaeopteryx* which had not been noted before. It was, said Huxley, actually lying face down on its slab and not face up as described by Richard Owen in 1862. Huxley took great delight in quoting from Owen's 1862 talk on the *Archaeopteryx* before contradicting it with his own new observations. Finally he demonstrated that apart from anything else Owen had got the legs confused. 'It seems that Professor Owen cannot tell his left foot from his right', Huxley drily commented. This was a very basic anatomical error and in the following few minutes Huxley made Owen look extremely incompetent. It was an error too far

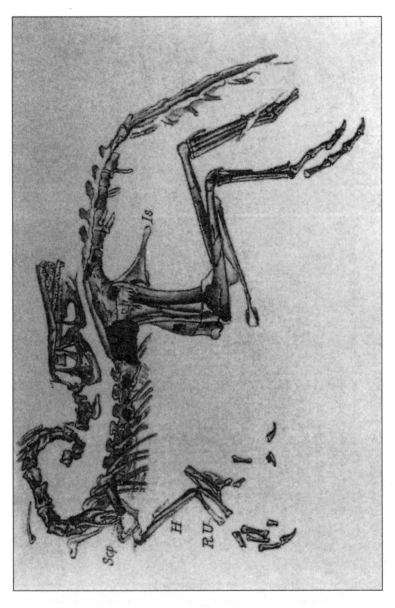

Compsognathus, *a small dinosaur found in the same quarries as*
Archaeopteryx. *Huxley claimed that the skeletons of*
Compsognathus *and* Archaeopteryx *shared similarities*

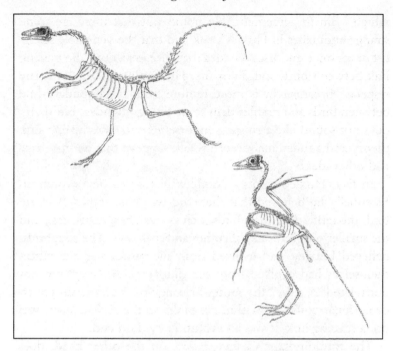

A drawing of Archaeopteryx*'s skeleton next to that of*
Compsognathus

on Owen's part and one that would not be easily forgotten by
his many enemies. Huxley had scored a major victory.

Huxley's demonstration of the missing links between birds and
dinosaurs was his making. From that day onwards he ceased to
be seen as a maverick evolutionist and atheist and was portrayed
as a great popular naturalist. There could be no further question-
ing of his status as Darwin's champion. The old man himself
approved of Huxley's interpretation of the *Archaeopteryx*. He had
long been perplexed by the patchy fossil history of the birds and
was delighted that they could now be linked to the dinosaurs.

But was the 1868 talk really what it appeared to be? Could it
in fact have been a smokescreen cleverly crafted by Huxley?

Adrian Desmond, author of the finest Huxley biography,
gives a new twist to this talk and its meaning and it is one with

which I am in agreement. He points out that there are some strange anomalies in Huxley's talk and that the venerable scientist never once endorses the idea that *Archaeopteryx* is the missing link between birds and dinosaurs. His comment that 'In many respects *Archaeopteryx* is more remote from the boundary-line between birds and reptiles than some living [flightless birds] are' does not sound like a ringing endorsement for the missing-link theory and a fuller analysis of his talk suggests that he may have had other ideas.

In fact, Huxley paints a complex picture of bird evolution. Essentially he believed that there are two main types of living bird, the ratites (flightless birds such as ostriches, emus, etc.) and the smaller songbirds like thrushes and sparrows. The songbirds, believed Huxley, had evolved from the ratites and the ratites themselves had evolved from the dinosaurs. *Archaeopteryx* was not related to either the ratites or songbirds but was simply an evolutionary offshoot within the birds. So the *Archaeopteryx* was not a missing link, it was an evolutionary dead end.

The tiny dinosaur *Compsognathus*, on the other hand, does show both reptilian and bird characteristics in its skeleton, even though it did not have feathers. According to Huxley *Compsognathus* is the missing link: 'a still nearer approximation [than *Archaeopteryx*] to the "missing link" between reptiles and birds'.

Desmond points out that a few years later, in 1876, Huxley is more specific as he lines up the ratites as the 'scanty modern heirs of the great multitude of creatures which once connected Birds with Reptiles'.

Far from endorsing the *Archaeopteryx* as a missing link, Huxley was actually still clinging to his belief in the persistence of life. At 150 million years old *Archaeopteryx* was too young for his missing link. He was looking much further back in time to the Triassic, 220 million years ago. Yes, the birds are descended from the dinosaurs but *not* through *Archaeopteryx*. Although he made it appear as though he was turning the *Archaeopteryx* into a missing link, he had already assigned this role to the large flightless birds. Huxley's belief in persistence was itself very persistent.

Somehow Huxley's ambiguous statements on bird evolution

got lost in the background and it was widely assumed that he had declared *Archaeopteryx* to be the missing link between living birds and dinosaurs like *Compsognathus*. Whatever the actual detail, Huxley had provided the world with its first definite statement on the issue of the origin of the birds and he would be forever remembered as the person who first suggested that the humble backyard blackbird was in fact a dinosaur in disguise.

The universal praise which Huxley received for his 1868 talk placed his star firmly in the ascendant. In contrast, Owen's was descending. Within a few years Huxley had been given Owen's title of Britain's greatest naturalist. Owen did not disappear from the scene altogether, he had too many influential friends for that, but he was increasingly seen as part of an old-fashioned and embittered scientific elite whose best days had long since gone.

The world of the late 1860s no longer wanted their scientists to be arrogant, unwaveringly correct and disconnected from ordinary society. This was an era of populism when complex ideas needed to be explained and the evidence presented for all to see. Owen's old guard had always despised the lower social ranks and kept themselves as far apart from them as possible. Most were gentleman scientists whose family fortunes and connections paid for their positions, work and field trips; they needed no help from the state and so, in their minds at least, owed the state no duty beyond publishing their discoveries.

Fortunately most in Huxley's generation saw things differently. Huxley and many of his contemporaries were not from the landed gentry and had had to fight hard to get themselves accepted into the scientific elite. They often had to give street-level lectures to earn money on the side while state museums and universities paid their bread and butter wages. Many, including Huxley, did not forget the duty they owed to the state and its people and would give lectures or write popular science books at every opportunity. It is little wonder that these 'friendly' scientists came to replace the self-appointed and distant idols of yesteryear. Huxley's talk on the 7th of February 1868 effectively marked the changing of the guard from the staid conservative-minded camp of Owen and his friends to the more progressive and free-thinking Huxley, Darwin *et al.*

Owen may have lost in this feud but he was still held in high regard by many and he was, after all, still a capable, if somewhat sneaky, anatomist. His name continued to appear in the papers and he was the favourite scientist of the ageing Queen Victoria but his once shiny reputation had been severely tarnished by Huxley. These days he was more often ignored by his peers and in his later years he took to rewriting much of his own past, at one stage claiming to have invented Darwin's theory of natural selection. When he heard of this, Darwin laughed.

The embittered Richard Owen eventually died in 1892 at the ripe old age of eighty-eight. Even now people are still trying to unravel the many parts of this complex man whose arrogance drove him to become famous and then discredited, his eventual downfall coming about because he had not noticed which way up the *Archaeopteryx* fossil was lying on its slab. One wonders if during his later years Owen ever regretted setting eyes on the wretched fossil.

Some of Owen's more bizarre lies managed to outlive him. It seems that somehow he convinced his grandson that he and Huxley had in fact been the best of friends during life. After Owen's death the grandson approached Huxley to see if he would write a critical review of Owen's work. Even more bizarrely, Huxley accepted. Perhaps it was his attempt to have the final word over the cantankerous old man with whom he had spent so many years battling.

One feud over the *Archaeopteryx* may have ended in victory for Huxley but the fossil's effect on Victorian society was not yet over. Inadvertently, Huxley had started another far worse battle across the Atlantic – and this one was to cost people their lives and fortunes.

The Toothed Birds

THE EFFECT THAT the *Archaeopteryx* can have on people is electrifying and instantaneous. It is a fossil that does not brook indifference from the scientists who have gazed upon it but inspires them to do quite unexpected things. Within the first few years of its discovery this small and delicate denizen of the Jurassic managed to radically alter the lives of Andreas Wagner, Hermann von Meyer, Richard Owen, Charles Darwin, Thomas Huxley and many others besides. These people were the front wave in the war which occurred over the understanding of the *Archaeopteryx*. Behind them were others eagerly waiting to enter the controversy that has bubbled around it from the time of its discovery to the current day.

One such battle had it roots way back in 1863 shortly after the publication of Owen's *Archaeopteryx* paper. In Germany, Edward Drinker Cope, a young American graduate, was being shown around the Munich Bavarian State Collection's palaeontology section by Alfred Oppel, the man who had surreptitiously made a sketch of the *Archaeopteryx* under the nose of Carl Häberlein a couple of years previously.

The American was especially keen on the museum's gigantic collection of Solnhofen fossils, about which he enthused to his family in letters back home. Evidently Oppel managed to impart some of his enthusiasm for the *Archaeopteryx* to Cope for one of his letters contained a reference to this fossil even though it had left Bavaria some months previously. Cope's travels took him from Munich to London, where he viewed the real *Archaeopteryx* specimen in the British Museum. As ever, the effect was profound.

That evening a friend called round at Cope's London residence to find the young man in a state of considerable distress and burning all of the drawings that he had made during his tour of Europe's museums. It was all his friend could do to stop him throwing on to the fire the notes which went with them. The young Cope had suffered a minor breakdown and was quickly shipped back to his family in native Pennsylvania where it took him several months to recover.

Cope's distress was of a religious nature. He was the son of a rich Philadelphian shipping magnate and had inherited not only his father's love of natural history but his strict devotion to the Quaker religion. Edward Cope had a particular love of fossils and so his father had paid for him to study at a number of local institutions before sending him on his fateful European tour. The Copes were a God-fearing family so although the idea of fossils themselves was tolerated, the idea of evolution was most certainly not. As Creationists, the Copes believed that the world with all its life had been made in seven days and was at best only a few thousand years old.

Edward Cope's tour of Europe left him with a deep theological problem. As he viewed hundreds of exotic fossils brought to the museums of Europe from around the globe, Cope realized that the Earth must be considerably older than the 6,000 years given by most biblical scholars. Viewing the *Archaeopteryx* (which he described as being 'nearer bird than reptile but is neither') made him see that all the talk of Darwin's *Origin of Species* might just be true. Here was an animal which directly contradicted his Creationist beliefs. While other religiously minded scientists, such as Owen and Wagner, had chosen to assimilate the *Archaeopteryx* into their own theologically influenced version of the evolution story, Cope's mind could not handle the contradiction. Hence the breakdown. After his recovery a donation by his father bought his son entry into Haverford College, Pennsylvania, where he became Professor of Zoology.

★

Professor Edward Drinker Cope. The London Archaeopteryx *was the cause of his first breakdown*

In 1863, during his European tour, Edward Cope had had the chance to meet with a fellow countryman of his in Berlin. This man was Othniel Charles Marsh and like Cope he was on a family-sponsored tour of the major European palaeontology museums. Marsh later wrote of this meeting that 'Cope called on me with great frankness, confided to me some of the many troubles that even then beset him. My sympathy was aroused, and although I had some doubts of his sanity, I gave him good advice and was willing to be his friend'.

After what sounds like a strained meeting, the two gentlemen went their separate ways. Cope went to London where his breakdown occurred while Marsh travelled down to Pappenheim, spending several weeks searching the Solnhofen quarries for fossils. Eventually he moved on to London where he too viewed the *Archaeopteryx* and, by all accounts, made quite an impression on the various scientists with whom he made contact. Unlike Cope, Marsh had shed all religious convictions and in the aftermath of his European tour became convinced that Darwin's doctrine of evolution through natural selection was the way forward for palaeontology. Marsh returned to America having gained both experience and vital contacts whilst abroad.

The similarities between Cope's background and that of Othniel Charles Marsh are remarkable. Although nine years older than Cope, Marsh too had been born to a well-established, well-to-do and strongly religious American family. While Cope's main benefactor was his father, Marsh's was his exceedingly rich uncle, George Peabody. The young Marsh too was a keen naturalist but a slow learner, only taking an interest in academic matters late in his twenties before gradually drifting into the field of palaeontology in the early 1860s.

After funding him through further education, George Peabody sent his nephew on a European tour only a matter of months behind Cope. The final coincidence was George Peabody's considerable donation to Yale University which resulted in the construction of a museum. Perhaps unsurprisingly, Marsh became its Professor of Palaeontology. Thus it was that by 1865, and despite the age gap between them, both Marsh

Professor Othniel Marsh, a close friend of Thomas Huxley and the sworn enemy of Edward Cope

and Cope were in an almost identical situation. Both had even sought out the *Archaeopteryx*, although the conclusions they had drawn from this fossil were completely different. Such differing opinions were to characterize the lives of these two academics, leading to an open hostility that makes Huxley and Owen's feud look quite tame.

During the mid-1860s America was only just beginning to hint at its massive potential for the field of palaeontology. Most of the continent's interior remained unexplored but the advent of the railroad and large numbers of immigrants hungry for farmland was rapidly opening up the frontiers of the 'wild west', usually to the cost of its native inhabitants. While Europe's well-known fossil quarries were being worked to death by over-keen Victorian scientists, the New World was still hiding its treasures.

Both Marsh and Cope were keen to make their mark on science, and as soon as possible. In order to do so both chose the well-trodden path to palaeontology fame of linking their names to exciting new fossil discoveries. The chief drawback to this strategy was that palaeontological expeditions were expensive and, in those days, a dangerous undertaking, given the periodic battles between the pioneers and native American tribes.

Fortunately, Marsh and Cope still had their wealthy family backers and were young enough to be oblivious to the possibility of danger. Soon both men were out in the field making small but significant discoveries. Although aware of each other's presence in the general field of palaeontology there is no real evidence of any animosity between the two men at this stage. All this was to rapidly change and the resultant falling out between Marsh and Cope would have a great effect on how the *Archaeopteryx* and, indeed, the whole concept of evolution would be viewed by future generations of scientists.

The first success went to Cope, who had discovered and studied a remarkably complete new species of dinosaur which he named *Laelaps* after the dog of the goddess Diana. Like Huxley, who at this exact time was sitting in the British Museum surrounded by Owen's dinosaur bones, Cope had had a great deal of trouble in reconstructing *Laelaps* in Owen's standard four-legged pose. Unknown to each other, Huxley and Cope had come to the selfsame conclusion – that some species of dinosaur actually walked on two legs and that there were remarkable similarities between the skeletons of birds and dinosaurs.

Huxley was easily the more famous of the two and it was his February 1868 talk that made the headlines, but when he became aware of Cope's work he published another paper on the subject, making it clear that Cope was a co-discoverer and praising his work. 'It is very satisfactory to me,' wrote Huxley, 'to find that so able an anatomist as Prof. Cope should have been led by the force of facts to arrive, simultaneously with myself, at conclusions so similar in their general character with my own.' It was to be the last time that Huxley would ever praise Edward Cope.

Cope, who was hungry for publicity, welcomed praise from somebody as respected as Huxley and became convinced that he was on the edge of worldwide fame. Events were, however, not to favour him.

While Cope had been steadily trying to make a name for himself through scientific endeavour, Marsh had a different tactic, choosing to try and impress the popular press with tales of high adventure and bravado. Marsh played on the wild west element of his fossil expeditions, spreading stories of dangerous encounters with 'Red Indians', wild animals and tornadoes and turning himself into some kind of Indiana Jones.

The press lapped it up and portrayed Marsh as being a cross between an intellectual and a cowboy. Photographs of him with a geological hammer in one hand and a gun in the other served to enhance this idea. The fact that he was dodging arrows while contributing to the scientific prestige of America was noted.

A classic example of Marsh's publicity-hunting came hot on the heels of Cope's *Laelaps* discovery. In 1869 the question of evolution was causing a stir in the Americas with the attitude towards it being even more sceptical than in Europe. In the autumn of that year the fossil of a giant man, over three metres tall, was dug up in the Onondaga Valley, New York. At once the fossil was claimed as clear proof that Darwin's *Origin of Species* was wrong and that humans had been alive on Earth millions of years ago.

The discovery created quite a stir and it was not long before the national newspapers were full of the story. Marsh must have spotted its publicity potential and as he was one of the few public advocates of *The Origin of Species* he decided to go along to the Onondaga Valley and take a closer look at the fossil. One glance confirmed his suspicions: the 'fossil man' was simply a crude figure sculpted from gypsum. Tool marks were still visible on its surface.

Marsh wrote several letters to the press announcing the forgery (it later turned out that the 'fossil' had been manufactured and buried by pro-Darwinians trying to fool local biblical scientists). The letters were printed locally, then reprinted nationally and eventually internationally. The 'Onondaga Giant' affair captured the public's imagination and Marsh's contribution was welcomed by both the press barons and the scientific establishment. From that moment on Marsh was regularly called upon by journalists keen to seek his opinion on scientific matters. On top of his image as an adventurer, he was now also a science populist.

Cope had always held ambitions for fame and was irritated to see that whilst his own serious fossil discoveries received a few lines at the back of the paper, Marsh could command headlines by simply proffering his opinion. Jealousy set in, which was not helped at all when Marsh wrote a letter to the *New York Herald* demonstrating that Cope had wrongly reconstructed an ancient long-necked plesiosaur by sticking the animal's skull on the end of its tail instead of its neck. Several tense letters were exchanged between the two. The rivalry had begun.

By 1870 both men had started to organize large self-financing expeditions into the American Midwest. They were searching for the giant marine 'sea serpent' fossils (plesiosaurs and mosasaurs) which were being recovered from this region. Working in the same part of the country and chasing after the same fossils served to crank up the competition between the two professors. A network of spies and double agents grew up in both camps, reporting every movement and discovery back to their respective paymasters. As time went on so the tricks became more dirty. False trails were laid, productive quarries were destroyed to prevent their use by anyone else and landlords paid to trick or refuse permission to dig to any rivals.

The event that was to turn Cope's jealousy of Marsh into hatred, which in turn would lead to all-out war, occurred in 1872. It was an event that was also to have a radical effect on the story of the *Archaeopteryx*.

That year Marsh had returned from an extensive fossil-collecting trip in Kansas. Among his haul was an excellent, but headless, skeleton of the ancient bird *Hesperornis*, a flightless two-metre-high giant which swam and hunted in the Cretaceous seas of 75 million years ago. After the controversial *Archaeopteryx*, *Hesperornis* was the second-oldest known fossil bird but no complete specimens had been found. For years odd bits and pieces of its bones had been recovered from Kansas. These bones were just about recognizable as being avian but the real nature of the beast had yet to be seen. Now Marsh's 1872 expedition had produced the first complete skeleton of *Hesperornis*.

Since his viewing of the *Archaeopteryx*, Marsh had been a fascinated by bird evolution and he knew the scientific appeal that the subject still held but his *Hesperornis* skeleton was without a skull and so would have to wait its turn to be studied. In the meantime he ordered one of his assistants to keep an eye open for any more specimens that might come to light. A few months later a box full of scrappy and unprepared fossils arrived on Marsh's desk, none of which looked terribly promising. Nonetheless, amongst the rubble were some skull and jaw fragments which were accompanied by a note:

> The hollow bones are part of a bird, and the two jaws belong to a saurian. The latter is peculiar, and I wish I had some of the vertebrae for comparison with other Kansas species.

Marsh ordered the bones to be cleaned. When the delicate specimens were returned to him, he was astounded. The bones were from a new type of ancient bird, which Marsh named *Ichthyornis*, but the fossil jaws were puzzling. Marsh was at first unsure, describing the jaws as being from a new type of reptile which he named *Colonosaurus* but something did not seem right and a few weeks later he returned to the specimen, ordering them to be further prepared. At last Marsh realized that the jaws and the bones of *Ichthyornis* actually belonged to the same animal. Although it resembled a modern bird, *Ichthyornis* had a jaw that was unmistakably filled with a row of tiny needle-like teeth. It was a eureka moment and one that would be the making of Marsh.

Ten years earlier the scientific establishment (including Thomas Huxley) had firmly rejected John Evans' discovery of the *Archaeopteryx*'s toothed jaw: a bird with teeth would have backed up the idea that the *Archaeopteryx* was a bird–reptile cross. Now here was evidence that simply could not be ignored. There were unquestionably birds with teeth living during the time of the dinosaurs.

Whereas the *Archaeopteryx*'s skeleton would have been described as being that of a reptile if it were not for the impressions of feathers around it, that of *Ichthyornis* was unmistakably a bird even though no fossil feathers had been found with it. However, having a toothed beak did give it a reptilian element and while the Darwinian community had lost the opportunity to claim the *Archaeopteryx* for themselves, *Ichthyornis* was in the hands of an accomplished self-publicist and avowed Darwinian. Marsh did not lose the opportunity and at once dashed off a preliminary paper to the scientific press in which he firmly stated what others had not been able to do with regard to the *Archaeopteryx*: 'The fortunate discovery of these interesting fossils,' wrote Marsh, 'does much to break down the old distinction between Birds and Reptiles, which the *Archaeopteryx* has so materially diminished.'

To Marsh *Ichthyornis* was an even better missing link and the ultimate proof of Huxley's assertion that the birds and reptiles did indeed share a common ancestor. Later he was to state this in even more unequivocal terms:

The teeth [of *Ichthyornis*] may be regarded as a character inherited from a reptilian ancestry. Their strong resemblance to the teeth of reptiles, in form, structure, and succession, is

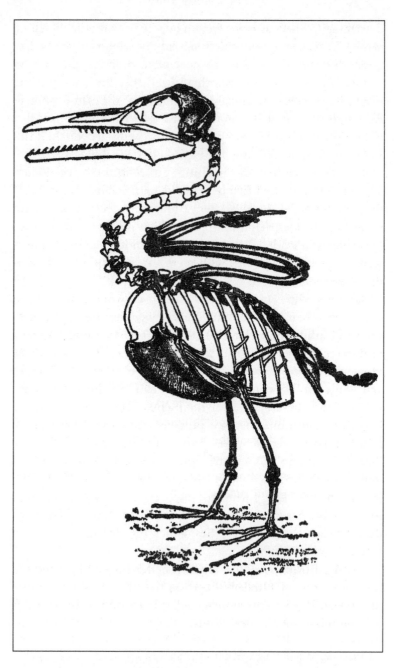

Ichthyornis, *one of Marsh's toothed birds which would be his greatest triumph and then later initiate his downfall*

evidence of this . . . [This bird] was carnivorous in habit, and doubtless was descended from a long line of rapacious ancestors.

From the moment that news of Marsh's discovery hit the street, praise began to pour in. One scientist said he was as 'startled, I might almost say, as the midwife who first looked into the mouth of the baby Richard Third'. Henry Osborne, a close friend of Cope's, later claimed it constituted 'the most important single palaeontological discovery of his life'. The popular scientific press and newspapers were equally kind.

Marsh had succeeded where practically every other Darwinian supporter had failed – in drawing the public's attention to the idea that there could really be missing links lurking in the fossil record and that the idea of evolution might not be so fanciful after all.

Not all the response was overwhelmingly favourable. A seething Cope damned Marsh with faint praise by describing his discovery as being 'simply delightful'. Not only was Cope distraught at the idea that his rival was once again stealing the limelight, but he was still unconvinced by the concept of evolution through natural selection. He preferred Owen's idea of God-inspired archetypes and thus had no truck with missing links. If the discovery of the toothed birds was the making of Marsh, it was also the start of the feud proper between himself and Cope whose attempts to find fame had so far been eclipsed by Marsh's outrageous success.

Probably the greatest success of Marsh's toothed bird discovery was that it finally got him noticed across the Atlantic in the all-powerful academic institutions of England, France and Germany. Already Marsh had many contacts in Europe but all the running in these relationships had had to come from his end. Suddenly the roles were reversed. One person in particular took an interest in Marsh's work and that was Thomas Huxley.

It had been several years since Huxley had vanquished Owen and the intervening time had seen him take Owen's place as the

foremost naturalist and palaeontologist in the world. Huxley still
held a deep interest in the evolution of birds and still harboured
the belief that whilst the birds were probably descended from the
dinosaurs, the link would be found through the giant flightless
birds and not the diminutive *Archaeopteryx*. Marsh's two-metre-
high flightless and toothed Cretaceous giants seemed to fit into
this view of bird evolution. A correspondence began between
the two. Huxley was later to write of Marsh's find that:

> The discovery of the toothed birds of the cretaceous for-
> mation in North America by Professor Marsh completed
> the series of transitional forms between the birds and rep-
> tiles, and removed Mr. Darwin's proposition that 'many
> animal forms of life have been utterly lost, through which
> the early progenitors of birds were formerly connected
> with early progenitors of the other vertebrate classes,' from
> the region of hypothesis to that of demonstrable fact.

We can be in little doubt as to the importance which Huxley
(and many others) attributed to Marsh's toothed birds.

The success of *Ichthyornis* and *Hesperornis* persuaded Marsh
that he needed more and better specimens so that he could write
a more detailed description. Fortunately for him, the fossil birds
of Kansas proved to be more abundant than those of the
Solnhofen quarries of Germany and in 1876 alone three beautiful specimens of *Hesperornis* came to light complete with their
toothed skulls. They arrived just in the nick of time, for in
August of that year Huxley was to make his first visit to the
United States having been tempted there by the offer of a
nationwide lecture tour. His fame was such that he was being
offered the magnificent sum of $1,000 per lecture. A press
entourage to report his every movement completed Huxley's
rock star image.

His tour brought him to Yale in the summer of 1876. He was
sufficiently friendly with Marsh to accept an offer of accommodation in Marsh's Uncle George's plush flat, and spent his evenings at Marsh's own large mansion on the edge of town. The two
scientists became firm friends, Marsh regaling Huxley with tales

of his wild west palaeontological adventures. These were relayed back to England in Huxley's letters to his wife, in which Marsh is described as 'a wonderfully good fellow, full of fun and stories about his western adventures, and the collection of fossils is the most wonderful thing I ever saw'.

Marsh's fossils were indeed spectacular and wholly different from anything to be seen in Europe. There were, of course, the specimens of *Hesperornis* and *Ichthyornis*, at which Huxley's mind boggled. He became even more convinced that Marsh had discovered the key evidence in favour of evolution.

Other surprises were in store. Marsh had also arranged for Huxley to see some giant bird footprints (which are actually those of a dinosaur) in a nearby rock formation. Such ancient footprints fitted well with Huxley's ideas of giant flightless birds having lived before the time of *Archaeopteryx*.

Most of the time was, however, spent in the lab, with Huxley asking questions about some animal or other and Marsh sending his assistants off to fetch various numbered boxes. 'At each inquiry,' wrote Huxley's son Leonard, 'Professor Marsh would simply turn to his assistant and bid him fetch box number so and so, until Huxley turned upon him and said, "I believe you are a magician; whatever I want, you just conjure up!"'

The biggest reaction of all was produced by a series of fossilized horse specimens which Marsh had been collecting for several years from rock formations of different ages. When put in order of age the fossils seemed to show something remarkable. The oldest horses (aged about 50 million years) were tiny cat-sized animals with four-toed feet, but as the specimens became younger in age the size of the horses increased and the number of toes decreased from four to three and then, eventually, to the one-toed animal we know now.

Huxley was astounded. If the toothed birds had been evidence of the reality of missing links, then Huxley found before him not a series of missing links, but a continuous and smooth series of fossils each slightly more advanced than the last, through to the modern horse. It was a revelation.

To say that Huxley's visit to Marsh was a success is an understatement. Many of his lectures were rewritten to include the

marvels he had witnessed in Marsh's collection. The distinguished English scientist acted as though he were Marsh's unpaid
publicist, promoting his name whenever the opportunity arose.
To one colleague Huxley wrote that 'I think that I am quite safe
in adding that no collection which has hitherto been formed
approaches that made by Prof. Marsh in the completeness of the
chain of evidence by which certain existing mammals are connected with their older Tertiary ancestry.'

Marsh basked in this glory. In 1877 he was asked to deliver a
keynote speech to the American Association for the
Advancement of Science in Nashville. Following Huxley's
example, Marsh chose to use the toothed birds as his ultimate
testament to the proof of Darwinian evolution:

> To doubt evolution today is to doubt science, and science
> is only another name for truth . . . The classes of Birds and
> Reptiles, as now living, are separated by a gulf so profound
> that a few years since it was cited as the most important
> break in the animal series, and one which that doctrine
> could not bridge over. Since then, as Huxley has clearly
> shown, the gap has been virtually filled by the discovery of
> bird-like Reptiles and reptilian Birds . . . the stepping stones
> by which the evolutionist of today leads the doubting
> brother across the shallow remnant of the gulf, once
> thought impassable.

Cope was in the audience that night and he must have seethed
as the applause for Marsh's talk rippled around him. The next
day the *Daily American* reprinted Marsh's talk in full, proclaiming
him to be the American equivalent of Darwin. In many respects
he was more than this, for while Darwin had shied away from
promoting his great idea Marsh had waded in and was as a result
converting key people in what was still a very sceptical country.

Marsh's hospitality to Huxley was returned a couple of years
later when he made a visit to London. Huxley took charge of
his schedule and ensured that he was well looked after and that
he met everyone who was anyone in British science.

The same was not true for Cope. When he went to England

a few months after Marsh he received a very different reception. Cope complained to his wife that Huxley had been indifferent to him, which he blamed solely on Marsh.

'Huxley has such influence,' Cope complained bitterly, 'not only on account of his writings but because of his readiness as a speaker and his quick wit, which I had occasion to hear several times.'

There is every possibility that Marsh had poisoned Huxley against Cope, but equally well Cope's loose alliance with Richard Owen may have been a cause. Huxley had also received at least one letter warning him about Cope and claiming that he deserved 'the contempt of all the scientific men of the country'. Huxley's rejection must have come as a particularly bad blow considering the praise he had once given Cope for advocating the dinosaur *Laelaps* as being a relative to the birds. His reputation was at a low ebb.

The feud between Cope and Marsh is most famous for the 'bone war' which occurred in the period immediately after Huxley had anointed Marsh and snubbed Cope.

Until this point the feud had largely been a paper one, with both Cope and Marsh using scientific conventions to subtly destroy each other's credibility. Marsh, for example, once proved that Cope had fiddled the dates on a series of papers he had submitted to a journal; Cope had caused Marsh to change the names of several of his new species after proving them to have been used elsewhere already. Subterfuge in the field had mostly been limited to spying, the laying of false trails and the spoiling of each other's fossil sites.

All this changed when, in 1877, Cope got word that giant bones had been found in the badlands of south-eastern Wyoming. He duly turned up with a digging party and found the most monstrous bones that science had ever seen: leg bones which were metres in length and vertebrae which took several men to lift.

Cope had found the world's first dinosaur quarry site, a bluff of hard sandstone which was thick with gigantic bones. He began to assemble a giant four-legged *Diplodocus*-like dinosaur the size of which was, in those days, hitherto unimagined. The science community took notice and at last Cope began to get the favourable press he desired.

Incensed that his rival had stolen a march on him, Marsh acted immediately and, by chance, caught wind of a rumour of similar bones having been found at a small place called Como Bluff near Laramie in Wyoming. A visit surpassed his wildest dreams. The hillside was packed full of giant bones which proved to be more numerous and of better quality than Cope's. They were also easier to extract from the rock and within a very short time Marsh had removed and assembled a wide range of Jurassic giants. The names he gave to some of them have since become household terms, *Stegosaurus*, *Brontosaurus*, *Diplodocus* and *Allosaurus*.

Cope too was finding and naming new specimens but the process was a costly one and so both Cope and Marsh began to sell casts of their assembled skeletons to museums across the world. As people gradually got to see these giant monsters a new phase of dinomania began to take hold of the public.

Jealousy between the two palaeontologists led them to scour the hills of Wyoming and Utah for new and exciting dinosaur finds. Each skeleton would be hastily dug from the ground, sketched, named and rushed into print in an attempt to steal the other's thunder. This frantic burst of activity has not been matched since. Within only a few years Marsh and Cope had managed to find and name sixty-six dinosaur species (Cope named twenty-nine, Marsh thirty-seven) plus dozens of pterosaur, crocodile and other fossils. Many mistakes were made (*Brontosaurus*, for example, was assembled by Marsh with the wrong skull on it and later had to be renamed *Apatosaurus*) but after the scrappy bones collected from England and elsewhere, the world was at last being introduced to complete and gigantic dinosaur skeletons.

Looking at the upright, two-legged reconstructions of Cope and Marsh's carnivorous dinosaurs, it was immediately obvious to all and sundry that Huxley had been entirely correct in his belief that these animals were bipedal. Thanks to the hatred generated between two scientists, the dinosaurs had shaken off Owen's Crystal Palace image and had come of age.

It must have been obvious to both Cope and Marsh that their feud could not go on for ever and that one day one of them would be taken beyond breaking point. It was Cope who was first to admit defeat. He had spent a fortune on his field expeditions and had made a number of unwise investments in mining firms. Despite his run of success with the dinosaurs, by 1880 he found himself very low on money, his personal fortune now standing at next to nothing. It was the beginning of the end for this rather sad character.

First his field expeditions had to cease, forcing him home again. Then his wife and child left him, perhaps as a consequence of his being about the house again after years absent on fieldwork absence. The financial crisis continued to bite deep and he was forced to sell his grand house and move into smaller rented accommodation. Debts mounted and by 1889 Cope was on the verge of destitution and would surely have gone that way had he not been offered a token professorship by the University of Pennsylvania. It was not a grand salary but it was enough to live on and to allow him to continue his palaeontology research.

Marsh had also blown much of his personal finance on fieldwork but he had found a new and important source of cash and prestige. While Cope was slowly going downhill, Marsh had become an instrumental figure in the United States Geological Survey (USGS) which at the time was headed by John Wesley Powell.

The USGS was a well-funded institution which Marsh used to his full advantage, becoming its chief palaeontologist. The downfall of Cope seems to have triggered megalomania within Marsh and he started to treat everyone around him like slaves. He refused to give credit for any work performed by his assistants, and forced them to work long hours for minimal pay. He also made sure that Cope received no grant money from any of the institutions with whom he was connected (especially the USGS), adding further misery to his rival's plight. The bitterness of years of battling had turned Marsh from a jovial if egotistical character into a power- and publicity-hungry monster who would brook no criticism or rivalry.

Marsh viewed the USGS more or less as his own publishing house and used it to print lavish monographs of his work. It was this privilege that in 1880 finally allowed him to publish what is arguably his most famous monograph, which dealt exclusively with the toothed birds *Hesperornis* and *Ichthyornis*. The publication stirred many memories of his earlier work and brought a flood of congratulatory letters, including one from a now aged Richard Owen who described it as 'the best contribution to Natural History since Cuvier'! Even Darwin, also in his seventies, got in on the act saying that: 'Your work on these old birds and on the many fossil animals of North America has afforded the best support to the theory of evolution'.

Marsh's success continued to rankle with Cope. Fed up with Marsh's manipulation of the USGS, which had just tried to block several of his own monographs, Cope wrote a 23,000-word report to the United States Congress (the USGS' paymaster), alleging that Marsh was committing gross acts of fraud. It was ignored. Finally Cope took what he felt was the only action left available to him. He went to the press.

The 12th of January 1890 would be a day that few in the American scientific community would forget in a hurry. For there on the front page of the *New York Herald* was a screaming headline:

SCIENTISTS WAGE BITTER WARFARE
Professor Cope, of the University of Pennsylvania, brings serious charges against Director Powell and Professor Marsh of the Geological Survey. Corroboration in plenty. Learned men come to Pennsylvanian's support with allegations of ignorance, plagiarism and incompetence against the accused officials. Will Congress investigate?

The lengthy article that followed was dynamite. Cope had got together with the journalist William Hosea Ballou to produce a piece which expressed the anger, jealousy and frustration that had been building within Edward Drinker Cope for years.

'For some time past a volcano has been slumbering under the Geological Survey,' wrote the *Herald*, 'and of late there have been indications that the time for eruption is not far distant.' Beneath was printed a lengthy and vitriolic interview conducted by Ballou, in which Cope sought to demonize Marsh and Powell with all the spite that he could muster. In terms of their work at the USGS the pair were charged with plagiarism, bribery, nepotism, dereliction of duty, empire-building, embezzlement, and more. Given the tone of the article, it would not have been entirely surprising if Cope had accused Marsh and Powell of being baby-eating Devil-worshippers in disguise.

Particular invective was aimed at Marsh's scientific work: it was claimed that that this had been stolen from others, including Cope, who accused Marsh of having stolen his toothed-birds work from one of his assistants and his fossil horses from Professor Kowalevsky of Russia. Here Cope was hitting at Marsh's weak spot for these were the two things for which he was best known and for which Huxley had praised him. Against these, the accusations of destroying fossils in the field, barring access to the Yale collections and making simple scientific errors, paled into insignificance.

The article finished with a series of quotes from other scientists about Marsh none of which were complimentary. 'I never knew him to do two consecutive honest days' work . . . He has never been known to tell the truth when a falsehood would serve the purpose as well . . . he is ignorant of the best-known facts of geology'. Some of these allegedly came from Marsh's own maltreated assistants.

Cope's case had been made, and in some style. Although the article was a thinly disguised attempt to tell the world how hard done by Edward Cope was, he must have hoped that it would also alert the American government to Marsh and Powell's USGS activities. He was to be sorely disappointed.

The feud between Marsh and Cope had begun partly because of Marsh's masterly ability to get himself on to the front page while Cope would always languish somewhere near the adverts at the

back. To try and wrongfoot Marsh using the media was to fight
him very much on his own territory and a very dangerous tactic.

Marsh's reply was swift. One week later the *New York Herald*
carried a different set of headlines:

MARSH HURLS AZOIC FACTS AT COPE

Yale Professor picks up the gauntlet of the Pennsylvania
palaeontologist and does royal battle in defence of his
scientific reputation.

Unfortunately for Cope, much of what he and Ballou had
written the week before was either not provable or simply plain
wrong. In a calm and straightforward manner Marsh tackled all
of Cope's points, dismissing them one by one. Not once did he
lose the opportunity to put the boot in.

Cope had accused him of restricting access to his collections.
That is partially true, explained Marsh, but security had had to be
tightened after Cope had stolen a series of his fossils in 1882 and
later published information on them himself. Other charges made
against Marsh were thrown back at Cope with greater measure.
It was Cope who was the destroyer of fossils in the field. It was
Cope who had stirred some of his assistants into trying to publish
their own material when they had no formal palaeontological
training. It was Cope who had faced expulsion from at least one
national scientific body because of his serious misconduct.

Marsh's denials were packed full of the names of the great and
good of American science some of whom had been quoted by
Cope the week before but who now issued denials of ever having
spoken to the press. It seemed as though Ballou had embellished
or even made up a few of the interviews.

Cope's accusations of plagiarism regarding the toothed birds
and fossil horses were also dealt with head on. First there was a
statement from an assistant who had worked on the fossil birds
with Marsh and who confirmed that Marsh was indeed the
author of this famous work. As for stealing the fossil horses from
Kowalevsky, Marsh denied ever having read any of this man's
work. Besides which, he pointed out, Kowalevsky had the same
reputation for dirty dealing and plagiarism that Cope did.

'Kowalevsky,' wrote Marsh, 'was at last stricken with remorse and ended his unfortunate career by blowing out his own brains. Cope still lives, unrepentant.'

The formalities over with, Marsh could at last dispatch Cope once and for all. At that time the *New York Herald* was most famous for having sent Henry Stanley to the Congo in search of the fabled Dr David Livingstone. Marsh drew on this analogy in his most furious outburst. 'Little men with big heads, unscrupulous in warfare, are not confined to Africa,' spat Marsh, 'and Stanley will recognize them here when he returns to America. Of such dwarfs we have unfortunately a few in science.'

Marsh's status and eloquence easily won the day. As news of this war of words spread through the newspapers of the world Cope was always portrayed as a bitter and twisted man jealous of Marsh's scientific prowess. Marsh looked very much like the wounded party forced to defend himself against an illogical and slanderous enemy. Like many of his plans, Cope's vindictive attempt at trying Marsh via the media had ended up rebounding, leaving him in a much worse position than when he had started. Cope had been made to look like an unstable lunatic and many of his remaining colleagues tried to distance themselves. They did not want to make enemies of Marsh or Powell and risk being sidelined like Cope.

To Cope his enemy Marsh must have looked like the original Teflon man to whom no mud would stick no matter how hard it was thrown. It was to be his last serious attempt at revenge. He was now an ill and poverty-stricken man who chose to while his days away in Philadelphia accompanied only by his fossils and a few close friends.

In 1897 Cope died of kidney failure alleged by some to have been caused by syphilis. He left his skeleton to the Anthropometric Society so that it might become the reference specimen for all humankind, a request that was ignored but which reveals something of Cope's ego, even after death.

★

After surviving a very public trial by the *New York Herald*, Marsh might well have had cause to believe himself to be invincible. There is, however, one final twist to the Marsh and Cope feud and one which centres on the very creatures that made Marsh's name – the toothed birds.

Marsh's fall from grace was not to be at the hands of Cope, the *New York Herald* or the many other enemies he had made during the preceding few years. It was to be at the hands of politicians.

In 1890, following a drought and economic recession, Congress needed to acquire land and expand into new sections of the American Midwest. However, the USGS had been vetoing all attempts at unplanned settling, insisting that settlements should be built only after careful investigation of the physical and human consequences (chiefly to the Native American tribes). Fed up with this behaviour, Congress decided to rein in the USGS and, for the first time, insisted on a breakdown of the Survey's annual expenditure for the 1880s.

The American government was looking for an excuse which could be used be to hang the USGS out to dry. There, in the expenditure budget, stood an obvious target – Marsh's lavish 1880 monograph on the toothed birds. Not only had the monograph cost a fortune to produce, but it had the audacity to suggest that there was truth behind Darwin's *Origin of Species*. Most politicians considered Darwin's theory of evolution through natural selection to be ridiculous and atheistic. The politicians believed that they had found the USGS' weak point.

The charge was led by Senator Hilary Herbert from Alabama who, during the debate about the USGS' budget, held up a copy of Marsh's toothed bird book for all to see and then ridiculed the idea that such animals could exist. He complained that the taxpayer's money was being used to fund atheistic rubbish about two-metre-high birds with teeth.

Birds with teeth? Congress had never heard anything so silly in their lives. The phrase 'birds with teeth' became synonymous with corruption in the USGS and after a short campaign Herbert got his way. The USGS' budget was slashed and the palaeontology section all but closed down. Marsh was forced to resign immediately, with Powell going a couple of years later.

For Marsh it was the first real public humiliation that he had ever received but the collapse of the USGS had a far deeper effect than the wounding of his pride. Like Cope, Marsh's personal finances had been exhausted by the years of feuding; now, without access to the lucrative USGS, he suddenly found himself seriously lacking in funds and consequently had to apply to Yale University for a salaried position. His power base gone, Marsh started to sink slowly into obscurity and ended his existence, not as a famous palaeontologist, but as an ordinary university researcher. Like Cope, Marsh's health had been damaged by years of rough fieldwork and the strain of the feud. In 1898 he died of pneumonia a relatively forgotten figure but one whose contribution to science had been vital.

Cope and Marsh made a significant contribution to the story of bird evolution, Cope postulating the link between dinosaurs and birds with his *Laelaps* dinosaur and Marsh offering proof of that link with his toothed birds. The vast number of dinosaur specimens that the pair turned up in the 1870s and 1880s finally corrected Richard Owen's ill-begotten notion of these animals as pseudo-rhinocerotic beasts.

The palaeontology world had travelled a long way during the thirty years since the discovery of the first *Archaeopteryx*. As things stood, the link between birds and reptiles, as illustrated by both the *Archaeopteryx* and the toothed birds, offered the only tangible proof that Darwin's theory was correct. More proof was needed and the Solnhofen limestone was about to provide it.

A Second Specimen

DURING THE AUTUMN of 1876, as Thomas Huxley was in America being wowed by Marsh's fossil menagerie, a Bavarian named Johann Dörr was gazing at a fossil that had been handed to him by one of the workers in his small Eichstätt quarry.

The fossil in Herr Dörr's hand was a second *Archaeopteryx* but he could not recognize it as such. It was still in a rough and unprepared state with only a few bones visible through the smooth limestone covering. Even though it may not have been readily identifiable this fossil looked like a good one. The Solnhofen fossils had not lost any of their value in the sixteen years since Carl Häberlein's big dealing days. They could still be a significant side industry for most quarries.

The fossil had a skull, body and all four limbs. Dörr believed it to be a good example of a pterodactyl and as such probably worth quite a tidy sum. He wrote a letter to one of the few local fossil collectors who he felt could afford to buy it.

A few days later saw the arrival of a distinguished, professional-looking gentleman in his late fifties who had travelled from nearby to view Dörr's new find. This was Ernst Otto Häberlein whose father, Dr Carl Häberlein of Pappenheim, had died a few years previously at the ripe old age of eighty-four. Like his father, Ernst Häberlein had chosen a solid middle-class profession and was a noted revenue officer in the region. He had his family's penchant for Solnhofen fossils and, together with his partner Dr Redenbacher, had amassed a considerable number of them in a private collection.

Häberlein junior examined the new fossil and agreed with Dörr that it was most probably a pterodactyl and a good one at that. It looked as if there was plenty of scope for further preparation too. Pterodactyls were the most desirable of the Solnhofen fossils (after an *Archaeopteryx*, of course) and could be guaranteed to fetch a high price. Some hard bargaining was called for by Häberlein. A few short minutes later and a deal had been done. Häberlein would pay 2,000 marks (about £3,750/$6,000 now) for the fossil – a high price but one which could certainly be recouped later if necessary. In a world where stocks and shares could rise and fall in the blink of an eye, a good-quality Solnhofen fossil would always be a sound investment. Although he may have balked at the price, Ernst Häberlein had actually just bought the bargain of a lifetime.

Discovering the true worth of his 'pterodactyl' would take Häberlein some time, its valuable elements still being hidden beneath a thin layer of limestone. Ernst Häberlein was as skilled as his father in the art of fossil preparation but he was also a busy man and the new fossil would have to wait its turn. It was several weeks before it was unwrapped from its cloth and laid out in front of Häberlein.

The first tentative explorations of a new specimen are always a mixture of apprehension and excitement. The hammer and chisel must be used sparingly at first, delicately probing around the fossil to see what else might lie underneath. Use too much energy on a blow or position the chisel in the wrong place and the results could be catastrophic. Gentle, persistent work is the key.

Häberlein's first few chisel blows were around the edges of the visible bones. Little real damage could be done there and it would allow Häberlein to get a feel for the quality and strength of the rock with which he was working. Hours later, the shape of the animal was beginning to emerge from its rock tomb.

In terms of quality this fossil was exceptional. The skeleton was very complete and lying in a favourable position. In fact, it looked as though the animal had been pinned out on a dissecting board, the spine running down with the arms coming out at 90 degrees, as though the creature were having a lazy stretch when it died. The legs were separate from each other and there

Ernst Häberlein who, like his father, found himself in possession of an
Archaeopteryx *specimen*

appeared to be a long tail sweeping away from the base of the
spine. Possibly the most important feature of all was the presence
of a skull attached to the end of a long, flexible neck. This was
going to be a spectacular fossil, even for the Solnhofen limestone.

Häberlein's moment of delight came as he chipped away at the
tail. As the small bits and pieces of rock came away, Häberlein recognized the pattern emerging from underneath. He had seen his

father's prize specimen, the *Archaeopteryx*, during the months in which it had been in his house, waiting for the Munich Bavarian State Collection to make up its mind. There, attached to the tail, were the unmistakable impressions of feathers. It was a second *Archaeopteryx* and it was in far better condition than the first one.

Interested as he was in the *Archaeopteryx* for its scientific value, Häberlein was a financier and had seen the monetary gains made by his father from just one single fossil. Science be damned, Häberlein was going to sell his new fossil – and for considerably more than the 2,000 marks he had paid for it.

Häberlein was not experienced in brokering fossils and did not at first know to whom he should turn. The logical first step was to try the Munich Bavarian State Collection which had by far the best selection of Solnhofen fossils, including many purchased from Häberlein senior during his prospecting days. A letter was duly dispatched asking if Munich was interested in purchasing the new *Archaeopteryx*.

The reply was favourable. Yes, the museum was interested, but it would need to see the fossil and had to have an idea of the price involved.

Häberlein was certainly agreeable to his fossil being viewed. He knew its scientific value and had no intention of indulging in the cloak and dagger tactics that had surrounded the selling of the first *Archaeopteryx*. Besides, his preparation of the fossil had ceased and only a few feather tails were actually visible although it was obvious that there were more awaiting discovery. It would be up to the Bavarian State Collection to finish chipping away at the slab. The price was another matter entirely. Häberlein had seen his father's *Archaeopteryx* and he knew that his new specimen was in better condition and more complete. It also had the all-important skull, a feature which had been so contentious in the first specimen.

Taking this, plus the fossil's celebrity and rarity and fifteen years of inflation into consideration, Ernst Häberlein came up with a price for Munich. It was not cheap. In fact, it was extortionate. The second *Archaeopteryx* had a price of 25,000 marks on its head, the equivalent of about £47,000 ($75,000) in modern money.

Munich protested. It pleaded. But all in vain. Häberlein was convinced that his fossil was worth at least that much. Regretfully, Munich had to turn him down. There was no way that they could afford such a sum. In fact, no state-funded institution was likely to have this type of cash available. It seemed probable that the new *Archaeopteryx* would end up as a centrepiece in the private collection of a member of the landed gentry or a *nouveau riche* industrialist. For scientists anxious to examine the fossil, this would be a disaster.

Häberlein too realized that if Munich had turned him down then most other museums were likely to do so as well and that the fossil would have to be sold to a private individual. However, such collectors were demanding and did not purchase fossils for their scientific potential but for their rarity and beauty. To prove that it was worth such a sum Häberlein would have to finish the preparation himself.

The task took months of eye straining work but the result was better than anyone could have hoped for. Not only were the tail feathers there, but also those on the wings. In its fully prepared state the new *Archaeopteryx* looked magnificent, its feathered wings and tail spread outwards for all to see. It vaguely resembled a Christmas tree angel which had become trapped inside a limestone matrix.

In the spring of 1877 he announced to the world that not only did he have a new and near perfect specimen of the *Archaeopteryx*, but that it was for sale along with the rest of his Solnhofen collection. No price was stated. Ernst Häberlein sat down and waited for the offers to come rolling in.

News of the *Archaeopteryx* spread like wildfire. Within days people in France, London and the United States were aware of Häberlein's find and knew that he would want a vastly inflated sum for it. The timing was good. Fossils were still very much in the public's eye; almost every scientific institution would have jumped at the chance to own an *Archaeopteryx* specimen but the high price tag meant that most could only dream of it. However, some foreign institutions did begin to organize themselves to make a bid.

In June 1877 Othniel Marsh received a letter from an old

friend of his working in Germany who had read Häberlein's press announcement:

Dear Professor Marsh

Are you aware – probably it is an old story to you – that Ernest Haeberlein [*sic*], of Pappenheim near Solnhofen, has discovered his second *Archaeopteryx*, said to be more perfect than the first, as having the head?

The German journals express the hope that this may not be brought away from that country. Now is your chance for a cable dispatch, to send the specimen regardless of cost!

Yours truly,

Spencer F. Baird, June 8th, 1877

Marsh, it seems, had not been aware of the new specimen, for within twenty-four hours he had cabled Professor Geinitz, a friend of his in Dresden, with the specific instruction to get first refusal. Marsh had just wowed the world with his toothed birds and the idea that this new *Archaeopteryx* had a skull excited him greatly. If it also had teeth then his ideas on bird evolution could be proved right. At this time Marsh was beginning to show the early signs of a Richard Owen style of megalomania and felt the need to own every important fossil on the planet for himself. An *Archaeopteryx* would be the crowning glory of his collection. Used to throwing money at a problem, Marsh felt confident that the new fossil would soon be his. 'Telegraph me the amount before finally completing the purchase,' he naïvely told Geinitz, only adding as an afterthought, 'If there is time to write, please also inform me how perfect the fossil is.'

The reply came a few days later. The new specimen, Geinitz informed him, was a good one, complete with a toothed skull, but he had not yet secured it. He had offered 1,000 marks to Häberlein but the offer had been refused (not surprising, considering that he had laid out 2,000 marks for the fossil in the first place). Geinitz warned Marsh that the sort of sum being asked for by Häberlein was extortionate: he advised him not to get involved in the matter but to wait and see if the price would drop with time. Marsh heeded this advice. It was clear that the *Archaeopteryx* was not going to be sold in a hurry.

Interest was being shown in London too. Richard Owen was still with the British Museum and had at last persuaded the government to build a separate and gigantic Natural History Museum on some waste land in South Kensington. The building had been under construction for some years. He was fascinated by the idea of a new *Archaeopteryx* that was better than the specimen for which he had fought so hard. However, Owen's power-mongering days were long past and he had neither the will nor the means to get drawn into an unorthodox auction with Häberlein junior. Instead he wrote to a German friend of his, asking him to keep an eye on proceedings.

News of all this interest from abroad was not greeted with joy in Germany. There was still considerable annoyance at the loss of the first *Archaeopteryx* to London and, more recently, the loss of a fantastic Solnhofen pterosaur specimen to Marsh at Yale University. Within a matter of weeks of Häberlein's announcement a newspaper campaign was organized to try and persuade the German federal government to buy the specimen on behalf of their people. German palaeontologists petitioned the Ministry of Education pleading with them to take action before another national treasure was lost abroad. The Ministry explained that it had no jurisdiction over museums: these were the concern of the state governments and so any money would have to be found locally. Munich's Bavarian State Collection was one of the better-funded German museums of the day, yet it had been unable to get hold of 25,000 marks. Now the rumour was that Häberlein was asking for 36,000 marks. No museum could afford such a sum.

As a last resort Kaiser Wilhelm I was petitioned, but he too dismissed the idea. One scientist commented, 'Ah! If, instead of a bird, a petrified cannon or gun had been concerned!' – a none too subtle reference to the military ambitions of the German government.

All negotiations with Häberlein had come to nothing. He had refused a large number of offers including one of £3,000 (about £137,000/$215,000 today) from Professor H. Lemming of

London who may in fact have been negotiating on behalf of the British Museum. After a year with no agreement on the sale, Häberlein must have wondered whether he had aimed too high with his price. Faced with increasing local pressure, he agreed to give the Freie Deutsche Hochstift of Frankfurt a six-month option on the fossil. This institution had managed to buy other national treasures but Häberlein's price was too high even for them and the money simply could not be raised. In the opening months of 1879 the Frankfurt option lapsed and there started a renewed and vigorous attempt at buying the fossil.

Professor Lemming of London opened the bidding by offering £2,500, less than his initial offer. Then Othniel Marsh came back to the fray. Häberlein wrote to him offering the specimen for $10,000 (about £106,000/$170,000 now) but this was still too high and the offer was not taken up. According to some, Marsh's miserly streak showed itself at the last minute, and Yale was denied the fossil.

A more hopeful bid was organized by Karl Vogt of the University of Geneva. Vogt was a fiery character whose extreme left-wing beliefs had led to his self-imposed exile in Switzerland, whence he could abuse the German state without fear of persecution. A zealous Darwinian who would brook no criticism of the theory of natural selection, he was well known for his quick temper and his inability to control his mouth. This had led to many fallings out including a spectacular spat with Andreas Wagner whose description of the first *Archaeopteryx* contained a direct warning to Darwinists.

Vogt saw the new *Archaeopteryx* as a Darwinian icon and determined that it should be placed in the hands of the people. He manoeuvred behind the scenes to persuade the University of Geneva to buy the fossil from Häberlein for the reduced, but still expensive, price of 24,000 marks. The university was agreeable and the deal was announced in the German press. In order to seal the agreement, Vogt was asked to explain the importance of the *Archaeopteryx* to the 1879 Swiss National Congress in St Gallen so that they could approve the purchase. A simple enough task, considering the *Archaeopteryx*'s fame. Unfortunately for Vogt, he could not control his political feelings for even a few minutes. When on stage he spoke only briefly about the *Archaeopteryx* but at length about the injustice and problems of the German federal state. His mannerisms became frantic, his voice rose to shouting pitch as he launched into attacks on Bismarck, the Kaiser, Germany's empire-building and the disgrace of its scientific policy. As he ranted at his audience, Vogt became incomprehensible. Nothing was spared his revolutionary zeal. At last he was silenced by the chairman but the audience was not amused. There was no applause and no support for Vogt. The next day Geneva withdrew its support for his purchase of the *Archaeopteryx*.

The trouble caused by Vogt did have one benefit. This very public failure encouraged Werner von Siemens to take an interest in the *Archaeopteryx* sale. Siemens was a powerful industrialist whose legacy lives on in the electronics manufacturing giant that still bears his name. Siemens approached Häberlein directly and offered him 20,000 marks for the fossil. It had been nearly four years since Häberlein had first bought the specimen and it must have been apparent to him that it was overpriced. Siemens was offering cash in hand and, at last, Häberlein accepted. The second *Archaeopteryx* was now in private hands.

Any thoughts that Siemens was buying the *Archaeopteryx* for himself disappeared when, a few weeks later, he gave the specimen to the Humboldt Museum in Berlin on permanent loan. His motive had been patriotic: to secure the valuable fossil for Germany. It also gave the Berlin Museum time enough to raise the money to buy the fossil from Siemens at cost price, which it duly did a couple of years later.

The second *Archaeopteryx* confirmed what many had suspected. More beautiful and more complete than the London specimen, it had a toothed skull, confirming John Evans' discovery of a toothed jaw in the London specimen and adding weight to Huxley and Marsh's proposed link between the birds and the reptiles. The picturesque fossil rapidly overtook the London specimen as an evolutionary icon.

Despite its completeness, studies of the *Archaeopteryx* were

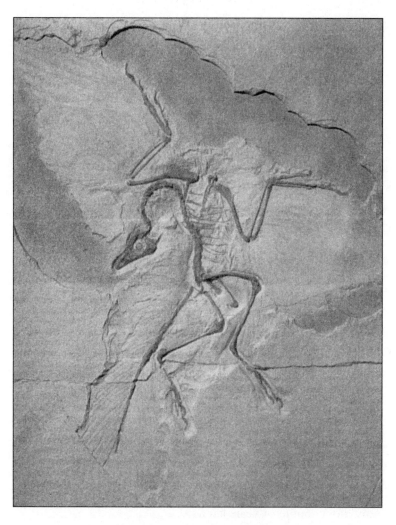

The Berlin Archaeopteryx. *It is generally thought to be the most beautiful of the seven known specimens*

slow and laborious. Many eminent scientists viewed the specimen, including Vogt and Marsh, but the amount of information published on it was relatively thin. Not that the Humboldt Museum cared, for it had secured a palaeontological treasure and one whose scientific significance was plain. The reptilian nature of the birds could now not be doubted. It was time for the palaeontological community to move on to other problems associated with the evolution of birds.

10

The Origin of Birds

BY THE 1880s the so-called 'golden era of palaeontology' was coming to an end. Many of the major players had either retired or were dead. As the years progressed so the famous names who had fought hard to found the concept of scientific investigation that we know today became fewer in number. Darwin died in 1882, Owen in 1892, Cope in 1897, Marsh in 1898 and Huxley in 1895.

The older generation had made way for younger blood and, as always happens, the new scientists seemed to be ignorant of the previous battles which had been fought for their benefit. Evolution itself was no longer the controversial topic it once had been. Huxley, Darwin, Marsh and others had done an admirable job of persuading younger scientists to look favourably upon the idea of natural selection. By the turn of the twentieth century the majority of scientists (but certainly not the public) were on the side of Darwin, a total reversal of the situation in 1859 when *The Origin of Species* had been published.

That the battle to own the Berlin *Archaeopteryx* had occurred because the fossil was seen as a symbol of evolution, rather than a controversial piece of evidence in favour of it, shows how far opinion had shifted in the fifteen years between the discovery of these two fossils. The general agreement on the idea of evolution meant that scientists were now free to direct their attention elsewhere. Thanks to the patient work of Huxley and Marsh few questioned the link between the reptiles and the birds: the two *Archaeopteryx* specimens and Marsh's toothed birds had settled that one. However, the exact nature of this link was still proving problematic and was increasingly causing problems. Were the birds descended directly from the dinosaurs, as Huxley believed, or from some totally separate reptile group altogether?

As the nineteenth century drew to a close, differing positions were held by the various important contributors to the debate over bird evolution.

Huxley's belief in the persistence of animal groups through the fossil record followed him to his grave. To him the birds must have evolved long before *Archaeopteryx* was on the scene, which meant the Solnhofen fossil could not be a missing link but must be some weird form of bird. He favoured a dinosaur ancestry for birds, but not through *Archaeopteryx*. His early birds were giant ostrich-like creatures whose fossil remains had yet to be found.

Marsh went further than this and uncharacteristically disagreed with his close friend, Huxley. Marsh saw the *Archaeopteryx* as a direct link between the dinosaurs and living birds. After all, remove the feathers from *Archaeopteryx* and you were left with a dinosaur skeleton.

A different position altogether had been taken by Cope, who favoured the idea put forward by palaeontologist Harry Seeley, an ex-pupil of Richard Owen's and a firm believer in Owen and Cope's God-directed evolution. With a pedigree like that, it is not surprising to find that Seeley and Huxley did not get on at all. Seeley took exception to Huxley's bird–dinosaur link and proposed his own, slightly eccentric theory that the ancestors to the birds were the pterosaurs; he even suggested that the pterosaurs might have been warm-blooded. Even Richard Owen did not hold with Seeley and Cope, both of whom were friends of his, and did his utmost to demolish this idea. For once, Huxley was in agreement.

This three-way split marked the start of a new phase in the quest to understand bird evolution. It was no longer a case of proving whether or not the birds and reptiles were linked. It was now a matter of finding out the real origin of the birds. Are the birds just dinosaurs in disguise or were they descended from some other reptile group, known or unknown?

★

A bizarre example of how famous the *Archaeopteryx* and the bird evolution debate had become was given in 1898 by the French writer Alfred Jarry, creator of literary monster Père Ubu, a grotesque whose wild adventures were featured in several plays. In a play entitled *Ubu cocu, ou l'Archéoptéryx* Jarry makes the fossil bird the son of Ubu's wife and her lover Barbapoux. The *Archaeopteryx* does not actually do much in the play, appearing several times but never speaking. According to palaeontologist Eric Buffetaut, Jarry appears to be using the *Archaeopteryx* as 'a kind of nonsensical symbol of the bizarre and the hybrid', a view borne out in this quotation from the play: 'It seems prehistoric to us, a cross between a vampire and an archaeopteryx, ichthyornis, with many qualities of the chiropters, the leporids, the birds of prey, the palmipedes, the pachyderms and the pigs.'

Although this may not be the most accessible play ever written, it does show the extent to which the *Archaeopteryx* had filtered into the consciousness of the western world. Other snippets come from closer to home. My grandmother-in-law, who went to school in England during the 1910s, distinctly remembers being taught about the *Archaeopteryx* in class, a major step forward in an age when evolution was still considered by many to be heretical.

The issue of the origin of the birds was a difficult one to resolve given the serious lack of known bird fossils. There was a brief flurry of excitement in 1907 when it looked as though another *Archaeopteryx* specimen had been recovered from the West African country of Guinea but on closer inspection it turned out to be a false alarm.

A new direction in the bird evolution debate began in South Africa with the discovery of a new group of primitive reptiles which were collectively named 'thecodonts'. The thecodonts lived during the late Permian and Triassic periods (about 250 to 230 million years ago) long before either the birds or dinosaurs are known to have existed.

The thecodonts show evidence of being related to a vast array of later reptiles including the crocodiles, dinosaurs and ptero-saurs, and many have assumed that they were the common ancestor of all of these. However, a brilliant Scottish palaeontol-ogist named Robert Broom looked at the thecodonts and believed that they might be the common ancestor to both the birds *and* the dinosaurs, based on similarities in their skeletons. If so then Huxley and Marsh's neat line from the dinosaurs to the birds would be broken. According to Broom, one could not be descended from the other; instead the birds and dinosaurs were cousins, descended from the same distant relative. Broom's ideas were radical but his was only one opinion of many floating around during the opening decades of the twentieth century. There was no real consensus as to where the birds had originated. Coherence was needed and it was to come from a most unex-pected source.

Gerhard Heilmann was born in Skelskør, Denmark, in 1859, only a matter of months before Darwin published his *Origin of Species*. The history of his early childhood is not well known although it seems that he grew up in a provincial town in a relig-ious upper middle-class family. Heilmann's interest in natural history was apparently sparked when his family obtained a copy of Christian Lütken's *The Animal Kingdom*, a book which fasci-nated and entranced him to such a degree that in a later inter-view he claimed to have been a supporter of Darwin by the age of fourteen. Even then his fascination with the evolution of birds was emerging as he himself says:

> One of the questions that [Lütken] treated was whether the birds descended from the crawling animals, and his conclu-sion was that he did not believe so. That came as a bitter disappointment to me, and it drove me to addressing the issue myself.

The young Heilmann soon developed quite a scientific bent and rebelled when forced by his parents to publicly announce his belief in the Devil. It may also have been family pressure that

*Gerhard Heilmann, the artist with an interest in
fossils whose ideas were to find acceptance
in the scientific world*

pushed him into medical training rather than his preferred career as a naturalist. But later, fed up with his studies, in 1883 Heilmann quit medicine and became an artist's apprentice instead, much to the annoyance of his family.

Heilmann's artistic career turned out to be a fruitful one. For many years he was a painter at the Royal Porcelain Works in Copenhagen before leaving in 1902 to become a successful freelance artist. Among other things Heilmann became responsible for the design of Danish banknotes, and he was a noted book illustrator as well. His interest in the natural world and birds in particular may have been rekindled when he was asked to provide illustrations for a whole series of books on natural history. Soon he became noted for his ornithological sketches and was much in demand by the Danish Ornithological Society, even designing their logo.

It cannot be certain what exactly inspired Heilmann to begin taking an active interest in the evolution of birds once more. His work as a natural history illustrator would have taken him to many museums at home and abroad and thus afforded him the chance to view hundreds of bird specimens, fossil and stuffed, as well as dinosaurs and other fossils. Heilmann seems to have been quite parochial in his ambitions and so when his first few papers on bird evolution appeared in the relatively obscure journal of the Danish Ornithological Society, few people took much notice. Between 1913 and 1916 he produced several such articles, all heavily illustrated and all dealing with the question of the origin of birds.

Not a single eyebrow was raised in the scientific community, even when the articles were collected and published in book form as *Vor Nuvaerende Viden om Fuglenes Afstamning*. It appeared that the global scientific community was not interested in anything that was published in Danish. In those days English, French and German were the languages of science (these days it is really just English) and to get oneself noticed one had to publish in one of these languages.

Heilmann too must have realized this as during the next few years he spent a great deal of time trying to persuade various English-language publishers to undertake a translation of his book. None of the big publishers would touch it unless Heilmann himself was prepared to bear the cost, which he was unable to do. As the rejection letters piled up, Heilmann's famous temper got the better of him. 'None of these publishers understand the content of my book!' he bitterly complained.

Finally, and after much help from Arthur Smith Woodward of the British Museum, a small London publisher took a gamble and said yes to his manuscript.

Heilmann spent a considerable time revising his original work, visiting Berlin to see the *Archaeopteryx* held there and requesting photographs and casts of the London specimen and Marsh's toothed birds. The resultant book, published in 1926, simply entitled *The Origin of Birds*, was a 200-page monograph crammed with literally hundreds of Heilmann's exquisite and remarkably realistic drawings as well as some of the finest photographs ever taken of many famous bird fossils, including the two *Archaeopteryx* specimens.

Like Marsh's monograph on the toothed birds, produced nearly half a century earlier, *The Origin of Birds* was a masterpiece and its effect on the scientific community was to be just as profound.

Heilmann divided his book into four main parts. The first three look at the evolution of birds based respectively on evidence from the fossil record, from their embryos and from living birds. In these chapters Heilmann drew together a staggering wealth of evidence. Most of the first chapter is devoted to the two *Archaeopteryx* specimens. His conclusion was blunt: that 'from its remains *Archaeopteryx* might be characterised as a reptile in the disguise of a bird'. It was, however, Heilmann's fourth chapter that was ground breaking and would be the final word in bird evolution for more than half a century. Having exhaustively illustrated and compared the bones and other bits of fossil birds and reptiles, Heilmann was justifiably able to state in capital letters near the start of this section that:

WE CAN THEREFORE WITH ABSOLUTE CERTAINTY MAINTAIN THAT THE BIRDS HAVE DESCENDED FROM THE REPTILES. OF THIS WE CANNOT, IN FUTURE, ENTERTAIN THE FAINTEST SHADOW OF A DOUBT.

Proavis, *Heilmann's reconstruction
of his hypothetical earliest
tree-climbing bird*

This most scientists had already decided for themselves thanks to the work of Huxley and Marsh but Heilmann wanted to go one step further. He wanted to answer the big question over which science was still divided: from which group of reptiles did the birds evolve?

To answer this Heilmann focused on the two *Archaeopteryx* specimens, still the oldest known fossil birds and therefore the closest in time to the point of origin of the birds. Heilmann possessed a systematic mind and his method of working was to compare every single feature of the *Archaeopteryx* specimens, and those of some other birds, with all the known fossil reptiles to see where the similarities and dissimilarities lay. The results were surprising.

It must be remembered that there had really only been a few theories put forward regarding the origins of birds. In simple terms these were that: (1) they evolved from the pterosaurs or (2) that they evolved directly from dinosaurs, or (3) from some as yet undiscovered common ancestor that predates both the dinosaurs and the birds but gave rise to both groups. Heilmann tackled each of these possibilities in detail.

The pterosaurs were given short shrift: there were just too many dissimilarities, leading Heilmann to conclude that any resemblance was 'merely due to adaptations for the flying purpose'. This view was in agreement with that of almost every other palaeontologist to have studied the origin of birds problem apart, of course, from Harry Seeley whose grand bird–pterosaur idea had gone to the grave with him nearly a decade earlier. Excluding the pterosaurs really left the question of the dinosaurs.

By the mid-1920s studying the dinosaurs was no longer the easy task that it had once been. Whereas Huxley and others had only a handful of scrappy bones to work with, Heilmann now had to consider hundreds of specimens, some almost totally complete.

The turn of twentieth century had seen yet another wave of dinomania, largely thanks to the Carnegie Museum in Pittsburgh having distributed multiple casts of one of Marsh's *Diplodocus* skeletons to museums across the world. The dinosaur had also entered the public's imagination via the first popular palaeontology textbooks, such as *Extinct Animals*, by Ray

Lancaster (once a maverick pupil of Huxley's). It was this book which inspired Sir Arthur Conan Doyle's 1912 dinosaur classic, *The Lost World*, the first treatment of dinosaurs in popular fiction. So by the time the first Danish edition of *The Origin of Birds* was published in 1916 the western world was already *au fait* with the idea of dinosaurs and there were dozens of named species to choose from. It also had a new species, the monstrous *Tyrannosaurus rex*, which had been found in Montana in 1902 by Barnum T. Brown.

All of this activity meant that dinosaurs were no longer seen as one coherent group of reptiles but had been split up into several subgroups. Some of these subgroups could be instantly dismissed by Heilmann as potential ancestors of the birds. For example, the gigantic and four-legged sauropods, such as *Diplodocus*, could never be compared to *Archaeopteryx*, or any other bird for that matter. Their skeletons are just too different. The same is true for most of the other four-footed dinosaurs such as *Stegosaurus*, *Ankylosaurus* and *Triceratops*, whose skeletons are also fundamentally dissimilar to those of birds.

Excluding all of these left Heilmann with very few choices within the dinosaurs. It boiled down to the ornithopods, characterized by *Iguanodon*, one of the animals so badly reconstructed by Richard Owen and later put right by Huxley, and the theropods, characterized by the bipedal terrors *Megalosaurus* and *Tyrannosaurus*. Again Heilmann's treatment of these two groups was systematic and thorough.

Heilmann quickly concluded that the ornithopods and 'the Jurassic birds . . . have hardly any points of resemblance between them'. Reading his systematic comparisons between the two groups can leave one in no doubt that he is entirely correct in this. With the ornithopod dinosaurs out of the way, only the theropods could be left as the possible ancestors to the birds.

Huxley's moment of revelation regarding the link between the dinosaurs and birds came while staring at the skeleton of the theropod dinosaur *Megalosaurus* in the Oxford Museum. He had also convincingly demonstrated that the tiny Solnhofen theropod *Compsognathus* had a near-identical skeleton to that of *Archaeopteryx*.

Heilmann had many more new theropod species to study, and compared bones, skulls, jaws and teeth that Huxley could only have dreamed of having at his disposal. Like Huxley, Heilmann's comparisons between the theropods, *Archaeopteryx* and living birds were favourable. The skeletons were almost identical, as were certain aspects of lifestyle, behaviour and even footprints and yet, surprisingly, Heilmann still found against a direct connection between the birds and the theropod dinosaurs. The problem was an obscure geological rule known as Dollo's Law.

In 1893 Louis Dollo had used his extensive study of fossils to declare that once evolution had removed a biological feature from an animal then it could never be regained. For example, humans currently have the organ known as the appendix. Millions of years ago this organ was used to help digest tough plant matter but nowadays it is redundant and should, in time, disappear from the body altogether. Once we lose our appendix, it can never return in exactly the same form. Even if humans started to eat tough plants again the appendix would still not reappear to help in digestion: evolution would have to find another way round the problem.

Of course, we now know that whilst certain physical characteristics can disappear, the genetic code used to create them continues to lie dormant inside the DNA. Occasionally such dormant genetic features are reactivated, producing things such as horses with three toes or whales with back legs, a feature known as atavism. Even humans are affected by atavism, as in the birth of ultra-hairy babies or babies with short tails. Even allowing for this, Dollo's Law still by and large holds true and in Heilmann's day it was sacrosanct. But how could it be successfully applied to the problem of the origin of the birds?

Heilmann's logic was simple and devastating. He noticed that although most features of the skeletons of birds and dinosaurs were identical to one another, the one big difference was that whilst the birds' skeleton had collarbones (clavicles), the theropod dinosaurs did not. The first reaction of many scientists to this news would have been, 'So what?' but Heilmann instantly knew this meant that the two groups could not be directly related. His argument goes something like this.

The collarbone is an ancient skeletal feature which occurs in reptile fossils far, far older than either the dinosaurs or the birds. The birds have a collarbone and yet the dinosaurs do not, which means that at some point the dinosaurs must have 'lost' theirs through natural selection. If, therefore, the birds did evolve from the dinosaurs then they must have subsequently had to re-evolve their collarbones. Dollo's Law states that this cannot happen, which means the dinosaurs cannot have been the direct ancestors to the birds. Heilmann himself sums up his argument by saying that '. . . it would seem a rather obvious conclusion that it is amongst the [theropods] that we are to look for the bird-ancestor. And yet, this would be too rash, for the very fact that the clavicles [collarbones] are wanting would in itself be sufficient to prove that these saurians could not possibly be the ancestors of the birds'. In other words, were it not for the matter of the collarbone, the theropod dinosaurs could undoubtedly be considered the ancestors to the birds.

This logical, if somewhat complex, argument leaves only one possibility for the origins of birds. Both birds and dinosaurs must have evolved from the same distant collarboned ancestor, diverging along separate paths, with the dinosaurs losing their clavicles whilst the birds hung on to theirs.

Heilmann concludes his study by following the work of Robert Broom (which came out at the same time as Heilmann first published this idea in Danish) in endorsing his idea of a thecodont ancestor for both birds and dinosaurs. Heilmann finishes with a speculative description of what the earliest bird might have looked like based on all the evidence gathered in his book. He sketches both the skeleton and a fully feathered reconstruction of this postulated animal, suggesting that it may initially have used clawed arms to climb about branches, and feathered wings to glide between trees as the modern flying squirrels do. Finally, he gives this speculative animal the name Proavis, saying that the term 'covers a form intermediate between reptile and bird; hence, a form that is no more a reptile, but which has not as yet become a bird. We must suppose the animal to be partly covered with scales, but these are in certain places beginning to change into feathers.'

That, in essence, was Heilmann's thesis. An artist with only a smattering of formal anatomical training had taken the issue of bird evolution by the scruff of the neck and shaken it until all the loose pieces had fallen into place. His conclusion was emphatic. There was no dinosaur–bird connection except through a distant missing link which he nicknamed Proavis. So according to Heilmann, *Archaeopteryx* was not, after all, the missing link between the birds and the reptiles. It was merely a primitive bird some way down the evolutionary tree from 'Proavis', an animal that might have lived 250 million years ago or more. *Archaeopteryx* is only 150 million years old.

Heilmann's efforts to get his work published in English paid off. His Danish book and papers may have been steadfastly overlooked for more than a decade but from the instant *The Origin of Birds* hit the shelves, it became a success. Almost all reviews were favourable. One later assessment of *Origins of Birds* states: 'The impact of Heilmann's book cannot be exaggerated. On the question of bird origins, its impact has been second only to the discovery of *Archaeopteryx*.'

In one stroke a normally fractionated scientific community united behind Heilmann's book. It was almost as if they had been waiting for an authoritative study such as this to settle the long-standing problems surrounding the origin of birds. One wonders if this wasn't in some part due to Heilmann being a total unknown and thus not party to any of the various feuds and vendettas that normally riddle the scientific community. In fact, one wonders if the scientific community was even aware of Heilmann's lack of formal scientific training. Would *The Origin of Birds* have been the success it was had it been known that its author was a man whose training was at a porcelain works and not at a university?

It is impossible to say. Certainly, the impact of the book would have been lessened had it not been for Heilmann's hundreds of individual drawings, hammering home the points

Gerhard Heilmann used his artistic talents and knowledge of fossil birds to make this reconstruction of Archaeopteryx

made in the text. These illustrations are undoubtedly the book's strength.

Best of all, perhaps, are the life reconstructions done by Heilmann. At the start of the book is a coloured painting of two *Archaeopteryx* courting, the colourful male displaying its tail and wing feathers to an uninterested and rather drab-looking female. Another colour plate shows that other great fossil bird, Marsh's toothed *Hesperornis*, sunbathing on rocks near the shore of a Cretaceous sea. These birds too are colourful with stripy backs not unlike that of the Disney fawn, Bambi. The black and white sketches also try to bring alive the subjects of Heilmann's text. Dozens of dinosaurs are depicted (many of them looking slightly overweight, a feature of dinosaur illustrations of the time), as were pterosaurs, other fossil birds and Broom's thecodonts.

Given that it was a cross between a scientific monograph and a highly illustrated encyclopaedia of prehistoric life, it is not surprising that *The Origin of Birds* was not only a success but also a bestseller. It was the making of Gerhard Heilmann: from being a noted natural history artist he became an acknowledged expert on dinosaur and avian palaeontology. Even so, he was apparently treated with contempt in Denmark, something that was put down, in one of his obituaries, to 'narrow-minded envy in certain academic circles'. His days of intensive palaeontology research had actually long since passed; *The Origin of Birds* was essentially based on work that he had performed over ten years earlier.

By all accounts Heilmann's indifferent treatment by Danish academics left him with a bad taste in his mouth and it was some time before he again put pen to paper. When he did, the result was another classic, *The Universe and Tradition*, of 1940, a popular book on Darwinian evolution running to some 500 pages and with over 1,100 illustrations. This work is peppered with Heilmann's anti-religious feelings, for which he was to become known during his later years and which gave him the image of being a rather cantankerous old man. Heilmann died in 1946. Despite the thousands of drawings (and his banknote designs) that he left behind, he is still best known for that one great work, *The Origin of Birds*, a volume that was a turning point in palaeontology.

11

The Wilderness Years

UNUSUAL AND UNEXPECTED though it may have been, Heilmann's *Origin of Birds* was to draw a line underneath the issue of bird evolution for some decades afterwards. This was not only because of the logic that Heilmann had applied to the subject but also because the whole field of bird evolution was about to go totally out of fashion.

There are as many fads in science as there are in high street clothes design. Topics become fashionable to study and then just as quickly become unfashionable again. This was as true in the past as it is today. We have already seen that there were at least three phases of dinomania between the 1850s and 1920s, each of which was sparked by a wave of scientific interest in dinosaurs. Another wave of interest in dinosaurs followed the release of Steven Spielberg's 1993 blockbusting film *Jurassic Park*. Similarly, the 1980 theory that an asteroid hit the Earth 65 million years ago, wiping out the dinosaurs, led to a scramble for research grants that lasted for fifteen years, with scientists of all persuasions coming up with ever more inventive way in which life on Earth could have been atomized by a natural disaster.

By the 1920s the subject of the origin of birds had been extremely lucky. It had received attention for an abnormally long period of time. In fact, interest had been almost continuous from the discovery of the first *Archaeopteryx* in 1861 until the publication of *The Origin of Birds* in 1926.

Not long after the initial excitement caused by Heilmann's book had died down the world found itself plunged into a deep economic recession, quickly followed by a devastating world war. By the time the world had stabilized again, the issue of bird evolution was no longer a hot topic. Apart from anything else, there was a general agreement that Heilmann had got it right and that the birds were not descended from the dinosaurs but from the postulated missing link, 'Proavis'. The scientific community believed that it would just have to wait until a specimen of Proavis turned up in the fossil record.

Although the issue of bird evolution may have entered its wilderness years, this is not to say that there weren't occasional additions or breakthroughs. One of the most important came from a series of daring and productive expeditions led by the adventurous palaeontologist Roy Chapman Andrews.

By the 1920s much of the western world had been explored for its fossils, and new finds were becoming a rarity. Andrews, a former taxidermist who had joined the American Museum of Natural History in New York, became convinced that the last great treasure store of fossils must lie in the hitherto unexplored and dangerous Gobi Desert of Mongolia. He was especially convinced that the missing link between humans and apes must lie within this region.

His employers were less than convinced but when Andrews managed to raise $250,000 from local businesses and benefactors they reluctantly let him lead an expedition there. One critic at the time said: 'They may as well look for fossils in the Pacific Ocean as in the Gobi'.

In April 1922 Andrews' first expedition, which consisted of three cars, two trucks, seventy-five camels, tons of fuel, food and water and a lot of guns and ammunition, set off from China toward the Mongolian desert. Within weeks the expedition was digging up the bones of dozens of giant dinosaurs and mammals, (from the post-dinosaur Tertiary era) hitherto unknown to science. The success of the first expedition was such that Andrews and his team, which included Edward Cope's protégé Henry Osborn, were sent back to Mongolia in 1923. This time the expedition members hit the palaeontological jackpot when they stumbled across a bright red sandstone formation that they nicknamed the Flaming Cliffs. The sediments here had been laid down about 70 million years ago, right at the end of the era of the dinosaurs, and immediately they began to produce cartloads of bones.

Especially numerous was a small four-legged and horned dinosaur called *Protoceratops* which looks a little like a shrunken version of its more famous American cousin *Triceratops*. Over a hundred skeletons of this animal were recovered, earning it the name of 'sheep of the Cretaceous'. Other new species were also found, including the bizarre looking *Oviraptor* and the now internationally famous *Velociraptor*.

The best discovery was, however, made by the palaeontologist George Olsen who was searching among the Flaming Cliffs when he came across an unusual rounded object eroding out of the sediments. Further digging revealed more of these rounded objects. The puzzled Olsen took them back to the camp, where another palaeontologist identified them as fossilized eggs, a rare find in the fossil record.

The same spot the next day revealed yet more eggs and as the expedition members fanned out across the slopes it became apparent that the entire landscape was full of these eggs eroding out of the hillside. The only fossils that had been found in that region were those of dinosaurs plus some very small shrew-like mammals. The eggs were several centimetres in diameter and so could only really have come from a dinosaur. As *Protoceratops* was by far and away the most common dinosaur there, it was assumed that the eggs must belong to them (although we now know that many must have belonged to *Oviraptor* too).

This was a revelation. Being reptiles, it had long been assumed that the dinosaurs laid eggs (and some probable dinosaur shell fragments had been found in France) but until that day there was no absolute proof of this. Furthermore, the Mongolian eggs weren't just occurring individually but had been preserved in entire nests containing a clutch of a dozen or so. When these excavated nests were viewed in their entirety they looked very similar to those of living birds. The nests were shallow and circular depressions with the eggs having been deliberately arranged inside them. Based on this evidence it looked very much as though the Gobi dinosaurs had made themselves a nest, laid their eggs in it, arranged them and then probably stayed near the nest until they hatched.

This behaviour is different to that of most living reptiles, which simply bury their eggs in a pit and then either leave them to it or, in the case of crocodiles, return only when they have hatched. The Gobi dinosaurs' behaviour is, however, very reminiscent of way in which birds nest and look after their young. This analogy did not attract much attention at the time. It was a missed hint that the dinosaurs might be more bird-like than perhaps Heilmann had supposed.

Andrews' Mongolian expeditions continued for several years and were a scientific success and a public relations coup for the American Museum of Natural History, to which the returned Gobi specimens belonged.

Andrews himself became a celebrity and cultivated the image of an adventuring palaeontologist, battling the elements and local bandits in order to bring home the fossils. More recently there have been some doubts as to how great Andrews' actual scientific contribution to these expeditions was. While Andrews was unquestionably a brilliant leader and courageous adventurer, some people now paint a picture of him as being more in love with his gun than with fossils. While his palaeontologists hunted the desert floor for bones, Andrews was apparently more likely to be out shooting dinner. He even shot himself in the leg on one occasion. Even so, Andrews managed to write a number of best-selling books based on his adventures and it has long been rumoured that the swashbuckling movie archaeologist Indiana Jones was based on Roy Chapman Andrews, although Jones' inventor George Lucas denies this.

Political instability at the end of the 1920s brought an end to the Mongolian expeditions. It was to be decades before the Flaming Cliffs would again be explored for their fossils.

In the years after Andrews' expeditions the world collapsed into World War Two. Unresolved political issues created an aggressive Germany which invaded, occupied and eventually fought for control of the whole of Europe. Unlike World War One, in which armies squared up against each other on elongated fronts, this conflict was all-inclusive. Waves of aeroplanes from either side bombed cities, towns and landmarks, leading to horrific structural damage and loss of civilian life. The aerial bombing was not accurate and as well as military targets many cultural buildings were hit, including museums.

During my time as a research palaeontologist I would periodically need to borrow fossil specimens from German institutions. Sometimes all I would receive was a letter explaining that the specimen I wanted had been destroyed during the war. Between 1939 and 1945 Europe lost countless scientific specimens, works of art, historical documents and buildings to stray bombs, rockets or tank shells, proving that it is not just human life that can be lost in wartime.

At the start of World War Two the three *Archaeopteryx* specimens were probably in the worst locations possible. The 1861 specimen was in the Natural History Museum in central London, the 1876 one in the Humboldt Museum in central Berlin whilst half of von Meyer's fossilized feather was in the Munich Bavarian State Collection (the other half being in Berlin with the 1876 *Archaeopteryx* specimen). All three cities were large and industrial and therefore high on the enemy's target list. By 1945 large areas of Berlin, Munich and London were almost totally flattened.

Within these cities all three museums were on the receiving end of aerial bombardment. The London Natural History Museum, under which a concrete-lined government bunker had been built, only took a glancing blow that merely damaged its eastern façade. The Berlin Humboldt Museum was not so lucky. The central hall of its elongated building received a direct hit, separating the west wing from the eastern one. When I visited the Humboldt in the 1990s the museum was still in two halves, the central hall remaining in its collapsed state awaiting the money to repair it. The outside of the museum also bore scars of the street fighting that took place at the end of the war. Munich too suffered extensive Allied bombing, with large areas of the city being laid waste.

In London many of the Natural History Museum's most

valuable specimens were shipped to warehouses in the country-side for safe keeping. The *Archaeopteryx* was probably among them and thus spent the war isolated from the horrors of aerial bombardment. The Berlin and Munich specimens apparently stayed put and a miracle must have preserved the Berlin *Archaeopteryx* from being either annihilated or stolen during the war, especially considering the direct hit taken by the Humboldt Museum. A few metres in the wrong direction and the Allied bomb would have deprived the world of one of its great fossil treasures.

For some time it was believed that the Munich feather had not been so lucky and that the specimen had been destroyed in the bombing. In 1954 the British palaeontologist and director of the London Natural History Museum, Gavin de Beer repeated the news of its destruction only to receive a letter from the head of the Munich museum explaining that the specimen was safe and well and on display. In an age of destruction and looting, the *Archaeopteryx* specimens, the icons of evolutionary theory, had survived intact.

For the London and Munich specimens, surviving the war was the end of their brush with destruction but in post-war Berlin the Humboldt Museum found itself inside the Russian sector. As world war turned into Cold War, so the Humboldt's location within viewing distance of the Berlin Wall effectively removed the best *Archaeopteryx* specimen from the gaze of western scientists for nearly half a century.

Not that post-war western or eastern scientists were especially bothered by the question of bird evolution. In fact, palaeontology as a whole lost its popular appeal: even the dinosaurs were temporarily removed from the spotlight. The only place for dinosaurs now was as the animated stars of science fiction movies. In 1955 Sir Gavin de Beer produced a highly detailed 70-page monograph about the London *Archaeopteryx* which drew together all the known information about this specimen since its discovery nearly a century earlier. It was the most detailed work on the specimen since Huxley's examination of it in 1867. De Beer notes that no fewer than thirty-eight different people have tried to speculate as to exactly where the *Archaeopteryx* lies in relation to fossil reptiles and living birds.

De Beer followed the now standard line as laid out by Heilmann, i.e. that *Archaeopteryx* is a true bird and that the birds were not descended from the dinosaurs but from a distant common ancestor. De Beers' monograph is still the most detailed and accessible document available on the *Archaeopteryx*.

It is a mark of how out of vogue fossil birds were among scientists that when, in 1956, another *Archaeopteryx* specimen was found, it barely raised a ruffle in the scientific community. The new specimen again came from the Solnhofen limestone and from the same quarry as the original London specimen but about 200 metres further along and six metres higher in the rock face. This specimen was discovered by chance by a student from the University of Erlangen when he was poking about in a shed. Like all fossils found in the quarries, the slab had been placed to one side awaiting proper examination to see if the specimen was worth selling. In this respect little had changed since the days of Carl and Ernst Häberlein, and Solnhofen fossils were still highly prized by museums and professional collectors.

One might imagine that the fame of the first two *Archaeopteryx* specimens would have ensured that the discovery of a new specimen would be instantly recognized by the workers at the quarry face. Had the new specimen been of the same quality as its predecessors then this would undoubtedly have been true. Unfortunately it was not. The skeleton is incomplete, missing its head and several other major bones, and the feathers form only the faintest of impressions in the rock, not immediately visible to the naked eye. Unlike the first two *Archaeopteryx*, this animal must have rolled around on the seabed for some time, its body decomposing and bits being eaten or washed away before its burial. The new *Archaeopteryx* is neither pretty to look at nor revolutionary in its implications. Perhaps it is little wonder that the science community barely lifted its eyes in recognition of this new discovery.

The specimen itself was eventually described in 1959 and remained in the hands of the quarry's owner, Eduard Opitsch of Pappenheim, who allowed it to be displayed in the nearby and privately owned Maxberg Museum. Consequently the specimen became known as the Maxberg *Archaeopteryx*.

Opitsch recalled his specimen from the museum in 1974 and it joined his tightly controlled private collection of Solnhofen fossils, unavailable for viewing by anybody other than its owner. Removing the *Archaeopteryx* from its visible position in the Maxberg Museum proved to be a disastrous move. After Opitsch's death in 1991 the Maxberg *Archaeopteryx* could not be found anywhere. It had been stolen and probably sold at vast expense to another private collector keen to own a slice of palaeontological history. The Maxberg *Archaeopteryx* remains missing to this day, leaving the scientific world with only a few photographs and two plaster casts.

After so long in the doldrums, at some point the fortunes of the *Archaeopteryx* had to take a turn for the better. This was to happen in the late 1960s when this fossil bird would once again become the centre of scientific controversy. As with all aspects of the *Archaeopteryx* story, the start of this new phase of interest would be down to the actions of one person.

Dinosaurs of a Feather

PROFESSOR JOHN OSTROM is one of those rare individuals whose work has led to a U-turn in general scientific thinking. His ideas have also been the cause of a serious falling out between two scientific disciplines and have been at the centre of some of the bitterest confrontations since the heady days of Darwinism. As one person, who is closely involved in this field, commented to me: 'The study of bird evolution is not for the faint hearted.'

John Ostrom's background is standard enough. He was for many years a research palaeontologist at Yale University's Peabody Museum of Natural History built, it may be remembered, using money provided by George Peabody in order to propel his nephew Othniel Marsh into the heart of academia.

In 1964 Ostrom was on a field trip in Montana, exploring the 110-million-year-old Cloverly Formation rocks that outcrop along the semi-arid hillsides and cliffs there. All palaeontology fieldwork is a combination of educated guesswork and good luck. The educated guesswork often leads the palaeontologist to an area which has fossils. The luck comes from being in the right spot at the right time to find a fossil eroding out of the rock face.

Although it is not on the same scale as some of Marsh and Cope's quarries, the Cloverly Formation is known for dinosaur fossils, and during this particular expedition Ostrom's luck was very favourable. After days of searching, digging and scrambling among loose layers of mudstone, he chanced upon a fossil claw eroding out of the cliff face. The claw was unusual. It was large, highly curved and lethally sharp, quite unlike anything he had seen before. Further digging revealed more parts of the skeleton which, it soon became clear, belonged to an entirely new type of theropod dinosaur (the theropods include all the bipedal carnivorous dinosaurs such as *T. rex* and *Compsognathus*). Ostrom and his team carefully excavated their new find and were delighted to see that the skeleton was almost entirely complete. It was removed to Yale for further study.

It was to take Ostrom years of painstaking work to properly reconstruct his dinosaur. Many features of its skeleton were totally new to him. It was small, only a metre or so in height, lightly built, and attached to its foot was the lethal claw. In honour of this last feature, Ostrom named the beast *Deinonychus* meaning 'terrible claw'.

He realized that the claw of *Deinonychus* was attached to the foot in a strange way. Most theropods have three toes which allow the animal's weight to be evenly distributed across the foot. However, with *Deinonychus* the large claw on its second toe meant that this toe had become raised off the ground, putting the weight on the other two toes. This large claw was also attached in such a way that in life it would have been highly manoeuvrable like those on a modern cat. This had not previously been seen in dinosaurs.

Ostrom deduced that the sharp claw could only have been used as a weapon, in defence or attack, but only if the animal raked its legs downward across the body of another animal. This would mean *Deinonychus* being able to jump high and to run fast. If it used its claw effectively, *Deinonychus* would have been a swift and dangerous hunter.

A fast hunting dinosaur may not seem that unusual today but in the 1960s theropod dinosaurs were still seen as being rather slow and stupid animals that spent their lives lumbering across the landscape, occasionally stopping to bite the head off a passing *Stegosaurus*. It was normal for reconstructions (even those by Gerhard Heilmann) to portray dinosaurs as a uniform drab grey or brown. When they fought each other both predator and prey would be shown standing still biting at each other's necks like giant sumo wrestlers locked in stationary combat.

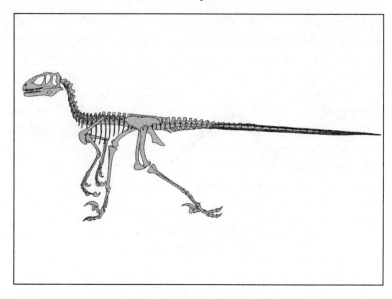

Deinonychus, *John Ostrom's vicious*
dinosaur which showed some
bird-like characteristics

However, the more that Ostrom saw of *Deinonychus* the more he became convinced that this small dinosaur was no stupid, lumbering giant. It must have been a fast and quick-witted animal which hunted by pursuing its prey at speed before attacking by jumping up and gouging at the stomach and flank with that terrible claw. Ostrom was seeing dinosaurs in a totally new light, making them look less like slow mechanical crocodiles and more like speedy hunting cheetahs.

Ostrom published his research on *Deinonychus* in 1969. The dinosaur was different enough to warrant the creation of a new subgroup of theropod dinosaurs. Ostrom named them 'dromaeosaurs', whose chief characteristic was their large claw.

This new and terrifying creature was greeted with interest by a scientific community which, after the post-war wilderness years, was slowly beginning to revive its interest in the dinosaurs.

Ostrom, however, wanted to look towards newer horizons.

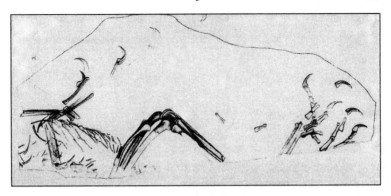

The Teyler Archaeopteryx *whose
wrist bones are similar to
those of Deinonychus*

He had spent years researching *Deinonychus* and after completing his study he decided to embark on an all-encompassing study of the world's pterosaurs, a group of fossil reptiles which had been ignored for several decades. Such a study would inevitably mean looking at the fossils from the Solnhofen limestone. After the *Archaeopteryx*, pterosaurs are the second most famous type of fossil to have come from the quarries around Pappenheim and it was from these animals that Carl Häberlein had made his first palaeontological fortune. Like the *Archaeopteryx*, the pterosaurs were often excellently preserved, not only fully articulated, but also with their delicate wing membranes intact. Moreover, there are considerably more preserved pterosaurs than *Archaeopteryx* specimens from Solnhofen.

In 1970 Ostrom embarked upon a tour of Europe's museums in search of his pterosaur specimens. His journey eventually took him to the Teyler Museum in Haarlem, Holland, where some of the Solnhofen specimens had been deposited during the mid-nineteenth century.

Not all of the Solnhofen's pterosaurs are shining examples of preservation. Many are just fragments of skeleton or even scraps of bone hidden away in the dusty corners of museums. In the

Teyler Museum Ostrom had come to study just one such scrappy specimen, a tiny piece of rock with a few bones in it which had been sitting in a glass cabinet since 1860. It had been placed there by Hermann von Meyer, the man who announced the discovery of the original *Archaeopteryx* specimen. Von Meyer had labelled it *Pterodactylus crassipea*.

Ostrom's study of this specimen began normally enough. Given its small size, he must have expected to look at it briefly, perhaps just long enough to confirm von Meyer's identification of this as a new species of pterosaur. Once it was out of its glass case Ostrom set about examining the few preserved bones on the small slab of Solnhofen limestone. The specimen consisted of a few arm and leg bones yet it was apparent that there was something unusual going on.

The closer Ostrom looked at the animal's arm bones, the more complex they became. There were three long fingers, each ending in a sharp claw. The middle finger was longer than the other two and all three were attached to a flexible wrist. This was certainly no pterosaur wing. In fact, the more he examined the fingers and wrist, the more Ostrom was reminded of the arm bones he had seen in *Deinonychus*. They were very nearly identical.

Deinonychus is a metre-high monster which lived tens of millions of years after the Solnhofen limestone had been deposited. It could not possibly be responsible for this fragile fossil, and yet the fossil looked distinctly dinosaurian in nature. Could it be some other type of small theropod dinosaur such as the Solnhofen limestone's other famous resident *Compsognathus*? Apparently not. Ostrom noticed surrounding the arm bones some very faint impressions which reminded him of feathers. The penny dropped. During his European travels Ostrom had also taken time to study the Berlin, Maxberg and London *Archaeopteryx* specimens in some detail. Of course he had seen these arm bones before. He was staring at a fourth *Archaeopteryx* specimen.

Ostrom was jubilant. He had managed to find an example of one of the world's rarest and most contested fossils. It was with some reluctance that he informed the Teyler Museum of his discovery, expecting to have the specimen instantly removed from his grasp and locked in the nearest bank vault. Luck was again with him. Not only was the museum delighted but they agreed to loan the specimen to Yale University in order to permit Ostrom to study it further.

The discovery of a new *Archaeopteryx* was of course to be welcomed but this particular specimen brought with it a problem. The Dutch specimen had been given the name *Pterodactylus crassipea* in 1857, several years before von Meyer coined the name *Archaeopteryx*. According to the laws of taxonomic nomenclature, the oldest name given to a fossil animal is the most valid. *Archaeopteryx* would have to change its name to *Pterodactylus*, a term which is not only anatomically wrong, but which sounds out of place when attached to a fossil with such an important scientific history.

For a few months it looked as though the complex rules surrounding the naming of fossils might actually succeed where Richard Owen had failed by giving the *Archaeopteryx* a new name that did not reflect its crucial evolutionary status. Fortunately, John Ostrom was on the case and spent much of his time defending the name *Archaeopteryx* which his discovery had suddenly rendered invalid. The lobbying paid off. The powers that be did eventually see sense and the *Archaeopteryx* was allowed to keep its famous and appropriate title.

This problem dealt with, Ostrom could begin to study his new specimen. His success was in more than just the identification of a new *Archaeopteryx* specimen which, after all, was not really going to threaten either the London or Berlin specimens in terms of completeness or beauty. What excited him most were the similarities he had seen between this *Archaeopteryx* and his new dinosaur, *Deinonychus*. Could this similarity really be coincidence? If it was not, then could current scientific thinking, which dismissed a direct link between birds and dinosaurs, be wrong? Ostrom became determined to find out. His results would open a real can of worms.

For almost half a century science had accepted Gerhard Heilmann's idea that birds had not evolved from the dinosaurs, as Huxley had suggested, but from the more ancient thecodont

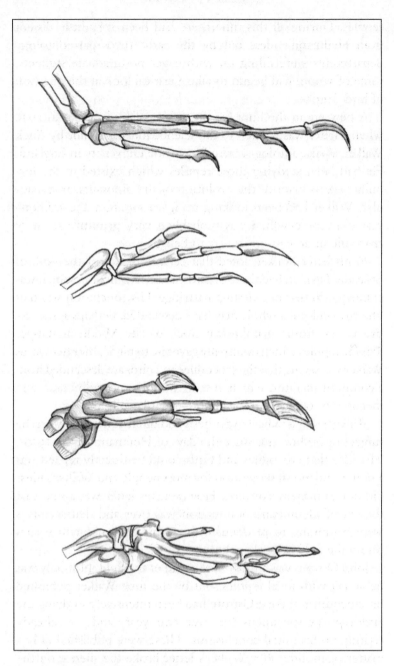

The wrists of Archaeopteryx, Deinonychus, *a juvenile hoatzin and a modern bird*

reptiles. During all this time there had been very little dissent from Heilmann's ideas but by the early 1970s palaeontology departments were filling up with eager postgraduate students, some of whom had begun to take a critical look at the question of bird origins.

A new era in the hunt for the origin of birds began in 1972 when a letter was written to the science journal *Nature* by Alick Walker, a palaeontologist from Newcastle University in England. He had been studying those reptiles which existed in the few million years prior to the evolution of the dinosaurs. In particular, Walker had been looking at *Sphenosuchus*, a 230-million-year-old reptile which was probably a very primitive form of crocodile or at least on its way to being one.

In his letter Walker noted that certain aspects of the skull of *Sphenosuchus* matched those of birds, as did its inner ear, which was compared to that of a nesting partridge. His conclusion was that 'the crocodiles as a whole may have descended, perhaps as successive waves, from an unknown stock of late Middle to Upper Triassic reptiles which eventually gave rise to birds'. In other words Walker was saying that the crocodiles and birds are descended from a common ancestor, which, if true, would remove dinosaurs and thecodonts totally from the picture of bird evolution.

Walker's was a radical hypothesis and the first new view on the subject of bird origins since the days of Heilmann in the 1920s. The idea that crocodiles and birds could be directly related was a rather outlandish suggestion for most people and Walker's ideas did not gain many converts. However, his letter was a sign that the era of Heilmann's domination was over and that scientists were beginning to re-evaluate the complex issues which surround the field of bird evolution.

John Ostrom was already way ahead of the field. Not only was he *au fait* with fossil reptiles, but by the time Walker published his crocodilian theory, Ostrom had been intensively studying the *Archaeopteryx* specimens for over two years and was already writing up his initial conclusions. These were published only a matter of months after Walker's letter broke the silence on the issue of bird origins. Where Walker had found one fossil reptile, *Sphenosuchus*, with some bird-like features, Ostrom declared that he had found hundreds. His thesis was very simple and harked back to the debates of the late nineteenth century. Birds, said Ostrom, are nothing more than feathered dinosaurs.

Ostrom had fused his study of *Deinonychus* with his study of *Archaeopteryx* and concluded the two skeletons showed marked similarities to one another. Not only were the fingers and wrist very similar but so too were the shoulder-blades, hips, thighs and ankle. Ostrom had even found Heilmann's missing collar-bone, which was small but nonetheless present, not only in *Deinonychus*, but also in a specimen of *Velociraptor* recovered from Mongolia a few years earlier. In the coming years collarbones were to be reported from most theropod dinosaurs, including *Tyrannosaurus*.

Finding dinosaurs with collarbones removed Heilmann's one serious objection to birds having evolved directly from the theropod dinosaurs. His strict use of Dollo's Law, which stated that dinosaurs without collarbones could not have evolved into birds, which had them, could be revoked. In an instant *The Origin of Birds*, a book that had been the palaeontologists' bible for half a century, became outdated.

For nearly a hundred years scientists had disregarded *Archaeopteryx* when looking at the origin of birds. The original Darwinian idea that *Archaeopteryx* was half reptile/half bird had been abandoned by almost everyone who had dabbled in bird evolution. Owen, Huxley, Seeley, Heilmann and others did not see this unique fossil as a missing link. Instead, they saw the *Archaeopteryx* as a type of bird already many million years down the line from the time when the first bird evolved. Of all the people we have encountered so far, only Othniel Marsh held fast to the idea that *Archaeopteryx* was a true missing link between the birds and dinosaurs.

After being on the sideline for many years, the *Archaeopteryx* was now in the spotlight again and, according to Ostrom, the initial Darwinian interpretation of this fossil had been entirely correct. To him it is indeed a halfway house between the reptilian dinosaurs and modern birds. Without its feathers, said

Ostrom, *Archaeopteryx* would have been identified as a small theropod dinosaur very similar to *Compsognathus*. Ostrom's revival of *Archaeopteryx* was not based on a whim. It was not even based on his having found the elusive dinosaur collarbone. To him the similarities between *Deinonychus*, *Archaeopteryx* and living birds were numerous, undeniable and progressive through time. As an example, let us take a quick look at one of the strongest pieces of evidence which is commonly cited in favour of birds having evolved directly from the dinosaurs.

The factor that led John Ostrom to identify his new specimen as an *Archaeopteryx* was the arrangement of bones in its wrist. Those in the Teyler specimen did not match that of a pterosaur but did look very similar to that of *Deinonychus*. Over the coming years Ostrom took this study of the arm and wrist further.

The wrists of ancient fossilized reptiles from before the time of the dinosaurs were a rather basic affair. They were a jumble of bones and ligaments designed purely to allow the animal to walk. The wrist can flex backwards and forwards and that's about it; refined movement was not possible. After all, the animal only needed to be able to place one foot in front of the other. Living birds are different. They have wrists designed to swivel along precise planes, giving them the refined movement necessary to control their wings both in the air and on the ground. Their wrists contain a series of delicate, rounded bones which move against each other along predetermined lines. Thus birds' wrists are very distinctive.

When Heilmann began to search for the ancestors to modern birds he knew that the wrist was one of the key features that had to be taken into consideration. A look at the *Archaeopteryx* specimens showed that it had a wrist that was nearly identical to that of modern birds. However, and no matter how hard people looked, nothing approaching a bird wrist could be seen in any ancient fossilized reptiles. The dinosaurs known to science at the time did not have it, nor did the pterosaurs, crocodiles or any other type of ancient reptile. Even Broom and Heilmann's thecodonts still had a primitive reptilian wrist. With no comparison in the fossil record, birds' wrists were assumed to be unique and it was thought that this type of wrist must have evolved very suddenly indeed. The wrist of living birds was thus not expected to be found in any other type of animal, living or extinct.

Except that it had been found. The flicker of recognition that crossed Ostrom's face in the Teyler Museum came about because he instantly knew that he was staring at the wrist of a bird, not a pterosaur. It was also because he knew that he had also seen the wrist arrangement in a most unexpected place – in *Deinonychus*.

Deinonychus belonged to a group of dinosaurs which had yet to be properly studied in Heilmann's day. In fact Ostrom was one of the few people ever to have studied them in detail. Although not identical to *Archaeopteryx*, the wrist of *Deinonychus* shows an extraordinary similarity. Both have three clawed fingers leading to a wrist made from a series of small and rounded bones, allowing the wrist to swivel in a near-identical manner. To Ostrom this could not have come about by chance. The birds must have evolved from a dinosaur from within the same group as *Deinonychus*, and to judge by the skeleton of *Archaeopteryx*, which Ostrom considered to be more dinosaurian than bird, that ancestor probably lived just before the time of the Solnhofen limestone.

One further piece of evidence could be pulled into the equation, and this time from a living animal. Heilmann and many others had long known about a strange bird called the hoatzin which lives in the flooded swamps of South America. The adult bird is a colourful and eccentric-looking beast but it is the chicks which have attracted the notice of palaeontologists. Hoatzin chicks are scraggy and drab in colour but they have one unique feature which sets them apart from other living birds – they have three distinctive claws emerging from their wings. These are present only in the juveniles and are used by the chicks to help them climb back into their nests after falling out (hoatzin chicks are hyperactive, and tumbles to the ground are frequent).

When the flesh and feathers are stripped away, the clawed wing of a young hoatzin looks little different from that of *Archaeopteryx* and *Deinonychus*. Later in life the hoatzin claws become reduced and fuse together to produce an adult wing that looks little different from that of all other living birds. Could these claws be an example of a genetic throwback to the hoatzin's dinosaur past?

They have certainly been read as such by many palaeontologists but at the very least the hoatzin brings into question the validity of Dollo's Law of irreversibility on which Heilmann relied so heavily in his *Origin of Birds*. As the ancestors to the hoatzin do not appear to have had clawed wings, the hoatzin is seen by some as a neat link between modern birds, *Archaeopteryx* and *Deinonychus*. As well as the wrist, features in the feet, legs, shoulders and pelvis of *Archaeopteryx* and *Deinonychus* are also near-identical, something that Ostrom also took delight in pointing out. He finished his initial study by confidently stating that:

> The skeletal anatomy of *Archaeopteryx* is almost entirely that of a coelurosaurian dinosaur [such as *Compsognathus*] – not thecodont, not crocodilian and not avian. Indeed, if feather impressions had not been preserved all *Archaeopteryx* specimens would have been identified as coelurosaurian dinosaurs. The only reasonable conclusion is that *Archaeopteryx* must have been derived from an early or mid-Jurassic theropod.

Ostrom's timing was perfect. The publication of his theory in 1973 coincided with a new wave of young up and coming palaeontologists whose minds were open to new ideas about bird evolution. They too were studying fossilized birds and reptiles and in many cases Ostrom's ideas fitted in with the evidence that they themselves were seeing.

In the same way that Heilmann's *Origins of Birds* had managed effortlessly to convert a generation of scientists to the idea that birds could not have evolved from the dinosaurs, so a series of influential papers from Ostrom began effortlessly to convert people back again. Whereas Heilmann's argument had relied upon a few differences between the birds and dinosaurs, linking them both to a missing ancestor in the fossil record, Ostrom's relied on dozens of similarities and concluded that the ancestor was already there to be seen in the form of the theropod dinosaurs. It is little surprise that by the late 1970s the idea that birds are descended from dinosaurs was being seen as the new standard theory of bird origins by most palaeontologists.

This theory was taken much further by many people. Birds are warm-blooded and highly active animals. Until the discovery of *Deinonychus* the dinosaurs were mostly seen as being slow, plodding reptiles. However, some palaeontologists asked the obvious question – if birds *are* descended from dinosaurs then could the dinosaurs themselves not have been warm-blooded and active?

Huxley himself had once suggested that the dinosaurs were warm-blooded (although he may have based his idea on Harry Seeley's vision of warm-blooded pterosaurs) but this was roundly ignored at the time. Now the notion was being taken more seriously. A few years further on and it is now accepted the dinosaurs were highly active animals (although not necessarily warm-blooded), a view which is reflected in the modern crop of animated dinosaur features such as *Jurassic Park* and *Walking with Dinosaurs*.

Strong support came from the dinosaur specialist Dr Bob Bakker, who was once described to me as 'the *enfant terrible* of the dinosaur world'. Bakker is certainly a larger-than-life and somewhat controversial figure whose talks are guaranteed to pull in the crowds at conferences and to generate heated arguments afterwards.

In 1974, less than a year after the publication of Ostrom's original paper, Bakker and a colleague, Peter Galton, wrote an influential letter to *Nature* suggesting that following Ostrom's work the birds and dinosaurs need no longer be seen as separate animal groups. Instead he suggested that they both be placed in a new class of animals called the dinosauria. 'Bats are not separated into an independent class merely because they fly,' observe Bakker and Galton. 'We believe that neither flight nor the species diversity of birds merits [their] separation from the dinosaurs.'

Bakker himself was later to forcefully put forward his own ideas concerning fully active and warm-blooded dinosaurs, earning him his reputation as a maverick. Although not everybody follows Bakker's point of view in every detail, there is general agreement within the palaeontology community that prior to the 1970s the behavioural capabilities of the dinosaurs had been severely underestimated. The view of both dinosaurs and birds was changing and all thanks to John Ostrom and his fascination with the *Archaeopteryx*. However, not everybody was so convinced.

'If you mount a dinosaur skeleton and a chicken skeleton next to each other and then view them both through binoculars at fifty paces then they look very similar. However, if you look at them in detail then you suddenly find that there are huge differences in their jaws, teeth, fingers, pelvis and a host of other regions.'

These are the words of Alan Feduccia of the University of North Carolina, to whom I spoke at length about his opposition to the bird–dinosaur theories of Ostrom, Bakker and others. Feduccia is an academic ornithologist who has become heavily involved in the area of bird evolution. Like many in the ornithological community he has a deep dislike of the idea that birds could have evolved directly from dinosaurs, preferring to follow Heilmann's idea of a Triassic common dinosaur and bird ancestor.

Feduccia's conversion to the anti-dinosaur cause was typical of many ornithologists. Initially he had not the slightest interest in the question of bird origins, preferring to study living neotropical birds from Central America. Aside from a couple of papers on fossil birds, Feduccia did not enter the foray until the late 1970s when he was researching a chapter for a book on bird evolution. It was then that he became acquainted with Ostrom's ideas and started to see what he believes are 'serious holes' in the idea that birds are simply feathered dinosaurs. He published a paper saying as much and found that by doing so he had taken sides in what was already deepening into a violent schism between two established branches of science.

Feduccia found that he was not alone and that many of his fellow ornithologists also had problems with Ostrom's ideas. In fact, there seemed to be a neat split between the palaeontology and ornithology disciplines on the question of the origin of birds. The palaeontologists almost exclusively believe in a dinosaur ancestry for birds while ornithologists took to Heilmann's idea of an ancient common ancestor for both groups. There are different ideas as to why this split should form so neatly along the lines of scientific discipline. One ornithologist, who wished to remain anonymous, explained to me that palaeontologists are incapable of seeing the differences between birds and dinosaurs. She explained that they are 'coming at this from the wrong direction. They start with a dinosaur skeleton and assume that it must be related to birds simply because they already know that all birds are dinosaurs. They can see the general similarities . . . but ignore the specific differences.'

In return many palaeontologists view the ornithologists as being stubborn and refusing to give in to the inevitable.

Mark Norell, a palaeontologist and a keen advocate of Ostrom's ideas, believes that the debate over the origin of birds has effectively finished. 'It's done,' he says with certainty. 'There's just a couple of people holding on who happen to be particularly vocal in their commentary about it but in the professional community it's definitely a minority and a very small minority at that.'

There can be no doubting the strength of feeling over this issue but how did such a standoff come about, and which side is nearer the truth?

Opposition to Ostrom's ideas did not arise spontaneously but slowly built up during the 1970s and only formed into a coherent movement during the 1980s. We have already seen that the opening shot in the bird evolution debate came from Alick Walker who advocated the crocodiles as the ancestral group to the birds. Walker himself continued to promote this hypothesis during the 1970s but later abandoned it after spending some years closely examining the *Archaeopteryx* specimens. In 1985 he concluded that the 'original concept of a particularly close relationship between birds and crocodiles has become so tenuous that it is very difficult to sustain'.

However, the idea of crocodilian birds was later adopted by others, most notably Larry Martin of the University of Kansas who carried on Walker's quest without him. Others, including Alan Feduccia, preferred to continue with Heilmann's original idea of an ancient reptilian ancestor for both dinosaurs and birds.

After a shaky start the various anti-bird–dinosaur factions began to get themselves more organized. They were, and still are, fewer in number than Ostrom's advocates but some of them are highly vocal and adept at using the media to make themselves heard. By 1985 this movement had been given an unofficial nickname: BAND, an acronym that stands for Birds Are *Not* Dinosaurs.

In overcoming Ostrom's ideas the BAND scientists had several big problems. Ostrom's theory had the advantage of a named reptilian ancestry from which the birds could have evolved. He was able to stand in front of a theropod dinosaur skeleton, such as *Deinonychus*, and point out the similarities between it and the *Archaeopteryx*, the conclusion being that *Archaeopteryx* and *Deinonychus* had skeletons which were so close to each other as to make them direct relatives. He could then stand in front of an *Archaeopteryx* fossil and a living bird and point out the similarities between the two, thus forming a neat lineage from living birds to the *Archaeopteryx* to the dinosaurs.

BAND's task was far more difficult. They did not have an actual fossil which they could say was the ancestor to both the dinosaurs and *Archaeopteryx* but believed that there had been one, be it a crocodile or some other reptile. Its fossil just hadn't been found yet. For the time being the BAND argument would have to be based on disproving the link between birds and dinosaurs. Effectively this meant that their argument was centred almost solely on the *Archaeopteryx*, which BAND members considered to be a true bird (and not a feathered dinosaur). They had to prove that this famous Solnhofen fossil was unrelated to the theropod dinosaurs.

The arguments put forward by the various BAND members are based on anatomical studies which seek to highlight the differences between bird skeletons, especially *Archaeopteryx*, and those of the dinosaurs. This is part of the fundamental BAND belief that birds and dinosaurs resemble each other only superficially because of a form of evolutionary coincidence known as 'convergent evolution': this means that two totally unrelated animals come to resemble each other because they have a similar lifestyle.

There are dozens of examples of convergent evolution in the fossil record. Modern dolphins look identical to the ancient ichthyosaurs that swam in the Jurassic seas and yet one is a reptile, the other a mammal. Dolphins and ichthyosaurs look similar not because they are directly related, but because they are both aquatic predators that need to chase their prey and are hence streamlined. Another often used example is that of the Tasmanian tiger, an Australian marsupial mammal which became extinct during the 1920s but which is the spitting image of the wolf, a placental mammal from the northern hemisphere.

According to the ornithological community, convergent evolution is responsible for the apparent similarity between the skeletons of birds and dinosaurs. The dinosaurs and birds look similar because they both run on two legs and because they both led nimble cursorial lifestyles. Look closely at the skeleton of *Archaeopteryx* and that of a dinosaur, argue the ornithologists, and you will find some fundamental differences that preclude a relationship between the two. Again, some of the strongest evidence presented by the BAND scientists focuses on the hands.

Palaeontologists have long known that the reptilian ancestors to the dinosaurs all had five fingers on each hand. Indeed, Richard Owen was so keen on the idea that all animals have (or had) five fingers that he used it as one of his vertebrate 'blueprint' characteristics; since then this has been soundly disproved by the recent discovery of a 360-million-year-old, eight-fingered amphibian.

Although their ancestors may have been five fingered, *Deinonychus* and its theropod dinosaur relatives have only three fingers on each hand. This means that at some stage in their history the theropod dinosaurs lost two of their fingers through evolutionary adaptation. But which two had gone?

This question was first asked in 1980 by Samuel Tarsitano and Max Hecht, two BAND adherents. They looked at the evolutionary history of the theropod dinosaurs from the time of *Archaeopteryx*, about 150 million years ago, to the oldest known dinosaurs, which occur about 225 million years ago. They noticed that the oldest dinosaurs had five fingers, while some that were slightly younger had only four fingers and some that were yet younger (such as *Deinonychus*) had only three. Thus through time five dinosaur fingers could be seen to have reduced to three. By looking at the sequence of finger loss it was possible to deduce that the theropod dinosaurs had probably lost their two outer digits (i.e. the little finger and ring finger), leaving them with a thumb, index and middle finger.

Tarsitano and Hecht then looked at the three fingers possessed by *Archaeopteryx* and all modern birds (whose fingers are fused together). According to Ostrom's theory the finger arrangement of modern birds should be identical to that of the theropod dinosaurs. In order to gauge whether this was so, Tarsitano and Hecht studied the way in which the fingers of a bird develop during its growth inside the egg. (It has long been believed that the development of an embryo to one degree or another reflects the evolutionary history of the animal concerned. For example, many vertebrate embryos go through a brief stage where they have gills, a reflection of their fish ancestry.)

Several earlier studies of bird embryos, including some that date back to Heilmann's day, have tried to trace the development of the wing and have reached varying conclusions. More recent studies have settled on the idea that the three remaining fingers on living birds are the index finger, middle finger and ring finger. They have thus lost their thumb and little finger, keeping their middle three digits. If this is so then it means that the finger arrangement in theropod dinosaurs and birds is totally different. Dinosaurs like *Deinonychus* have the first three fingers (starting with the thumb) whilst birds have the middle three fingers starting with the index finger. If this is so then the birds are unlikely to be descended from the theropod dinosaurs as it would mean their re-evolving and then losing certain fingers which, whilst not impossible, is unlikely to have occurred in the brief gap of 20 million years or so that Ostrom places between *Archaeopteryx* and its true dinosaur ancestors.

The issue of fingers has probably caused more problems than any other between BAND supporters and Ostrom's pro-dinosaur followers. Mention the subject of dinosaur fingers to a palaeontologist and you run the risk of hitting a raw nerve.

Some palaeontologists accept that there is a discrepancy between the hands of birds and dinosaurs but point to the hundred or so similarities between the two groups. Some just dismiss the argument as irrelevant. Ornithologists use this argument more than any other in favour of the BAND belief that dinosaurs and birds are just an example of convergent evolution.

Ostrom argues that comparing adult dinosaur skeletons with bird embryos is wrong because, as we do not have any theropod embryos, we cannot tell exactly which fingers the theropods have lost through time. He also argues that using older dinosaurs to tell which fingers are disappearing is irrelevant because the ones chosen may not be ancestors of the theropods which gave rise to the birds.

In return Feduccia accuses the palaeontology community of taking the attitude that 'birds are dinosaurs and therefore birds and dinosaurs must have the same finger arrangement'. On the issue of bird and dinosaur fingers, both sides have what they feel to be convincing arguments but there is currently no way of proving which is the more correct.

Given the strong feelings on both sides it is perhaps little wonder that the matter of bird evolution rapidly reached stalemate. By the mid-1980s the palaeontologists had the weight of numbers on their side and the support of the scientific and popular press. On the other hand, the ornithologists were vocal and very persistent.

The battle between BAND and Ostrom's followers was only just beginning and would hot up considerably in the coming years. There were times when the relationship completely broke down. Speakers were shouted down at conferences and papers were blocked from publication after being deliberately sent to 'enemy' reviewers. I have even heard one person describe the opposite side as Nazis. Could these two fighting factions ever agree on anything?

As it turned out there was something that they could all unite over. The story of the *Archaeopteryx* was to be stepped up a gear. Things were about to become very strange indeed.

The Demon Fossil

IT MUST BY now be apparent that the *Archaeopteryx* has the uncanny knack of being able to attract trouble. From the discovery of the first specimen, this feathered enigma has spent most of its time being tugged between various scientific and religious groups each with its own vested interest in the way in which this fossil should be interpreted.

The mid-1980s saw the *Archaeopteryx* already embroiled in a feud between palaeontologists and ornithologists but as the decade wore on so others were to add their twopence worth, and in a totally unexpected way.

Had this fossil been sentient, the 1980s would have instilled a sense of *déjà vu* in the *Archaeopteryx*. Its immaculate timing had brought it into a Victorian scientific world which was trying to come to grips with the evolutionary (and then revolutionary) ideas put forward by Darwin. For the first few decades of its existence the *Archaeopteryx* became a pawn in the battle for and against the idea of evolution and its causes. As we have seen, Darwin eventually won the day and the issue shifted away from *Archaeopteryx*'s evolutionary status and on to the question of the origin of birds.

From this it might be imagined that the big debates over evolution had all but disappeared at the end of the nineteenth century and for years this was true. Although most religious groups had never come to terms with the anti-Creationist ideal behind evolution, many had learned to live with it. Scientists and church leaders simply agreed to disagree over the issue of evolution. It was a status quo that held for many decades.

There was a brief while after World War Two when science could do no wrong in the eyes of the general public. Advances in domestic technology fuelled a consumerist society eager to have its household chores, such as cleaning, washing and cooking, automated and to have its leisure provided via television, radio or gramophone. Electronics, plastics and the increasing use of the combustion engine created the start of the suburban dream to which we all subscribe to this day.

But nothing lasts for ever and by the late 1960s what was once new and miraculous technology was being taken for granted. In the light of the Vietnam war and the stockpiling of nuclear arms, a youth-orientated society was more suspicious of science. Part of the problem undoubtedly came from a growing gap between the public and science itself. A century earlier it had been easy for Huxley to stand before his 'working men' and explain the latest progress of scientific thought most of which could be neatly summarized in a few sentences. The science of the late twentieth century was a different affair. The big discoveries were no longer just about new types of fossil or the latest means of recording music. They were in astrology, physics or chemistry and were very specialized.

Few of these discoveries were relevant to people's everyday lives, and to many the great scientific institutions became remote and monolithic, emblems either of the military or of a faceless state. This general distrust of science continued into the 1970s and became worse as people who had provided for all their physical needs began to look towards the spiritual void in their lives. They felt the need to 'find themselves', or at least find out what purpose their existence on Earth served. Some turned to new age and occultist beliefs, others back towards the religious establishment.

When asked about the question of evolution, one Church of England vicar explained to me that there was no need for the Church to deny what Darwin had said because the Bible and *The Origin of Species* are not actually incompatible. 'It simply means that God is in control of evolution,' he said; 'the story of Creation is metaphorical and so cannot be taken literally.' These are sentiments that many adopted over the years, including

Richard Owen. What is the point in picking a fight with evolutionists when theology can smooth out the differences
between science and organized religion?

However, some of the new generation of people being
attracted back to the Christian religion in the 1970s were not
interested in bending the words of the Bible in order to fit with
Darwin. To them the Bible had got it right first time and science
had got it wrong. This new brand of radical preaching declared
that the Earth and universe are only a few tens of thousands of
years old and that all fossils were buried during the Great Flood
of Noah. Science had fluffed its radiometric dating and, when
you put all this together, evolution itself could be dismissed as a
myth brought about by wilful determinism on the part of palaeontologists, biologists, geneticists and others.

This new way of viewing the progression of life was called
Creationism (because of its central belief that the world was
created by God) and it operated most conspicuously within the
new evangelical Christian churches that had sprung up in nearly
every small town in the Christian west. By the early 1980s the
rise of popular evangelical Christianity was beginning to
threaten some of the more established churches. The movement
was also beginning to gain a measure of political power.

In the American deep south and in Queensland, Australia,
Creationist Christians in positions of local responsibility
managed to get the theory of evolution removed or demoted
within school science curricula. Their justification was that evolution was still just a theory and that children also had the right
to hear alternatives theories. Sometimes the alternatives were
given instead of Darwin's theory, with biology textbooks that
mentioned evolution being banned from the classroom.

Court orders flew backwards and forwards, turning and over-
turning the various decisions made in favour of either the
Creationists or the evolutionists. Reading the accounts of some
of the goings on in these battles one can almost hear the voice
of Senator Hilary Herbert shouting to Congress in 1892 about
Othniel Marsh's 'birds with teeth'! The battle continues to this
day.

Early on, many Creationists realized that in order to deal with the issue of evolution head on they would have to answer the biblical criticisms of palaeontologists and come up with counter-arguments that went beyond simply quoting the Bible. The end result was the establishment of several institutions which specialized in the study of 'Creationist science'.

Leaving aside the issue of geological time (which is not of direct concern to this book), the fundamental issue that Creationists had to deal with was the Darwinian belief that one species could evolve into another entirely separate species. It was this issue above all others that would need to be addressed if the layman was to be convinced of the reality of biblical Creation. It was a point that would be raised at church meetings and on doorsteps across the land.

When, in 1986, I first asked an evangelical preacher about the issue of evolution he replied that it could not possibly work because 'it would mean that a butterfly is related to a rhino, and that's just daft'. Since then the debate has moved forward. Creationists have largely adopted the position that Andreas Wagner and Richard Owen held in the 1850s. Yes, argue the Creationists, there are fossils but there are no missing links. Without missing links as proof, evolution is nothing. However, and also like Owen and Wagner, Creationist science had a major problem with that most tenacious of fossils the *Archaeopteryx* which, thanks to the activities of John Ostrom and others, was undergoing a scientific renaissance and was being heralded as *the* missing link between dinosaurs and birds. Some Creationists began to take a deep interest in this fossil.

A quick look at the book of Genesis revealed a fundamental difficulty with the *Archaeopteryx*. The Bible quite clearly states that the birds were made by God on the fifth day of Creation and the land animals were made on the sixth. Not only did this mean that the *Archaeopteryx* could not be a missing link between birds and land animals like dinosaurs (unless one assumes that God made *Archaeopteryx* at midnight between the fifth and sixth days) but it also contradicts the order in which evolution dictates birds evolved (i.e. from a land animal to a bird not vice versa as the Bible suggests).

Creationists still had a very big problem with *Archaeopteryx*. It was OK to believe that this fossil was a bird but not OK to say that it was a feathered dinosaur. This led to a rather bizarre situation in which Creationists adopted many of BAND's arguments against birds having evolved from dinosaurs. The BAND scientists were less than amused to find that they were being quoted in an anti-evolutionary context, especially as they believed that there was another as yet unfound 'missing link' between the birds and thecodont reptiles further back in the fossil record.

In the meantime the work by BAND followers was the only grip that Creationists had on the *Archaeopteryx* fossil. This was not exactly a great threat to the fossil's evolutionary status. Then out of the blue came support from a most unexpected direction.

That Darwin's view of evolution threatened Creationist science is not surprising. That it should turn out to threaten an internationally acclaimed scientist and knight of the realm is perhaps more so. In 1984 the story of the *Archaeopteryx* took a turn that would produce one of the more bizarre episodes in its history.

Central to this story are two figures both of whom, whilst being highly respected as scientists in their field, are also known for their alternative views on the causes of evolution. They are Sir Fred Hoyle and Professor Chandra Wickramasinghe, both readers in astronomy at the University of Wales and both with a string of accreditations and major discoveries behind them. During the mid-1970s their interest in matters astronomical gradually drifted into other areas.

Hoyle had for some time had a preoccupation with the manner and way that disease epidemics start and spread across the globe. He was particularly fascinated by the results of a study on the common cold performed by Christopher Andrewes in the early 1960s. Andrewes noted that new strains of the cold virus often appeared in several parts of the world at the same time. Theoretically a virus should appear in one place and then spread outwards from there like ripples spreading from a stone dropped in a pond. How could these new viruses suddenly appear in totally different parts of the world at the same time?

Hoyle's interest was further aroused when he met with Wickramasinghe, a man who held a long-term belief that small single-celled organisms were capable of living in space and of being dispersed throughout the universe by comets. Hoyle and Wickramasinghe combined ideas to produce a new and radical theory – that all viruses on Earth originate in space and that modern viral epidemics, such as the 1918 influenza outbreak, can be linked to the Earth passing through comet tails which contain these extraterrestrial viruses.

This theory, known as panspermia, has attracted some support from within the scientific community and it is now known that complex organic molecules do occur in space (although they could not by any means be described as life).

In 1978 Hoyle and Wickramasinghe took their theory one stage further, claiming that Darwin's theory of evolution through natural selection was wrong. Instead, Hoyle and Wickramasinghe claimed to be able to see a new pattern in the fossil record, one showing that animal evolution was not continuous but instead occurred in bursts at very specific periods in time. The cause of these sudden evolutionary bursts was not natural selection but extraterrestrial 'genetic storms' hitting the Earth.

During these storms large quantities of highly reactive viruses would rain down on the Earth. The DNA of these viruses would become absorbed into that of the plants and animals on the Earth and combine with it to produce a simultaneous wave of genetic mutations in the fossil record. Evidence of these genetic storms can, according to Hoyle and Wickramasinghe, be seen in the periodic mass extinction events that affect the evolutionary history of life when millions of pre-existing species die, to be replaced by newer forms.

There have been a large number of such events in the last 540 million years, some larger than others, but probably the most famous is the so-called K-T boundary event at the end of the Cretaceous period (about 65 million years ago). This was the demise of many types of large reptile including the dinosaurs, marine reptiles and pterosaurs. It also marked the start of the mammals' success on Earth. Traditionally, mass extinction events are linked to sudden global changes in environment or, in the case of the K-T boundary, catastrophic events such as an asteroid impact. Hoyle and Wickramasinghe begged to differ.

To them the K-T boundary event was the result of an especially large genetic storm from space. Also, and for reasons which are not clearly stated in their text, Hoyle and Wickramasinghe are insistent that the first birds could only have evolved at this point in time. They do not dispute that birds evolved from reptiles (although which group of reptiles is not stated), just that the transition must have occurred 65 million years ago during the K-T boundary event and not 180 million years ago during the early Jurassic, as most palaeontologists believe. If so, it would be impossible for there to be any bird fossils before this time, something that the feathered *Archaeopteryx*, at 150 million years in age, seems to flatly contradict.

Hoyle and Wickramasinghe's interest in the *Archaeopteryx* was kindled by a letter which they received in September from Lee Spetner of the Weizmann Institute in Israel. Spetner wrote: 'For several years I have had a strong suspicion that the *Archaeopteryx* fossil is not genuine. I suspect that the fossils were fabricated by starting with a genuine fossil of a flying reptile and altering it to make it appear as if it originally had feathers.'

At this stage Hoyle and Wickramasinghe were not actually trying to debunk the *Archaeopteryx* but they communicated with Spetner anyway. What they received convinced them that there was a case to answer. A few weeks later Hoyle, Wickramasinghe and Spetner, who had flown over from Israel, were standing inside a secure room in the London Natural History Museum. In front of them was the London *Archaeopteryx* specimen which Richard Owen had fought so hard to buy from Carl Häberlein.

The chief aim of the visit was not just to view the London *Archaeopteryx* but also to take their own set of detailed photographs. To this end the group of scientists was accompanied by a professional photographer who busily snapped away while they examined the fossil with critical eyes. The world did not have to wait a great deal of time to learn of their results. Viewing and photographing the specimen convinced the four men that they were indeed dealing with a fraudulent fossil. In February they told the London Natural History Museum as much, but met with scepticism.

The team's photographs were passed on to Geoffrey Crawley, editor of the *British Journal of Photography* and, according to Hoyle and Wickramasinghe, a noted expert on 'spotting frauds'. He immediately concluded that the fossil was indeed fraudulent and offered to run a short article on the subject in the March 1985 edition of his magazine. Accordingly an article entitled '*Archaeopteryx*, a photographic study' appeared in conjunction with a press release. The article alleged that the London *Archaeopteryx* was a forgery, based on several key observations such as the apparent presence of foreign substances on the fossil (interpreted as the forger's paste), inconsistencies between the slab and counterpart of the fossil and several other features such as the way in which certain natural features of the rock-like mineral veins suddenly appear and disappear.

The conclusion was that the London *Archaeopteryx* had been manufactured by taking a fossil of the small dinosaur *Compsognathus*, covering it in a paste made out of ground-up Solnhofen limestone, laying some modern bird's feathers on top of this and then sandwiching the slab and counterpart back together again. When the two parts were separated the feathers were removed leaving a *Compsognathus* fossil with feather imprints around it.

This thesis was not a new one. By all accounts similar claims were verbally circulating around London in the months after Owen purchased this specimen in 1862. Many other anti-Darwinists since, including some Creationists, have also hinted that the *Archaeopteryx* was a fraud. Perhaps the major difference here was that these allegations were not being made by just anybody but directly by two world-renowned scientists.

Before Hoyle, Wickramasinghe or the London Natural History Museum knew what was happening, the allegations of forgery were spread across newspapers throughout the world. In many people's minds the *Archaeopteryx* was, and still is, seen as being the only solid evidence in favour of Darwin's view on evolution. Demolishing it was regarded by people as tantamount to demolishing Darwin. The sudden rush of press publicity took

A cartoon from the Fortean Times *parodies the idea
that some of the* Archaeopteryx *specimens
may have been faked*

Hoyle and Wickramasinghe completely by surprise. The press wanted interviews, whilst the palaeontological community wanted their blood. The publicity nonetheless buoyed them up and convinced them to continue what they had started. The London Natural History Museum was contacted once more and permission was sought to examine the *Archaeopteryx* again.

Permission was given but this time the reception was not so warm. Before they were allowed anywhere near the *Archaeopteryx* the team was given an hour's pep talk in which it was made quite clear that the museum was less than delighted at the attention being focused on its star exhibit. Hoyle, Wickramasinghe and their photographer were given a further hour to examine the specimen. It would be the last time that they would be granted permission to do so.

Based on this study and on other research carried out on casts of the *Archaeopteryx*, several further articles were published in the *British Journal of Photography*. All the various pieces of research were collected in a book which was frankly entitled *Archaeopteryx – The Primordial Bird: A Case of Fossil Forgery*. Its publication in 1986 produced another spate of popular press articles. The book provided a reason for the forgery, something that had been missing from the earlier articles. It was claimed that the *Archaeopteryx* had been an expert forgery made because it was known that some scientists were on the lookout for a missing link following the publication of *The Origin of Species*.

Richard Owen bought the fossil from Carl Häberlein in the full knowledge that it was fraudulent. It was apparently Owen's aim to try and trick Huxley and Darwin into publicly supporting the *Archaeopteryx* as evidence of the reality of the argument put forward in *The Origin of Species*. Once in this public position, Owen could then pull the rug from underneath them by exposing the *Archaeopteryx* as the fossil forgery that it was.

Unfortunately for Owen, neither Huxley nor Darwin rushed in to defend the *Archaeopteryx* publicly and so the fraud was never exposed. A second forgery, it was claimed, was later ordered by Ernst Häberlein, probably for financial gain, but this deception too remains unexposed. On top of this scenario, Hoyle and Wickramasinghe allege other cover-ups throughout history, most notably by scientists who studied the fossils and realized that they are forgeries but have maintained a conspiracy of silence on the issue.

All in all these were quite serious charges against one of the most famous fossils in the world but can they be substantiated?

Since the beginning the palaeontology community had been completely wrong-footed by Hoyle and Wickramasinghe's allegations. The Natural History Museum had never expected them to be taken seriously and had ignored the threat completely.

Refuting allegations of forgery was extremely difficult because so little is known about the manner of the *Archaeopteryx*'s discovery and because most of the press articles leaned towards Hoyle and Wickramasinghe's point of view. The quoted scientists all appeared either to dismiss the allegations out of hand or to be desperate for the *Archaeopteryx* to be seen as genuine. The whole episode did not show the scientific community in its best light.

Had these views been expressed by the Creationist Christian community, they would probably have raised little more than an eyebrow but Hoyle and Wickramasinghe had a reputation behind them. Even though the allegations had not been made through the normal scientific channels (i.e. through a peer-reviewed science journal) it was felt that they warranted a formal reply. Hoyle and Wickramasinghe had directed their efforts at the London *Archaeopteryx* and it was the curators of this specimen that hit back the hardest. In May 1986 a long and detailed paper was published in *Science* authored by Alan Charig, the museum's Chief Curator of Fossil Amphibians, Reptiles and Birds, and five of his colleagues. The paper had been written in the weeks after the first allegations were made but the peer review process meant that it had taken a year to come to press. The title was emphatic: '*Archaeopteryx* is not a forgery'.

Across four pages the paper dealt with all of Hoyle and Wickramasinghe's arguments in favour of forgery, and in some detail. Charig and his colleagues could find no evidence of any paste having been used on the fossil as there is an absence of shrinkage (which would be expected after a century in storage) and air bubbles in the feathers. The slab and counterpart fit together perfectly and the actions of the mineral veins are perfectly normal and can be seen on other Solnhofen fossils. It was also pointed out that much preparation work was done on the fossil during its time in the museum, revealing further feather impressions, which would mean that Owen *et al.* would have had to have added to the forgery themselves. (Hoyle and Wickramasinghe later said that the forgers had deliberately covered some of the feather impressions with another layer of rock so as to give the fossil an additional look of authenticity.)

The *Science* paper was really a matter of protocol. Few scientists had offered Hoyle and Wickramasinghe any support and hence few of the readers of *Science* needed much convincing that the *Archaeopteryx* wasn't another Piltdown Man style hoax. It was a way for the London Natural History Museum to lay the matter to rest. The article had, however, really only dealt with the matter of the *Archaeopteryx* itself; the historical arguments and the arguments against birds having existed earlier than 65 million years ago were for the most part ignored.

Whilst I wish no malice towards Fred Hoyle (who, sadly, died during the preparation of this book) and Chandra Wickramasinghe (who initially agreed to be interviewed by me but later changed his mind), their historical and palaeontological arguments really do not stand up to much scrutiny.

My research (and that by others) into the purchase of the London *Archaeopteryx*, as laid out in the early chapters of this book, does not tally with their idea that Owen knew he was buying a fake. His motives are clear – he wanted to get his hands on the fossil for nationalistic reasons and so that he could be the first to describe it, which he duly did in 1862. This means that if he had exposed it as a fake then he himself would have been made to look stupid. Huxley's lack of interest in the *Archaeopteryx* was due to it being inconvenient to his belief in the persistence of birds. Initially, he would probably have been delighted to see it exposed as a fake.

Darwin's indifference was caused by his unwillingness to defend his own ideas in public although his letters reveal him privately to have been fascinated by the fossil. His only endorsement appears in the sixth edition of *The Origin of Species*.

In my view, Hoyle and Wickramasinghe make many other historical misinterpretations of the history of the *Archaeopteryx*, including the statement that it was found in a near pristine state, whereas Carl Häberlein actually did much of the preparation, and hinting that Andreas Wagner may have been deliberately killed because he 'knew too much' about the conspiracy.

I am not accusing Hoyle and Wickramasinghe of writing their articles and books for the sake of publicity and profit. Having had a brief communication with Wickramasinghe I can attest that his interest is sincere. I also suspect that, like the Creationists, their desire to see the *Archaeopteryx* disproved comes from their long-held belief that the birds must have evolved at a particular point in time 65 million years ago.

With regard to this last point, both Hoyle and Wickramasinghe show a worrying disregard for the whole host of other bird fossils known from before the great extinction 65 million years ago. Othniel Marsh alone had collected 175 individual toothed birds and many others have been found since. Hoyle and Wickramasinghe deal with this in a sentence, claiming that *Hesperornis* is 'clearly a wading reptile'. It, like the flight-powered *Ichthyornis*, is dismissed because no fossil feathers have been found with it. Other finds known at the time, such as some Cretaceous birds from Mongolia, are not mentioned at all.

Hoyle and Wickramasinghe continually cite Occam's Razor, the principle that the simplest explanation of a problem is probably the correct one. Yet their theory is vastly more complex than the supposition that the *Archaeopteryx* fossils are genuine. They also state that 'everything published should either be documented, or accompanied by an observational or experimental demonstration, or by mathematical proof'. Their book has no notes or bibliography, making it difficult to see where the information has come from although two of their most-quoted books, *Life on Earth* by David Attenborough and *Before the Deluge* by Herbert Wendt, are popular texts which do not directly concern the *Archaeopteryx* and whose authors do not claim to have performed original research on the history of the fossil.

As a highly experienced palaeontologist who has seen both the London and Berlin *Archaeopteryx* specimens in detail, I can state that they do not look like forgeries to me.

The accusation of forgery may not have gone down well with the scientific community, but it was greeted with open arms by Creationist scientists who had hitherto had trouble getting a handhold on this inconvenient fossil.

Hoyle and Wickramasinghe's work has been used as direct evidence of the fallacy of evolutionary science and is normally quoted in the same breath as other famous hoaxes such as Piltdown Man and Onondaga Man. Many have taken the research further, widening its scope to include the Berlin *Archaeopteryx* and other fossil birds. With idea of forgery in the air, there was no further need for complex arguments about the *Archaeopteryx* fossil having been wrongly dated by geologists.

In 1990 Ian Taylor, a Creationist scientist from Ontario, Canada, gave a long talk on the Berlin *Archaeopteryx* to a Christian Science conference on Creationism. The talk was unequivocal in its belief that the Berlin *Archaeopteryx* is also a forgery.

When I communicated with Ian Taylor about his work on the *Archaeopteryx* it became clear that it was inspired by that of Hoyle and Wickramasinghe. He even claimed to have had help from Fred Hoyle and Lee Spetner in the preparation of a later paper on the subject. Taylor's arguments very much follow in the footsteps of Hoyle and Wickramasinghe and show a high degree of biological knowledge, some of which he uses to present palaeontologists with some questions about the feather arrangement and the positioning of various bones.

Many of Taylor's points are dealt with in the correspondence that followed the publication of his paper but to argue against Creationist findings is to miss their point. These papers do not seem to be written to convert sceptical scientists but to convince the faithful that the Bible has answers to any criticisms that science might raise. As such, the underlying principle of Taylor's work appears to be that the *Archaeopteryx* cannot possibly be a genuine fossil because its presence contradicts the Creationist science cause.

Taylor's work is not alone. The innovation of the Internet has given many pressure groups a cheap means of publishing their material. A brief search of Creationist science web sites reveals hundreds of references to *Archaeopteryx,* most of which claim the fossil to be a forgery. Sometimes they cite Hoyle and Wickramasinghe. Sometimes they don't. All such references show the power that *Archaeopteryx* still has after nearly a century and a half of scrutiny. It is and remains an inconvenient fossil which is capable of being interpreted in almost any way at all, depending on which theory it needs to fit.

It may not have troubled the scientific community too much, but the press portrayal of Hoyle and Wickramasinghe's work did stick in many people's minds. During the research for this book it was surprising how many people who had no interest in science at all remembered the allegations of forgery levelled against the *Archaeopteryx*.

In the aftermath the London Natural History Museum tried to allay public fears by putting on a display in 1987 entitled 'The Feathers Fly' which was designed to allow people to see that the *Archaeopteryx* was not made out of bits of rock and glue. The original London specimen was even put on display – but underneath a thick layer of bulletproof glass.

This led to accusations that the museum had in fact displayed a replica of the original which had been touched up in order to hide the forger's tell-tale marks. As with many conspiracy theories, the museum would be damned whatever actions it took.

The *Archaeopteryx* specimens not only have a knack of attracting trouble, but also a knack of turning up in the right place and at the right time (or the wrong place at the wrong time, depending on your point of view). In November 1987, less than two years after the publication of Hoyle and Wickramasinghe's book, a sixth *Archaeopteryx* specimen was discovered in the collection of Friedrich Müller, the former mayor of Solnhofen and a keen amateur palaeontologist. (A fifth specimen had been found in a Solnhofen quarry near Eichstätt in 1973.) It had sat in the collection for years, misidentified as a skeleton of the dinosaur *Compsognathus*, again emphasizing the anatomical closeness of these two fossils. As it resides in the Bürgermeister Müller Museum in Solnhofen it is commonly known as the Solnhofen *Archaeopteryx*.

The privilege of describing the new find went to Peter Wellnhofer, a long-time *Archaeopteryx* enthusiast working for the Bavarian State Collection in Munich. The new specimen was larger than any of the others, lying on its side and headless but otherwise identical to the London specimen. Best of all, faint impressions of feathers were visible where the wings would have been. The discovery was not just important because of the *Archaeopteryx*'s rarity in the fossil record. It was important because this fossil could not have been a forgery.

Although no exact data were available, the fossil had been discovered about a century after the London specimen and had been in private hands ever since, yet it had feathers. Wellnhofer was very pleased to be to say that 'a question of a forgery in the new specimen does not arise, the impressions of the wing feathers are direct evidence that *Archaeopteryx* had feathers'. Like Wellnhofer, the scientific community greeted this new specimen with joy because it allowed them to stick their tongue out at those still making accusations of forgery.

Not that it has made any difference. The new fossil has simply been ignored, as has any other *prima facie* physical or historical evidence which goes against the idea of forgery. To some people the mere existence of the *Archaeopteryx* is a threat in itself.

A New Flock of Fossil Birds

HOYLE AND WICKRAMASINGHE'S accusations had served to unite both the palaeontological and the ornithological communities in support of the *Archaeopteryx* even though the fossil bird meant different things to them both. The discovery of the 1987 Solnhofen *Archaeopteryx* calmed a few ruffled feathers within the science community.

It also meant that it was back to business as usual for those on both sides of the origin of birds debate. The ornithologists still believed that the birds could not have evolved from dinosaurs while the palaeontologists believed that they had. It was an argument that had been in deadlock for nearly a decade. Both sides relied on the *Archaeopteryx* for their evidence, interpreting the fossil in different ways. What was needed were new fossil birds: some that weren't *Archaeopteryx* and weren't from the Solnhofen limestone.

Their prayers were answered. The next decade was to produce more fossil bird specimens than had been found during the entire previous century. Surely they would settle the origin of birds debate. Wouldn't they?

In August 1986, right in the middle of the forged fossil fiasco, there came news of a new and exciting discovery from Texas. A palaeontologist from Texas Technology University named Sankar Chatterjee claimed to have found a fossil bird of some 225 million years in age. If true, then this would radically alter the traditional palaeontological view that bird evolution took place just before the time of the *Archaeopteryx*, 150 million years ago.

Chatterjee had actually found the fossil in 1983 but it was just a series of bone fragments which did not look all that special and so he did not examine them closely for another two years. When preparation did begin Chatterjee immediately recognized what he thought were classic avian features in some of the bones. In particular, the skull appeared to be very bird-like, as did the arms and shoulders. However, when assembled the fossil animal was very incomplete and those bones that were present were not very well preserved. The evidence for this fossil being a bird was by no means conclusive.

At the time Chatterjee was working under a grant from the National Geographic Society, which had given him the money to clean up and study the bones. When they got wind of his find, they immediately became excited and started to talk of holding a press conference and other public relations exercises. Chatterjee was apparently nervous of this and later denied having had anything to do with the publicity organized by the National Geographic.

'But I never went to the press,' he said, 'I did not do the press release. I never called any journalists. We have to sign a form when we get a grant from National Geographic saying that they will do the press – we cannot do anything. It's entirely their ball game.'

All control was now out of Chatterjee's hands and he suddenly found that National Geographic had called in John Ostrom for a second opinion. Ostrom later recalled that he had been asked to provide an opinion on the fossils based on a cursory look at the bones. 'The bones were so smashed that you could make almost anything of them,' he says. 'I had only a few minutes with each bone. Chatterjee was telling me what things were, to save time, and I gave him the benefit of the doubt. But one has to approach this situation as free of prejudices as possible. I wish the circumstances had been different.'

With Ostrom having given a sort of positive response to Chatterjee's fossil, National Geographic produced a press release proclaiming to the world that Chatterjee had found the world's oldest bird fossil. The new animal was even given a name by

Chatteree, *Protoavis* and a daring description of the bird claimed that it had feathers, could fly and communicated by sound.

The release came at time when there was not much happening in the world and Chatterjee found himself being plastered over every front page across the globe. Ordinarily this would be every scientist's dream come true but for Chatterjee it was a nightmare of gigantic proportions.

The discovery of *Protoavis* was ground-breaking news that could potentially sink the idea that dinosaurs and birds are related to each other. *Protoavis* was older than all but the most primitive dinosaurs, which meant that if the fossil was a bird, then the birds as a whole must have evolved from a reptile group that was even older than the dinosaurs. *Protoavis* could stop the 'birds are dinosaurs' brigade dead in their tracks. It could be the early missing link for which many BAND people had spent a lifetime looking. As might be imagined, the palaeontological community did not greet this news with joy.

The first complaint was over the name. *Protoavis* not only presumed that this find was avian in nature, but also that it was very

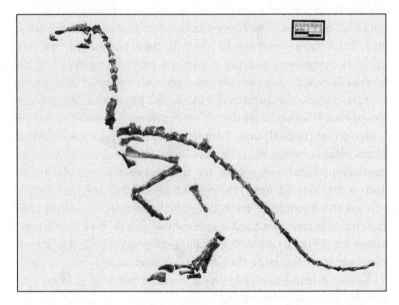

Could Protoavis *really be a 225-million-year-old bird? If so, then dinosaurs could not be the ancestors of the birds*

close to 'Proavis', a general nickname used by many people (including Gerhard Heilmann) to describe their vision of a hypothetical primordial bird. Even before any details were known *Protoavis* received a baptism of fire.

The second problem was a matter of scientific protocol. Whilst the National Geographic Society had released details of *Protoavis*, Chatterjee had yet to formally publish any pictures or a detailed description of the fossil. Generally, scientists announce their results just before they are about to be published in a journal, so that other scientists can look at the evidence put forward for themselves and comment on it. But Chatterjee did not do this so although everybody in the scientific community knew that *Protoavis* existed, they would have to travel to Texas to see it. Several people did just this. They were not impressed.

'I looked at it and didn't know what it was. The skeleton is just smashed and mashed and broken,' says Michael Parrish, who was one of the first to view *Protoavis*. 'I wish the elements identified as wings were better preserved. The material wasn't complete enough for me to be convinced.'

Others agreed and to date there are very few people who have publicly supported Chatterjee's belief that *Protoavis* is actually a bird. Even those who would like it to be a bird have been put off by the negative publicity which the issue has attracted. And when Chatterjee did publish his work on the fossil (five years later, in 1991), the issue was not settled and publication only served to stir up some of the old controversies again.

'It's a real roadkill,' says Timothy Rowe of the University of Texas. 'Palaeontologists walk a delicate line. We do have fragmentary material, and we do try to squeeze as much from the data as we can. There's always the temptation to go a little beyond the bounds of what the actual specimen will support, and that's the line that Sankar crossed badly. The basic argument is that he points to a lot of characteristics as being avian, but if you look at the skeleton, they're all contingent on his reconstruction. There are a bunch of ways you could put it back together. And he wants it to be a bird.'

A decade later and Chatterlee still very much believes that *Protoavis* is an early bird but he is wary of talking about it for, as he explained to me, he has 'had such bad experiences regarding the *Protoavis* controversy in the past'. One gets the impression that he feels he has been a victim of circumstance and of the power of the media. In an interview in 1992 Chatterjee defended his actions:

> I may be wrong, or I may be right. It's just a hypothesis that I found something that is the earliest bird. The thing is, nobody has discussed the material in my paper. Instead they are dealing with the peripheral subjects, which really bothers me. Some people who have never seen this specimen have made all kinds of comments. I'm really getting very tired.

The BAND scientists do not yet have their missing link in *Protoavis* but one does detect a hint of optimism in those who are searching for bird ancestors of that sort of age. 'It does have a remarkably bird-like skull,' remarks Feduccia whilst at the same time refusing to commit himself one way or the other.

It seems that for the time being no one is prepared to risk declaring *Protoavis* a bird in case it later proves to be not so. The humiliation would be too much to bear.

Hot on the heels of *Protoavis* came the discovery of yet another *Archaeopteryx* specimen, the seventh and, arguably, the most significant one to be found since the 1877 Berlin specimen. Behind the discovery was again the figure of Peter Wellnhofer who, with three *Archaeopteryx* to his name (he was also instrumental in the discovery of the Eichstätt and Solnhofen specimens), was rapidly gaining a reputation as *Archaeopteryx*-finder general.

The new specimen had come from a private quarry near Solnhofen where it was found in 1992. Unlike all the other *Archaeopteryx* specimens, this one was instantly recognized by the quarry workers and thus handled with some care. It was subsequently dubbed the 'Solnhofer Aktien-Verein *Archaeopteryx*' after the company which owned the quarry. This was a much

smaller animal than any of the other known fossils and was relatively complete lying stretched across its slab. Most importantly,
attached to the wings and tail are the unmistakable impressions
of feathers. If any serious suspicions remained that *Archaeopteryx*
was a forgery, then this would surely put an end to them.

Aside from this, there were certain other features which made
this fossil special. It has a sternum, a feature unknown in the
other specimens, a bone that in modern birds is attached to the
muscles used in flying. Additionally, the skull shows a set of bony
plates preserved on the inside of the lower jaw. These features,
known as interdental plates, are very reptilian, being found in
theropod dinosaurs and the older thecodonts. The new specimen was different enough from the other known *Archaeopteryx*
for Wellnhofer to declare it a new species, only the second one
known to science. It was duly named *Archaeopteryx bavarica* after
the German region in which the Solnhofen limestone, with its
extraordinary fossils, is found.

Solnhofer Aktien-Verein *Archaeopteryx* was a welcome addition to the fossilized bird stable but it did little to advance or
settle the ongoing battle over bird evolution. The sternum
revealed it to be more bird-like while the interdental plates
affiliated it to a reptilian ancestry – but which group of reptiles
was made no clearer than before. It was now more obvious than
ever that if this dispute was to be settled then it was not going to
be through the discovery of more *Archaeopteryx* fossils.

New fossils of different animals, from different times and
different places, were urgently needed but despite 150 years of
searching only a handful of ancient bird fossils were known.
Archaeopteryx was still the oldest known bird (leaving the disputed *Protoavis* aside) and by a margin of some 70 million years
or more. The gaps in the birds' fossil record were large, the problems apparently insurmountable.

Thus far we have focused on the physical evidence that has been
used to try and link the birds with the various reptile groups put
forward as candidates for their ancestry. However, a second argument had also rumbled on since John Ostrom revived the origin

of birds issue in the early 1970s. This argument again split along scientific disciplines, the palaeontologists on one side, the ornithologists on the other. The argument was over something very simple – how did the first birds take to the air?

The first time that this question arose was at the turn of the century but there was really very little evidence to support either cause. It was again Gerhard Heilmann who settled matters with his assertion that the first birds would have been gliders, climbing trees in order to launch themselves into the air. Typically, Heilmann accompanied this idea with a picture of his imaginary Proavis clambering up a tree while a second animal glides gently past in the background. This theory stated that powered flight came later. BAND ornithologists such as Alan Feduccia, Larry Martin and Storrs Olson are all promoters of this idea, which has since become known as the 'tree down' theory.

Palaeontologists, on the other hand, view the situation from the other way round. To them flight evolved from the ground upwards. Theropod dinosaurs are not exactly built to go clambering around in trees. Their arms, hands, legs and feet would not have been able to effectively grasp branches or pull their body weight upwards to any degree and yet the palaeontology community cites them as the ancestors to the birds. In terms of flight this can only mean one thing – that the first flying birds must have taken off from the ground. Ostrom's initial idea was that flight must have developed gradually over time. He envisaged feathers as having initially evolved as some form of insulation for his warm-blooded dinosaurs. As generations of these feathered dinosaurs ran around on the ground, their arms became more developed in order to help them catch their prey. The arms developed further still until wing-like structures evolved which would allow the first running dinosaurs to tentatively take to the air. From running dinosaurs to airborne birds in several easy steps, and with no need for tree-climbing.

Ostrom declared that *Archaeopteryx* itself would have been incapable of flying and was in fact a ground-dwelling animal which used its wings to help trap insects. The wings were the wrong shape for flying and not strong enough, and the feet would not have been able to grasp branches properly. 'I conclude,' said

Ostrom, 'that *Archaeopteryx* was not capable of powered flight other than that of fluttering leaps while assaulting its prey.'

Palaeontologists agreed on the idea of flight having come from the ground up but not all were convinced by the idea that *Archaeopteryx* was flightless. It was very quickly pointed out that both the London and Berlin *Archaeopteryx* specimens possessed feathers that were asymmetrical in shape, i.e. there would have been more filaments on one side of the central vane than the other. The isolated fossil feather first seen by von Meyer shows this asymmetry in even more detail.

In modern birds asymmetrical feathers are entirely synonymous with flight. The uneven shape of the feather acts like the curved wing of an aeroplane, giving the bird lift as it flaps its wings through the air. The only modern birds with symmetrical feathers are flightless ones such as ostriches, rheas and kiwis.

Archaeopteryx may not have been graceful in the air but it was most certainly a flyer: the presence of a sternum in the Solnhofer Aktien-Verein specimen was the final proof of that. Ostrom had to admit defeat and now concedes that the late Jurassic skies of Germany would have been host to the aerial antics of the *Archaeopteryx*. The date for the first bird flight was moved from being some time after the time of *Archaeopteryx* to some time before it.

Many BAND members take great delight in this revision of the *Archaeopteryx*'s behaviour. One drily commented that such backtracking by palaeontologists 'is the shape of things to come'.

Ground up or tree down? Again each theory has serious implications for the questions surrounding the origin of birds. There is a fundamental lack of fossils to help in the promotion of either idea but this has not stopped the debate on the origin of flight. This issue produced a surprising volume of literature, but by the mid-1990s it too was deadlocked.

Alan Feduccia summed up the situation when he commented that 'Ornithologists view *Archaeopteryx* as a tree dwelling fairly typical bird albeit primitive. Palaeontologists view these forms as feathered dinosaurs. So, in fact, the background of the various scientists involved has played a dramatic role as to how we interpret the fossil record.'

Popular opinion was definitely with the palaeontologists and the world at large was beginning to accept the idea that the sparrows and hawks in their back gardens were in fact dinosaurs in disguise. The ornithologists' opinions were considered by many to be marginal and insignificant, but the BAND scientists were not going to go down without a fight. However, whether it was the origin of birds or the origin of flight, by 1995 the palaeontology and ornithology communities had argued themselves to a standstill with each side incapable of giving an inch. The battle had been a draining one and looked set to become one of those issues that could rumble on for decades without making any further progress. Then something most unexpected happened, a discovery which would break the deadlock and take the scientific infighting to new heights.

Europe and North America have been turned inside out by geologists. The rocks have been collected, studied, dated and classified. The rock formations have been mapped and explored from top to bottom by palaeontologists on the lookout for new specimens. While specimens are regularly found, the big surprises are getting fewer by the year. Even the seabed surrounding some countries has been mapped in great detail in the continual search for underground oil reservoirs.

Other parts of the planet are more surprising. There are vast areas of desert, forest, tundra and open plains where geologists have yet to set foot, let alone study the rocks. Political instability and economic underdevelopment have kept yet more areas of countryside unexplored. It is from these remote or inaccessible regions that the next big palaeontological discoveries have long been expected to come.

Some isolated finds had already hinted at what could lie beneath the ground. In the early 1980s the palaeontologist Jack Horner found vast numbers of fossilized dinosaur nests at the appropriately named Egg Mountain in Montana. There was evidence that the dinosaurs had guarded their eggs and then fed their young – very bird-like behaviour. Renewed exploration of Roy Chapman Andrews' Mongolian cliffs produced a magnificent specimen of the dinosaur *Oviraptor*. It was still sitting on its nest as though incubating the eggs. Mongolia also produced the bizarre and tiny theropod dinosaur named *Mononykus* which has only one powerful claw on each hand. *Mononykus* has a skeleton that is so bird-like, including a sternum, that some palaeontologists have tried to classify it as a bird. Meanwhile from Australia came several Cretaceous fossilized feathers which, it was speculated, could have come from either dinosaurs or birds.

The palaeontology community took all these as signs of the similarities between birds and dinosaurs. The BAND ornithologists simply dismissed them as examples of convergent evolution. To them dinosaurs just happened to look and behave like birds. The stalemate continued.

The United States and China may not have much in common with each other in the modern world, but during the time of the dinosaurs they formed parts of a vast continental expanse with an extensive network of inland ponds and rivers. In both countries the large dinosaurs that roamed the land would die and their remains be washed into shallow, stagnant lakes. In America these lakes later emerged as the bone quarries exploited by Marsh and Cope during the 1880s and by many others since. In China such deposits lay untouched for a further century before Chinese scientists started to exploit them in the 1970s.

From Neolithic times onwards fossils have been a highly saleable commodity. Today a healthy black market in stolen or illegally exported fossils exists right across the globe. In the early 1990s Chinese palaeontologists became aware that some very good but fragmentary dinosaur fossils were occasionally turning up on the black market. Detective work led back to a remote farming region inside Liaoning Province about 400 kilometres or so north of Beijing. Here was a string of small quarries worked by the local farmers for building stone. These produced some unusual and good-looking fossils, some of which found their way on to the black market. The Chinese scientists travelled to Liaoning for a closer look.

The Liaoning quarries represent a very unusual geological situation. The sediments there were laid down in a freshwater lake near to a volcano. The lake must have been a quiet one, with few currents stirring its depths or waves disturbing its surface water. Periodically the volcano would erupt, sending clouds of choking ash and poisonous gases into the air. Any animals caught up in this toxic outburst were doomed. Flying animals would be knocked from the sky; land animals stopped in their tracks. Swimming animals too would have died as their watery environment was invaded by the volcanic ash. A small percentage of the bodies found their way into the freshwater lake where they sank into the still, deep waters.

Their remains were rapidly buried by a layer of volcanic ash, its fine particles working its way into all parts of the body and ensuring that the whole animal would be preserved in its entirety, protected from the attentions of scavengers and the degrading effects of oxygen. After 120 million years the bodies of these animals became exposed to the air once more by the actions of wind, rain and the hammering of geologists and local farmers.

The Liaoning fossils are remarkable. A complete cross-section of early Cretaceous life is preserved there. Fish, shellfish, plants, frogs, turtles, mammals, shrimps, pterosaurs and dinosaurs have all been recovered, the majority of species being new to science. However, it was not the range of life which caused the Chinese scientists to sit up and pay attention: these fossils were not just well preserved, they were excellently preserved. Not only were all the bones there but also in many cases the skin, fur and internal details. The fine volcanic ash had done its job superbly, producing a fossil locality every bit as stunning as the Solnhofen limestone, if not more so. A systematic study of the Liaoning fossils began in earnest.

The Chinese palaeontologists could spend only a few weeks of the year at the quarries collecting and studying the fossils and so the might of the Chinese state swung into action. Hitherto most of the collecting had been performed by farmers from neighbouring villages and so members of the local government went to the area and reminded people that it was illegal to hold or sell fossils without government permission. Any new finds were to be handed in to the police in return for a small reward. Breaking this law, the farmers were told, would risk a lengthy prison sentence.

The pep talk had at least some effect and slowly but surely specimens that would have been discarded or passed on to the black market began to find their way to the palaeontologists who were eager to study them.

It was in 1994 that the Liaoning fossil quarries began to reveal their scientific importance. The fossil-hunting farmers delivered three specimens to the Institute of Vertebrate Palaeontology and Palaeoanthropology in Beijing. These fossils were indistinct and only partially complete but there, surrounding the skeletal remains of what had once been a tiny animal, was the unmistakable outline of feathers.

A new fossil bird had joined the Mesozoic aviary and this one was only a few million years younger than the *Archaeopteryx*. Would it be able to settle the long-running dispute between the ornithologists and palaeontologists?

With the Cold War having diminished in severity it has for some years been common practice for academic institutions from behind the iron and bamboo curtains to involve western scientists in their study. Not only are the additional money and facilities most welcome, but it also provides them with access to publication in the American and European scientific journals, ensuring that any results will be read by practically every scientist in the world.

Two American scientists were called in to help in the study of the new bird. They were Alan Feduccia and Larry Martin, both of whom were highly vocal members of the BAND community.

The fossil bird turned out to be very different from *Archaeopteryx*. In fact, it was much more modern looking. In particular, it had a horny beak just like living birds, taking the known age of birds' beaks from 70 to 120 million years in one jump. It also had a pygostyle, a short bony remnant of a tail that supports the tail feathers. The animal was named *Confuciusornis* in honour of the Chinese philosopher.

Although it was initially thought to rival *Archaeopteryx* in age,

Confuciusornis is probably 20 to 30 million years younger, at around 120 million years. The fossil was a major find and was the first Mesozoic fossil bird to rival *Archaeopteryx* in perfect preservation and anatomical detail. It was not, however, much of a missing link.

That *Confuciusornis* was a true bird which could have flown was not doubted by anybody. It was feathered, beaked and had claws to help it perch in trees. There was little obvious reptile to be seen. However, there were some subtle differences in the way in which the pro- and anti- 'birds are dinosaurs' people interpreted the lifestyle of this animal.

Larry Martin and Alan Feduccia reconstructed its skeleton in an upright position, making it look like a squirrel standing on its hind legs. This was because they thought that *Confuciusornis* would have been capable of climbing up trees using the claws on its wings, a clear reflection of their belief in the 'trees down' theory and possibly hinting at a gliding ancestry for this bird.

Another study, by Luis Chiappe of the American Museum of Natural History and others, made *Confuciusornis* look much more pigeon-like, a clear reflection of their belief in the 'ground up' hypothesis.

Unlike the *Archaeopteryx*, this time the scientific community did not have to wait decades for new finds. Liaoning farmers were turning up this delicate bird's remain by the dozen. On one occasion over forty specimens were recovered from one bedding plane alone, giving the impression that a flock of these birds might have died as the result of a catastrophe, possibly a volcanic eruption.

Unknown to either Chinese or western scientists, fossils of *Confuciusornis* had actually been available on the black market for some time. Phillips Fine Art, an auction house in New York, had had a lot of specimens since 1993 but had refused to sell them until the animal had been formally named. As with Marsh and Cope's dinosaur skeletons, there was such an abundance of specimens it was not long before all the major museums had their own *Confuciusornis*.

This fossil was just a teaser. The Liaoning quarries were about to reveal their true scientific worth.

★

In the spring of 1996 the palaeontology rumour mill started to generate stories about a new type of dinosaur which had been discovered in China. Some said that it was half-dinosaur and half-bird, others that it was the missing link between the dinosaurs and birds. For months the rumours rumbled on.

It became known that as well as several key Chinese palaeontologists, Phil Currie of Canada's Royal Tyrrell Museum had also become involved in the project. It was also clear that he was going to remain tight-lipped on the subject, preferring to go down the traditional route of first publishing the results of his study and then talking about them. However, by the summer the Chinese scientists had broken their silence and had started to give vague hints as to the nature of their discovery to the Beijing press. It would only be a matter of time before the news crossed the Pacific Ocean and reached American ears. Faced with the inevitable, Currie and his Chinese co-worker, Chen Pei-Je from the Nanjing Institute of Geology, revealed news of their new fossil at the conference of the Society of Vertebrate Palaeontology in October.

Currie and Chen held up pictures of their new find to a stunned audience. John Ostrom was apparently so overwhelmed that, having stood up to get a better view, he had to sit straight back down again. The fossil was unmistakably a theropod dinosaur, and a small one at that, being not more than a metre or so in length. The dinosaur had been discovered by a Liaoning farmer (who thought that it was a dragon) and then taken to the Beijing Chinese Geological Museum where it was named *Sinosauropteryx* (meaning 'Chinese reptile wing') by its director Ji Qiang.

Currie had not yet had time to study the fossil in depth but the feature that had got him so excited and sparked all the rumours was apparent even from the photographs. The skeleton of *Sinosauropteryx* looked little different from that of *Compsognathus* and was like that of any small carnivorous dinosaur apart from one vital addition. There, running along the entire length of the animal's back and tail, was a dense black fringe. This fringe, claimed Currie, could be the remnants of preserved feathers. *Sinosauropteryx* is, said Currie, 'a little

Sinosauropteryx: *could this ancient fossil really be a feathered dinosaur?*

feathered dinosaur' and thus 'one of the most exciting finds in decades'.

For years some of the more vocal proponents of a bird–dinosaur link had been describing the London and Berlin *Archaeopteryx* fossils as 'feathered dinosaurs', an expression that was guaranteed to bring howls of outrage from the BAND ornithologists. Now with the arrival of *Sinosauropteryx* it looked as though they had got the real thing. That *Sinosauropteryx* is a dinosaur cannot be questioned, but can that fine fringe along its back and tail really be described as feathers? It is here that the trouble arises.

The fringe certainly isn't composed of the long and distinctive flight feathers seen on *Archaeopteryx, Confuciusornis* and all modern birds. This is not surprising as there is no way on Earth that *Sinosauropteryx* could ever have flown. It has the short and stubby arms of a dinosaur, not the long spreading wings of a bird. However, from a distance the fringe looks very much as though it might be made from soft, downy feathers of the type used to stuff duvets and pillows.

When Currie and others finally got to look at the fringe structures under the microscope they were disappointed. Whatever it was composed of, the fringe would have been very dense in life, and in death its many filaments had clumped together making it almost impossible to separate out any one single filament for study. Even in their clumped state it could be

Longisquama: *if those elongated features are really feathers then the palaeontology textbooks will need to be rewritten*

seen that these were certainly not feathers in the traditional sense of the word.

At first Currie believed that he could see some sort of divided structure in the fringe filaments making them look like downy feathers. Further studies have complicated this view somewhat. The filaments, which were given the complex title of 'integumentary structures', were certainly soft and pliable and varied between about four centimetres and five millimetres in length but the inability to study any one filament in detail has allowed controversy to creep in.

While Currie and the Chinese scientists argued that the fringe of *Sinosauropteryx* was composed of 'protofeathers', the BAND scientists have a different opinion. 'These are almost certainly not feathers,' Alan Feduccia told me. 'They are a product of the biogenic preservation procedures operating in Liaoning.' He went on to explain that it was by no means certain that these structures were on the outside of the body at all. They could well be degraded muscle fibres, something denied by the Chinese palaeontologists, who argue that the fringe shows every sign of being on the outside of the skin, not underneath it. Again the BAND scientists found themselves on the defensive, trying to explain away a new fossil find that fits the predictions made by palaeontologists. But this was not a simple case of arguing over small differences in the skeleton: this was far more serious. This was about why feathers should have evolved in the first place.

The 'trees down' theory put forward by BAND supporters dictates that feathers must have evolved specifically to enable animals to glide or fly through the air. This means that they evolved for one function only – flight. Feathers, the argument goes, require a good deal of the body's energy and resources to manufacture and to do so without a real need for them would be a waste of an animal's time and energy.

The palaeontology 'ground up' theory takes the reverse position. In this feathers must have evolved for some other purpose on a flightless dinosaur and then, in time, have been adapted to allow it to fly. In modern birds feathers serve several functions but they are chiefly used for flight and for insulation (and also for display purposes). If, wondered the palaeontologists, the dinosaurs didn't evolve feathers for flight, then could they have used them for insulation? The idea that birds evolved from dinosaurs has often led to claims that the dinosaurs, like birds, must have been warm-blooded. Animals which have warm blood need insulation to help trap heat next to their bodies to stop them from freezing to death. The mammals have hair and the birds have feathers, which extends their geographical range much further than that of ordinary naked and cold-blooded reptiles.

The fringe on *Sinosauropteryx* looked very much as if it could have been used for insulation. It is very reminiscent of the fossilized fur seen around the perfectly preserved 50-million-year-old mammals found in the German Messel oil shale deposits. Assuming that the fringe was indeed external and not degraded muscle, then *Sinosauropteryx* seemed to be good evidence that the dinosaurs were warm-blooded. This fitted in with the palaeontologists' view of bird evolution. *Sinosauropteryx* seemed to be saying that feathers evolved first for insulation and then later for flight.

BAND supporters argue that using feathers for insulation makes no sense because the amount of energy used to create them would be an example of 'evolutionary overkill'. An example of using a sledgehammer to crack a nut.

Convincing though *Sinosauropteryx* was to the palaeontologists, there was still room for doubt. It did not matter how many times the press called it a 'feathered dinosaur': that the fringe was indeed made of feathers or protofeathers had yet to be proven.

Even the recovery of a second, far more magnificent specimen of *Sinosauropteryx* did nothing to resolve this. This new fossil threatened to rival *Archaeopteryx* in its beauty, being preserved almost as if the animal were taking a stride when it died. The thin dark fringe can again be seen running from the top of the head across the back and down to the end of its tail. Distinctive and unmistakable but also still problematic. 'Much more work needs to be done to prove that the [fringe filaments] have any structural relationship to feathers' is the conclusion of the Chinese palaeontologists who studied this new wonder.

As well as a fringe the new fossil had two eggs inside it and the tiny jaw of a primitive mammal preserved where the stomach would be expected to be. After a century of speculation this was proof positive that the dinosaurs enjoyed dining on our ancient mammalian forebears.

Up until 1997 the only western scientist ever to have seen *Sinosauropteryx* was Phil Currie. This was to change when in March of that year a delegation of four scientists travelled to China to see the new supposed feathered dinosaur specimens for themselves. The team consisted of John Ostrom, Peter Wellnhofer and Alan Brush, all of whom are in favour of the idea of dinosaurs having feathers, and Larry Martin, who is not.

Reports of their trip brings back memories of Huxley's voyage to America. Huxley was amazed by Othniel Marsh's fossil collection in 1876, and now the various Chinese universities and museums pulled out all the stops to impress their colleagues. The Liaoning fossils had been steadily pouring in for a few years and the importance of this deposit could not now be questioned.

The western scientists were shown fossils of all kinds – mammals, lizards, insects, birds and dinosaurs.

As a public relations exercise the visit was terrific success. Like Huxley, the scientists returned to their institutions raving about what they had seen. The reviews were ecstatic. 'This is one of the most important palaeontological sites in the world,' said Martin. 'There is enough here to keep palaeontologists busy for a century,' added Ostrom.

It became apparent that *Sinosauropteryx* was just the tip of the Liaoning iceberg and that there was much more yet to come. After one hundred years of ambiguity and argument over just one fossil, the *Archaeopteryx*, the study of the origin of birds was about to be deluged with many intriguing new specimens, and all from this one Chinese locality.

While in China the western scientists had been given a peek at the shape of things to come. In a dark corner of the Chinese Geological Museum they were shown what their host Ji Qiang, the museum's director, called his 'special animal'. This turned out to be a turkey-sized skeleton which was laid out in some detail on a slab of Liaoning shale. It had long strong legs, wing-like arms, a toothed skull and, according to Ji, feathers. When the team saw the animal they were amazed. It was indeed a well-preserved dinosaur with the same kind of fluffy covering as had been seen in *Sinosauropteryx*. The 'special animal' immediately became the centre of attention, but a problem soon arose.

All four western scientists concluded that whatever the structures were, they were not feathers in the sense that we know them today.

Larry Martin, who is not keen on the idea of feathered dinosaurs anyway, told me the structures 'didn't have a single feature which we would normally use to diagnose a feather. All four of us agreed but the Chinese said that unless we announced these [features] as being feathers our trip was over.'

A dilemma indeed, considering that the delegation was scheduled to travel to Liaoning to visit the actual quarries. Diplomacy was called for.

'We put our heads together,' continued Martin, 'and agreed to call them "protofeathers". It didn't mean much since no one knows what a protofeather looks like. The only reason to think that they are feathers is if you think that birds are dinosaurs and therefore dinosaurs must have had feathers. To call it a feather it must have a feature like a feather.'

The political wording worked and the scientists were allowed to continue with their trip as planned. By all accounts the Liaoning quarries were every bit as spectacular as we in the west have been led to believe.

The 'special animal' was studied further by the Chinese and later named *Protarchaeopteryx*. The optimism they had expressed to Larry Martin and others came across in their subsequent conclusions about the fossil. Not only was *Protarchaeopteryx* considered to be covered in 'protofeathers', it was also nominated as being the missing link between feathered dinosaurs like *Sinosauropteryx* and primitive birds like *Archaeopteryx*.

Ji Qiang himself described the fossil as the 'missing link between dinosaurs and birds which we expected to find'. Its name actually indicates that it is an ancestor to *Archaeopteryx*, which cannot possibly be true considering that the Solnhofen limestone is nearly 20 million years older than the Liaoning rocks. It is this 20-million-year gap between *Archaeopteryx* and *Protarchaeopteryx* that has given room for dispute.

The BAND view is that *Protarchaeopteryx* is not a dinosaur but a primitive flightless bird. They feel that the time gap is long enough for the descendants of flying birds like *Archaeopteryx* to have grown large and flightless once more, producing large forms like *Protarchaeopteryx*.

A further analysis of the skeleton by Mark Norell of the American Museum of Natural History placed *Protarchaeopteryx* with the dinosaurs rather than the true birds. He, like many other palaeontologists, points out that while the body feathers are not brilliantly preserved, there are two unmistakable tail feathers associated with the fossil. These are almost identical to those seen on long-tailed modern birds. However, these tail feathers are not directly attached to the dinosaur's body and so some people claim that they are from a separate fossil bird.

Norell adamantly denies this. 'They clearly are feathers,' he says, 'and they do belong to it. They are attached. Anyway, other specimens like *Caudopteryx* [discussed shortly] clearly do have feathers and can be phylogenetically placed outside of the birds.'

Larry Martin drily comments that 'you have to put this in its proper perspective. To the people who wrote this paper [on *Protarchaeopteryx*], a chicken would be a feathered dinosaur.'

Another stalemate.

Hot on the heels of the indistinct *Protarchaeopteryx* came another discovery from Liaoning: that of a fossil named *Caudopteryx* or 'long tail'. It was very similar to *Protarchaeopteryx* in shape and appearance but this one unquestionably had true feathers. It also had a crop filled with small stones (called gastroliths) which would have been used to help break up its food, probably insects, for digestion. *Caudopteryx* proved that whether or not it and *Protarchaeopteryx* were dinosaurs, they did at least have feathers as we understand them today and that they were flightless.

In a matter of months yet more 'feathered dinosaur' specimens flooded out of China, many of which have still to be named. They came in quick succession but all followed in the footsteps of *Sinosauropteryx* with its furry fringe that could not be definitely identified as feathers. Finds were made from other parts of the world as well, such as in Madagascar, Montana and Spain. It was as if after decades of constipation the fossil record had decided to rid itself of its fossil birds. Nonetheless, that one vital specimen, the one that could prove one way or the other what the evolutionary relationship between the birds and dinosaurs is, was missing. To win the day for the palaeontologists the Liaoning quarries would need to produce a specimen that was unequivocally a dinosaur but which also had feathers unequivocally attached to its body. It had yet to be found.

A feathered dinosaur or just an early bird? The battle over the *Archaeopteryx* and the origin of birds was now moving in favour of the birds having descended from the dinosaurs. Although they may not have had their definitive specimen, each new bird or dinosaur specimen from Liaoning seemed to tip the balance in favour of the palaeontologists' point of view. By the turn of the millennium the BAND opinion was very much that of the minority.

The plain truth was that the palaeontologists were producing new specimens by the bucketload and all of them seemed to fit in with their view of bird evolution. The BAND scientists were fighting a rearguard action. Having no alternative specimens of their own, they were forced to create philosophical arguments as to why each new feathered dinosaur species could not possibly be *the* missing link to birds.

The strongest argument in their armoury still relied on the *Archaeopteryx* and the question of convergent evolution. At 150 million years old this fossil was agreed by all to be the earliest fossilized bird. All the new specimens from China and elsewhere were younger than this which meant that the transition between birds and dinosaurs must have taken place before the time of the *Archaeopteryx*. If this is so then how could the 120-million-year-old feathered dinosaurs from Liaoning possibly be 'missing links'? They are far too young and therefore must be the product of convergent evolution.

In other words the birds evolved from some unknown reptile that lived before 150 million years ago, and took their own evolutionary path. Then, around 120 million years ago, the dinosaurs started to evolve to look like birds even though there is no direct connection between them.

Even this argument was getting less persuasive with time. Gaps are common in the fossil record of many animals. It has, for example, been pointed out that until recently a similar problem existed with the fossil record of mammals. It was long known that marsupial mammals (such as kangaroos) and placental mammals (such as humans) were closely related to each other and that both were more distantly related to the primitive and egg-laying monotreme mammals (such as the duck-billed platypus). However, the oldest known monotreme fossil was only 20 million years old whilst those of the marsupials and placentals went back some 100 million years. This meant that the younger mammalian groups had an older fossil record than their more ancient cousins.

The same could be true of birds and feathered dinosaurs. *Archaeopteryx* is a bird 150 million years in age and yet the group of dinosaurs from which it supposedly evolved (the dromaeosaurs) is younger than it, at about 120 million years. The fragmentary nature of the fossil record does not by any means preclude the dromaeosaur dinosaurs from having a longer fossil record. Darwin used a similar argument to try and justify the initial lack of missing links in the aftermath of the publication of *The Origin of Species*.

The only trouble with this argument is that it is actually little different from that of the BAND community, who also argue that the fragmentary nature of the fossil record is hiding the missing link between birds and non-dinosaurian reptiles.

The truth is that most palaeontologists were not overly worried by the lack of a pre-*Archaeopteryx* dromaeosaur. They felt that their case had been all but made and that it was now up to the BAND scientists to find some solid evidence of their own. In the summer of 2000 they did just that.

The end of the Cold War brought about access not just to Chinese fossils, but also to specimens from the old Soviet bloc. One such specimen had been lying in a drawer of the Palaeontological Institute in Moscow since it had been collected in Kyrgyzstan in 1969. Fortunately it was loaned to a St Louis museum where it was put on display and then later spotted by Larry Martin, who thought that its teeth looked bird-like.

We have encountered Larry Martin before. He was one of the original people to see the *Protarchaeopteryx* in China. He is also a vociferous advocator of the BAND position and thus opposes the bird–dinosaur hypothesis.

In some respects Martin is a poacher turned gamekeeper. During the 1960s he was probably the only professional student of Mesozoic fossil birds in America working on the Kansas rocks which had once been a battleground for Cope and Marsh. He was finding new fossil birds but nobody took any interest. 'I was all alone,' he says, 'I had nobody to talk to but myself.' Like many other palaeontologists he went along with Ostrom's ideas but in the late 1970s changed sides after he saw features in Marsh's toothed bird *Hesperornis* which convinced him that Alick Walker's crocodile ancestry for birds fitted the evidence better than Huxley's dinosaur one. It did not take long before he became embroiled in the politics of bird evolution. However, the fossil he had borrowed from St Louis would change everything.

It was a 220-million-year old reptile, or at least part of one, called *Longisquama* which had some obvious and interesting features attached to it. These features were a series of elongate scales, up to five centimetres long, which cover the chin, neck and the back of the front limbs. The exact function of these long scales is unknown but the most commonly held theory is that they could have been used to allow the animal to glide through the air.

A picture of the specimen found its way to Terry Jones of Oregon State University who thought that the strange features looked less like scales and more like feathers. He organized a team of nine scientists to examine the specimen, which included some notable BAND members such as John Ruben and Alan Feduccia.

The team's conclusions were guarded. The 220-million-year-old *Longisquama* was said to have 'feathers' which were 'non-avian' and yet the description they give makes it clear that these scales look like, and probably behaved in a very similar way to, modern bird feathers.

'We avoided the term "feathers",' says Martin, 'because we knew this would bring the forces of damnation upon us.'

They may not have used the term feathers, yet it is quite clear that this is exactly what Martin believes them to be. When I spoke to him about it he reeled off dozens of points about *Longisquama*'s 'scales' which would make them feathers: they are hollow, they have a centre-line like a rachis, they have three layers, etc. In fact, he claims that they have thirteen or so of the features used to diagnose feathers while the Liaoning dinosaurs have none. High praise indeed for *Longisquama*. Other BAND members have been no less ecstatic: 'It's a stake in the heart of the dinosaur theory! It's extremely important, more important than the discovery of *Archaeopteryx*,' was Storrs Olson's comment. John Ruben adds: 'we now question very strongly whether there were any feathered dinosaurs at all'.

Needless to say, this mood of optimism did not spread to the palaeontology camp. The presumed feathers have since been examined by others who believe them not to be complex structures but a series of elongated and transparent scales each of which would have had the texture of the delicate wing of a dragonfly. The barbs are more likely to be wrinkles on the surface of these scales. Another claim, that the scales could have been opened and closed like the wings of a butterfly, is also disputed. Rather than a gliding mechanism, it is claimed that these scales are more likely to be for display purposes.

Although many palaeontologists have expressed their admiration for the unique fossil, few really believe that it has any bearing on the bird evolution issue. Like Chatterjee's *Protoavis* fossil, *Longisquama* is, at the very least, felt to be too ambiguous.

Mark Norell probably sums up the feelings of many in the palaeontology community when he talks of the difference between the Liaoning fossils and *Longisquama*. 'Here you have these animals [from Liaoning] which look like *Archaeopteryx*, which have feathers like *Archaeopteryx* but then people say that they're not. Instead they produce a fossil which looks nothing like either dinosaurs or birds but which has a few scales on its back.'

Not that the BAND people really expected that *Longisquama* would be taken all that seriously. One gets the feeling that they believe the world to be against them and that their argument is losing out purely because the palaeontology community has managed to get the media on their side, making it difficult for other opinions to be heard. That the palaeontology community has developed close links with the media is certainly true but this is not always a good thing. Sometimes it is a relationship that can end in tears.

Archaeoraptor: *The Piltdown Bird*

AT THE TIME of writing, dinosaurs are not just a scientist's plaything. They are also a financial treasure trove. In 1993 the planet Earth erupted into a new phase of dinomania from which it has yet to recover. Dinosaur images are everywhere: on breakfast cereal packets, on T-shirts, in films and on television. Their marketing is especially aimed at children.

According to a survey completed by one of my previous employers, it is children who largely drive dinomania. Young boys between the ages of five and eleven are especially fascinated by dinosaurs; after this age they presumably discover girls and football. We have reached a stage where as the magic of dinosaurs evaporates in each eleven-year-old boy so another five-year-old comes along to replace him.

This fascination is not, however, restricted to the young. The television industry long ago discovered that adults too will watch documentaries about dinosaurs in preference to almost any other type of factual programming. At the time of writing the most watched factual documentary on Earth is the computer-animated *Walking with Dinosaurs*, a television series produced by the BBC in 1999.

The recent arrival of factual-only cable television channels such as Discovery and National Geographic has led to competition for ever more sensationalist scoops to help grab audiences. A relatively easy way of guaranteeing scoops is to buy the rights to certain discoveries. Nowhere has this been more actively done than in the palaeontology community. Most scientists are (or

consider themselves to be) badly funded and so if a media institution comes along and offers to fund their research in return for
the exclusive rights to broadcast the results, few people disagree.
Unfortunately, the needs and wants of science and the media are
often at cross purposes.

The media likes to be up to date and sensationalist. Most scientists prefer to take their time and then, when the results are
available, hedge their bets as to what their research means. The
result has been an uneasy relationship between the media and
science with the participants in either field not really understanding each other's motives. Nonetheless, while media institutions hold the purse strings, science will always be there to take
the money but relationships built in this manner are a recipe for
disaster and can result in some dreadful misunderstandings.

One such misunderstanding unfolded over the period of a
year starting in 1999. As a newspaper report later phrased it, the
fallout left many people with *Archaeopteryx* egg all over their
faces. This is the story of *Archaeoraptor*, the flying feathered dinosaur which never actually existed.

The story of the *Archaeoraptor* begins in July 1999 in the same
region of Liaoning province which produced the birds and
feathered dinosaurs discussed in the previous chapter. A farmer
had given up working the land for the day and was gently splitting rocks in a nearby quarry in the hopes of finding a fossil
which he could later sell.

This turned out to be his lucky day for he found not one, but
two excellent fossils. The first was a tiny skeleton lying spread-
eagled across a thin shale slab. Many of the farmers in the region
had become unofficial experts at identifying fossils and he knew
that this one was that of a bird, complete with feathers, and thus
highly saleable. The other fossil was a few bones from a dinosaur,
found a few metres away from the bird.

Since time immemorial fossils have been tampered with to
make them look better or to fulfil some financial or religious
expectation. In the seventeenth century extra whorls would be
added to ammonite fossils to make them look larger and more

valuable. Even in modern museums it is a customary practice to build display skeletons from several different individuals. Very early on it was realized that many of the fossils emerging from the Liaoning quarries had been tampered with. What appear to be complete fossils turn out to be constructed from several different individuals, cleverly and skilfully knitted together by those who find them. Where a spare part wasn't available, a set of bones could be sculpted on to the skeleton using a mixture of sand and mortar. These 'pizzas', as such composite fossils are sometimes called, look excellent but are a menace to scientists, who can often only spot the joins using laboratory equipment. Fossils of *Confuciusornis* have suffered particularly badly from the forgers' art, probably because they are a relatively common find so many spare parts are available.

Our lucky Liaoning farmer did not know whether his fossil would be going to a scientific institution or to a private collector but, like many of his colleagues, he did know how to make it look more attractive. Although it was largely intact, the lower part of the bird fossil still had pieces missing. Without knowing that he was committing scientific heresy, the farmer slowly chipped away at his two finds until he could neatly fit the dinosaur's tail on to the lower half of the fossil bird's body. The fit was exact and so he glued it into place.

To complete the picture, two dinosaur legs were carefully added to the fossil bird. However, the added legs were in fact just one leg taken from a specimen which had been split in two creating a part and counterpart and thus preserving parts of the one leg on two separate slabs. The mirror images of this leg were carefully chipped out and fitted to the bird's body. The result was impressive, almost artistic.

China's attempt to keep all its fossils safe within its borders has never been entirely successful. The high rewards of the black market ensure that a few slip the net and end up being exported to the west. Such was the case with the composite bird fossil. The Chinese farmer took it to a local fence who bought it from him for what was probably a paltry sum, no more than a few dollars at most. The fence in turn would have sold the fossil to a third party, somebody who either had contacts in the Beijing scientific industry or who could get the fossil smuggled abroad.

In February 1999 it turned up without an export licence at the world-famous Gem and Mineral Show at Tucson, Arizona where fossil dealers and buyers gather annually to do business.

One visitor that year was Stephen Czerkas, an amateur dinosaur hunter who, together with his wife Sylvia, owned and ran a palaeontology museum in the small Utah town of Blanding. Fossils that have obviously been exported illegally are rarely displayed openly at such shows. However, they are always there and are available for viewing, but by invite only. Czerkas had got wind of one such specimen and was taken to a private hotel room in order to view it. What he saw amazed him. The farmer's talent at creating fossils meant that Czerkas did not spot the forgery before him. Instead, what he saw was every palaeontologist's dream, or every ornithologist's nightmare. It was a feathered dinosaur: nothing new there, but this one not only had feathers but also wings! It could have flown!

'It was stunning,' Czerkas later told a reporter. 'I could see right away that it didn't belong on sale. It belonged in a museum.'

As far as palaeontologists were concerned a flying dinosaur would be the last piece of the puzzle. It would not only further narrow the gap between birds and dinosaurs but it would also prove that flight arose from the ground up and not from the trees down.

Czerkas was convinced that he was looking at a fossil which would be as valuable to science as the *Archaeopteryx*. The tail was unmistakably dinosaurian whilst the wings, body and skull, which was toothed, were more avian. The features were far more convincing than in the *Archaeopteryx*.

Czerkas immediately wanted the fossil but the price tag was outrageous – $80,000 for the small slab of shale. Fortunately, he had good business backers for his museum one of whom, M. Dale Slade, agreed to provide the necessary funds after Czerkas phoned him from Tucson. The illegally imported fossil had a new owner and shortly afterwards left Texas for Czerkas' Dinosaur Museum in Blanding.

As I have already said, dinosaurs are now big business.

Czerkas' Dinosaur Museum is a commercial outfit and his new fossil would have to try and earn back some of its high cost. This would mean getting people to travel to Utah to see it. Czerkas was already convinced that he had found the new missing link, a fossil which could rival the *Archaeopteryx* in scientific importance. It was time to get some palaeontologists in on the act.

Although his was not a formal academic institution, Czerkas had many contacts in the academic community. One of these was Phil Currie, a palaeontologist from Canada's prestigious Royal Tyrrell Museum. For Czerkas' purposes Currie was a good choice as he was already very familiar with the Liaoning feathered dinosaurs, having been part of the team which first described *Sinosauropteryx*.

The fossil had only been with Czerkas for a few days when he spoke to Currie who, naturally enough, was very excited at the description being given to him. Like most palaeontologists, Currie was a firm believer in the birds are dinosaurs theory and so Czerkas' fossil was not by any means an impossibility. Czerkas asked him if he wanted to be co-author of a paper that he was planning about the fossil. Again, given the importance of this fossil, Currie was interested but he had a problem with its illegal importation into the United States. To be seen studying a smuggled fossil might seriously jeopardize his hitherto very good relations with the Chinese government. In order to be involved, Currie demanded that Czerkas agree to the return of the fossil after the study was complete.

Czerkas was extremely reluctant to concede this. After all, he had paid a small fortune for this specimen with the idea that it might put his museum on the map. However, he also knew that the fossil would not get celebrity status unless somebody with Currie's scientific credentials gave their full backing. It was a Catch 22. No scientific credentials and the fossil would forever remain obscure (or at least disputed) and would not draw the curious crowds. However, to get a scientist to look at the fossil would mean agreeing to send it back to China, which would deny the curious crowds the chance to see it anyway. Either way Czerkas was damned.

The deciding factor came when Currie decided to bring in *National Geographic* magazine for whom he had already worked on several similar projects. Currie had mentioned the new fossil to Christopher Sloan, the magazine's art editor, who had instantly seen the potential in the story. *National Geographic* is one of the most highly circulated magazines in the world, with a huge readership of professional and amateur naturalists and scientists. An article in the magazine would give the maximum publicity to the Dinosaur Museum and its new fossil. It was a suitable trade-off and Czerkas agreed to return the fossil after the scientific study was completed.

National Geographic is a popular magazine that prides itself on its accuracy and high production standards. It has a fine journalistic tradition and likes to make sure that its facts are straight before the presses roll. As such, it likes all its features on fossils to be based on specimens which have been part of studies whose results have been previously published in a peer-reviewed scientific journal.

Czerkas' fossil was to be no different. In order to get the *National Geographic's* support he too would have to get the fossil properly studied and the results published. Given the fossil's potential implications this should not be a problem. However, *National Geographic* was operating in an increasingly competitive market-place and wanted to run the article as soon as possible, in their November 1999 issue. This gave Czerkas and Currie only a matter of months in which to perform their study, write up the results and publish them. It was a near-impossible time scale but it was nonetheless agreed.

It was also decided that Currie's initial contact in *National Geographic*, Christopher Sloan, should be the author of the article. Although he had worked at the magazine for some time, this was his first venture into scientific journalism and he was being thrown into the deep end.

The association with *National Geographic* brought with it instant access to considerable cash funds. In early March Currie was flown out to the Dinosaur Museum for his first viewing of the fossil. From this point onwards a series of misunderstandings and communication breakdowns started to occur. The short deadline, Czerkas' enthusiasm to promote his find, Sloan's lack of journalistic experience, Currie's hopelessly overstretched time budget and a few other random events all conspired to produce one gigantic cock-up.

It must be remembered that the Chinese forgers were not amateurs. They sell their fossils, and their work is notoriously professional and difficult to spot with the naked eye, especially given the friability of the shale in which these fossils are embedded. Nonetheless, when the story of this fossil is stretched out it is clear that some key warning signs were either missed or ignored.

The first of these apparently came with Currie's first viewing. Later he alleged that he had spotted problems from the outset. He explains:

> I realized that all was not right because you couldn't see a connection between the tail and body and clearly the legs were part and counterpart. I told Stephen [Czerkas]. He agreed. It was obvious – you could measure the bones and see how they lined up.

Czerkas says he remembers things differently and that Currie only drew attention to one of the legs and that he did not express any grave concern. Either way, no further action was taken and the study of the specimen moved forward. A new member of the team was recruited, Xu Xing, a renowned palaeontologist and director of Beijing's Institute of Vertebrate Palaeontology and Palaeoanthropology. Although Xu was involved partly for political reasons, he was also extremely experienced with the Liaoning fossils. Unfortunately, he would not get to see the fossil until a few weeks after the study of it had finished.

With Currie having agreed to proceed with the study, *National Geographic* immediately ordered that news of the find be kept absolutely secret. They were investing money in this feature and wanted to maximize their return by making an announcement just before publication. Any sooner and there was a risk of the story's magic disappearing.

★

Archaeoraptor, *the faked Chinese fossil which for a while fooled the scientific world (light grey bones represent the forged tail and legs)*

With such a short time scale, the science team had to move very fast indeed. August saw the fossil, which had now been provisionally named *Archaeoraptor* (meaning 'ancient hunter'), being taken to Austin, Texas, to be CT X-ray scanned by Timothy Rowe, an expert in these matters. The resulting three-dimensional scans showed that the fossil had nearly one hundred individual fractures running through it, most of which looked perfectly natural. Some, however, did not.

Rowe's conclusions were damning. He explained to Czerkas that the fossil's tail was in no way connected to the body of the bird and was most likely from a separate fossil entirely. 'It was hard to do, but I told them that the fossil had been badly shattered and put together badly, deceptively, and that there was a chance that it was a fraud. They were badly affected.'

Currie again expressed his doubts but Stephen and Sylvia Czerkas apparently talked him and Rowe out of mentioning their reservations to anybody else. Later they privately expressed a distrust of Rowe's techniques. There does not seem to have been much love lost between Rowe and the Czerkases, even at this stage.

For some years Currie had been a man in demand and by September he had flown from America to the Gobi Desert, continuing in the footsteps of Roy Chapman Andrews. However, the *Archaeoraptor* was not forgotten and Currie sent Kevin Aulenback, one of his laboratory technicians, to the Dinosaur Museum to clean up the fossil in preparation for photography and for placing it on public display.

Aulenback's evidence should really have sunk the project. After only a few days he came to the conclusion that the fossil was a forgery and warned the Czerkases about his findings. They refused to accept them. Sensibly Aulenback e-mailed Currie, warning him that in his opinion the *Archaeoraptor* fossil was not one animal but in fact was composed of between three and five separate specimens.

At this point Currie, Rowe and Aulenback had all raised doubt about the fossil's authenticity but none of them seemed to be acting on it and, more importantly, none of them seemed to be speaking to anybody else about the matter either. In particular, Christopher Sloan was receiving very little news of the doubts being raised on the ground. Although he had been in contact with most of the people involved in the study, only positive comments were being relayed to him. It seems that although Rowe and Aulenback were sure that they were dealing with a forgery, the Czerkases were adamant that the fossil was genuine. Currie was caught somewhere in between and because he was the scientific leader of the study Rowe and Aulenback did not want to go behind his back. They had told him their opinion and it was up to him to act on it if he so chose.

A first attempt at getting the results in press was made in mid-August when the team submitted a paper to *Nature*. Although I have not seen a copy of this paper, it does allegedly draw attention to one of *Archaeoraptor*'s legs, which showed signs of having been tampered with before the fossil left China. It was claimed that this leg was from the counterpart and placed on the main slab. In other words *Archaeoraptor* had two identical legs – a fossil with two left feet! No mention is made of the tail, which both Rowe and Aulenback felt was unconnected to the body.

Rowe's name was on the paper but it seems that at the last minute he got cold feet. Before a copy of it had even reached *Nature*'s London offices, he had sent an e-mail to the editor complaining about the poor organization of the project and saying he felt that the *National Geographic*'s time scale was upsetting the project. He stopped short of asking for his name to be removed from the paper but in the event this was academic. Henry Gee, *Nature*'s editor, comments: 'This one looked like a real rush job. It seemed to be extremely amateurishly written. It didn't have any details of where [the *Archaeoraptor* specimen] came from, or how old it was, which you would normally expect.'

The paper was rejected. *Nature* explained that they would not be able to get it peer reviewed and into press before the October deadline set by the *National Geographic*.

With time now really tight, the paper was sent to *Science*, who immediately passed it on to be reviewed. The reviews raised several key problems with the paper and *Science* wrote back to the team explaining that they needed more evidence that *Archaeoraptor* was both bird-like and capable of flying. The paper was revised and sent back to *Science*, who again rejected it. Time had run out. It was October and the *National Geographic*'s presses were about roll off the November issue with the *Archaeoraptor* as the lead article. The editor was unhappy at the idea of running a story with no formal scientific backing. It was his magazine's place to report on discoveries, not to break the news. However, Currie and the Czerkases seem to have persuaded him that by the time of publication some scientific journal would have agreed to publish the paper. On this assurance the presses were allowed to roll. The die was cast.

D-Day was the 15th of October. It had already been decided that the fossil should be the centre display of a 'feathered dinosaur' exhibition to be held at the Society's Explorers' Hall in

Washington, DC and so this venue was chosen to host a conference announcing the discovery of the *Archaeoraptor* to the world's press.

As the scientific leader of the study, Currie was prominent in this conference and his comments were widely reported. The various snippets given in press articles show that neither he nor Czerkas had any doubts about the implications of the find for the bird–dinosaur debate.

'For me the debate's been over for ten years,' said Currie to reporters. 'We're looking at the first dinosaur capable of flying . . . It's kind of overwhelming.' Much had also been made of the likely feathered nature of all theropod dinosaurs, causing Currie to add that 'if Steven Spielberg was filming *Jurassic Park* today, he would have to add feathers to his *Velociraptors* and the young of *T. rex*.'

Stephen Czerkas was no less enthusiastic. 'We can finally say that some dinosaurs did survive,' he commented. 'We call them birds.'

On the face of it, *Archaeoraptor* did indeed appear to be the answer to the palaeontology community's dreams. It is hard to imagine how the BAND scientists could argue against a fully fledged feathered and flying dinosaur, but they did. On the day of the press conference Larry Martin made a very cryptic comment. 'The *National Geographic* is already committed but it will turn out to be an embarrassment.' Perhaps he had caught whispers of the problems with the fossil?

A fuller assault came a few days later in Denver at the Society of Vertebrate Palaeontology's annual conference. Some of the BAND people engineered a full-scale discussion on the fossil. Few people there had actually had the chance to study *Archaeoraptor* but rumours were already circulating that it might be a forgery.

Whether a forgery or not, there were some irregularities in the way the fossil had been brought to the attention of the scientific world. The first chance that most people would get to evaluate *Archaeoraptor* would be in the November issue of *National Geographic*, and not in a scientific journal. This was a most unconventional situation for a find with such important implications. It also meant that the name *Archaeoraptor* was not actually valid yet and would only be so when the *National Geographic* article hit the news-stands.

BAND adherents made much of all of this but the most damning comment of all came from one of *Archaeoraptor*'s own students. Timothy Rowe, who had expressed many private doubts about the fossil, chose the Denver conference to go public. 'I [have] found myself as an author of a paper returned to us, saying the specimen had been doctored. I take exception to that.'

Storrs Olson, a vocal member of the BAND community, campaigned heavily against *Archaeoraptor*, both at the Denver conference and later. He recalled that '*National Geographic* glorified this illicit specimen with their article. I told them that they should close the exhibition and conduct their own investigation. They just stonewalled . . . It is completely bogus. There is no such thing as a feathered dinosaur. It's like saying Elvis Presley is on the dark side of the moon.'

Despite the advice of Olson and others, the exhibition continued and the November *National Geographic* came out on time with its lead article entitled 'Feathers for *T. rex*'. The article was typical of the *National Geographic* and contained a large number of high-quality photographs and drawings interspersed with the magazine's distinctive text columns and extended captions. A glossy photograph of the *Archaeoraptor* fossil was afforded a double spread, the bones laid out in all their glory. Even when you know that there are problems with the fossil, it is hard to spot the joins. Only the feet look out of place. Other pictures show some of our favourite, and previously naked, dinosaurs, such as *T. rex*, *Deinonychus* and *Velociraptor*, clothed in feathers.

The text was also typical of *National Geographic*, a mixture of the history of *Archaeoraptor*'s discovery and comments from scientists who have a knowledge of the feathered dinosaurs. The more sensational comments are displayed in a bold font. It is these quotes, and their triumphant tone, that would later on provide the most embarrassment. 'This fossil is perhaps the best evidence since *Archaeopteryx* that birds did, in fact, evolve from certain types of carnivorous dinosaurs . . . we can now say that birds are theropods just as confidently as we can say humans are animals . . . it's a missing link between terrestrial dinosaurs and birds that could actually fly.' And so forth.

The *National Geographic* article brought forth more BAND criticism, most vocally expressed in a stinging open letter by Storrs Olson to the *National Geographic* Society. The editor of *Nature*, who rejected the *Archaeoraptor* paper, also received a tongue-lashing because of his previous support for the bird–dinosaur theory.

Olson's complaints are a more vocal expression of the beliefs of many of the BAND scientists. Namely that certain influential publications (especially *Nature* and *National Geographic*) have been ignoring their evidence against birds having evolved from dinosaurs. The unorthodox treatment of the *Archaeoraptor* issue was, to some, the final straw and proof positive that the system was biased against them. Ironically, many palaeontologists had likewise complained when Chatterjee's *Protoavis* made its first appearance in a *National Geographic* press release in 1986. Now the shoe was on the other foot.

While the titans of palaeontology and ornithology clashed, Xu Xing entered the proceedings. Xu had played a relatively minor role thus far, having seen the *Archaeoraptor* fossil for the first time at the October conference. He too had spotted problems with it and by December he was back in Beijing and doing some investigating of his own.

Xu soon discovered that *Archaeoraptor*'s tail had been found a couple of metres away from its body, which raised alarm bells. Such a distance meant that the two fossils were unlikely to be related, even if they were found on the same bedding plane.

Few Liaoning fossils are wasted and most end up in institutional or private collections in one form or another. Xu's search of several private collections finally produced a match for *Archaeoraptor*'s tail. It belonged not to a bird-like animal but to a small type of theropod dinosaur known as a dromaeosaur (the group to which *Deinonychus* belongs). On the 20th of December he wrote a doleful e-mail to Currie, Czerkas and others.

> Though I do not want to believe it, *Archaeoraptor* appears
> to be composed of a dromaeosaur tail and a bird body. I am
> 100% sure . . . that we have to admit that *Archaeoraptor* is a
> faked specimen.

These words shook *National Geographic* to its core. Although
Stephen Czerkas apparently tried to explain away Xu's findings,
Currie admitted defeat, perhaps realizing that he had missed too
many warning signs. As a means of alerting its readership, the
magazine printed Xu's e-mail in its March 2000 issue. In April it
decided to settle the issue once and for all and brought in a panel
of scientists, which included Storrs Olson, to examine the fossil.
All agreed that *Archaeoraptor* was indeed built from several other
fossils. It was the worst possible news for the National
Geographic Society, an organization that prides itself on its
attention to detail.

The international press had a field day, adding to the embarrassment of all concerned, but it was a nine-days wonder and the
fuss died down again. Although the media loves to see a scandal,
it would be difficult to make this one stretch any distance, probably because of its lack of sex. In May 2000 *Archaeoraptor* was
flown across the Pacific Ocean and back to Beijing, laying the
matter to rest.

In the aftermath of this affair it is not just the National
Geographic Society that has come out badly. Philip Currie, the
chief scientist in the study, was made to look very silly and even
he concedes that this episode was the greatest mistake of his professional career. The Czerkases do not come out of it well either.
Their undying enthusiasm for *Archaeoraptor* may have led to vital
clues being ignored or missed. The whole event is an example
of a communication breakdown, with the scientists being too
afraid to voice their fears to their media paymasters – but the
consequences go further than this.

Forgeries and frauds are not all that uncommon in the science
world. At the time of writing *Nature* has just refused to accept
papers from pharmaceutical companies which do not conduct

independent tests on their new medicines. Apparently in-house testing tends to produce results more in favour of the usefulness of the medicine. Then there are the palaeontological hoaxes. Piltdown Man was engineered to move the evolution of humans away from Africa and towards Europe. Onondaga Man was engineered to refute Darwinism. The *Archaeoraptor* episode can in no way be described as a deliberate hoax. It was more a case of misunderstanding. It was, however, on a subject very sensitive for scientists.

Had *Archaeoraptor* been a genuine flying dinosaur, it would have effectively sealed the argument in favour of birds being dinosaurs. It really would have been the modern equivalent of the *Archaeopteryx* in its scientific implications and would have drawn a neat line under the debate over the origin of birds. Instead the embarrassment felt by palaeontologists and the relief (and some gloating) of ornithologists has widened the gap, raising the stakes yet further.

The biggest reaction to the *Archaeoraptor* débâcle was not actually among the scientific community many of whom must have thought to themselves, 'There but the grace for God go I'. It was from the Creationist Christian movement which saw *Archaeoraptor* as nothing less than a fulfilment of one of their own prophecies.

For years the Creationist community had relied upon Fred Hoyle and Chandra Wickramasinghe's pronouncement of the *Archaeopteryx* specimens as forgeries despite the protests of palaeontologists. Now science had scored an own goal by offering them as a genuine missing link which turned out to be a fraud. In Creationist terms the *Archaeoraptor* joined that elite group of public frauds that apparently disprove the Darwinian view of evolution.

To them *Archaeoraptor* really is the Piltdown Bird. It is a warning about objectivity in science. It also underlines the differing needs of the media and science.

For a while it looked as though *Archaeopteryx* was about to lose its status as the fossil bird which is closest in form to the reptiles. Eyes were momentarily shifted towards *Archaeoraptor* in the search for a successor to *Archaeopteryx* but they were forced to look back again. After nearly a century and a half at the top, the *Archaeopteryx* is a fossil that is not going to be easily disposed of.

The irony is that even without its tail, *Archaeoraptor* is still an interesting and valuable fossil. As Larry Martin comments, 'Once you cut out the dinosaur part, it probably will be an interesting bird.'

Epilogue

A CENTURY AND a half ago a limestone quarry worker pulled the first *Archaeopteryx* specimen from its 150-million-year-old tomb. The scientific climate of the time ensured that it would receive a baptism of fire. However, nobody could have expected that the arguments surrounding the *Archaeopteryx* would continue on into the twenty-first century.

Archaeopteryx is both a frustrating and an enigmatic fossil that has left a very turbulent wake in history. Its various characteristics have been used to support several mutually exclusive causes: the same time the *Archaeopteryx* can be a primitive bird, a feathered dinosaur or a crude fake, depending on your point of view.

In terms of the popular consensus regarding the evolutionary origins of birds, the *Archaeopteryx* has also managed to change sides several times. Owen thought it was descended from a pterosaur, Huxley preferred the dinosaurs, Heilmann the thecodonts, Ostrom the dinosaurs again, Walker and Martin the crocodiles, etc., etc.

Who, if anyone, is right?

I started this book with the common palaeontological belief that birds are descended from dinosaurs and I must state now that I still hold to that theory. However, there were times during the research for this work when my faith wavered. Over the eighteen months or so which it took to put this book together, I had to sift through literally hundreds of papers on every aspect of bird evolution. It readily became apparent that since the 1970s there have been two bitterly opposed views on the subject. These can be neatly described as (1) those who are in favour of birds evolving from dinosaurs, and (2) those who are not. To research this topic effectively I decided to put my preconceived ideas to one side and to enter the affray with an open mind.

To be honest, I expected to be easily convinced of the bird–dinosaur theory but there were many times when the points put forward by the BAND scientists seemed to hold water. Quickly I was sucked into the world of palaeontology minutiae, looking at tiny features on photographs of ancient skeletons which might, or might not, prove their ultimate ancestry. It was easy to be swayed one way or the other by the points being put forward.

This process became even worse when speaking to the individual scientists involved in this debate. Many people were kind enough to grant me an interview and all were highly charismatic and very sure of their own ideas, offering a wealth of information for or against the idea of birds being related to the dinosaurs. It is very clear that the problem lies in whether or not it is valid to compare the skeleton of a bird with the skeleton of a dinosaur. The palaeontologists say that it is. The ornithologists say that it isn't, preferring to look at the biology of living birds rather than just their skeleton.

To my mind the arguments are more finely balanced than is sometimes portrayed in the press. The ornithologists do have some pertinent questions which have not, as far as I can see, been fully addressed by the palaeontology community.

However, at the end of the day the palaeontology point of view does have much solid evidence going for it. There are similarities between bird and dinosaur skeletons which cannot be ignored. There are fossils being pulled from the ground which fit the predicted path of bird–dinosaur evolution. These are positive contributions to the debate.

The ornithologists, on the other hand, seem to have spent much of their time offering up reasons why birds cannot have been dinosaurs. Some of this is persuasive but equally well much of it is hypothetical.

Compared to the dozens of fossils which the palaeontologists cite as evidence for a bird–dinosaur link, the ornithologists only have *Longisquama*, and that is by no means a clear-cut fossil to interpret. By the time I had finished the research for the book I felt sure that the balance of evidence favoured the palaeontologists' case even if it could not yet be proved beyond all reasonable doubt.

There may be many disagreements about the *Archaeopteryx* but there are some areas of agreement too. Most now feel that the *Archaeopteryx* is actually a type of primitive bird rather than a feathered reptile or feathered dinosaur. It is thus most commonly referred to as the oldest confirmed bird in the fossil record. Most also do not think it to have been the ancestor of the living birds. Instead it is commonly portrayed as being on an evolutionary side branch which eventually became extinct. This of course means that *Archaeopteryx* is not technically a missing link between dinosaurs and living birds, as it is often portrayed, but is an evolutionary dead end.

There are other areas of agreement too. Everybody is agreed that this fossil is one of the most important scientific icons of the modern era and even those who believe it to be a forgery cannot help but admire its beauty.

Love it or hate it, the *Archaeopteryx* is a remarkable fossil with a remarkable tradition. I suspect that it will still be talked about for many centuries to come.

Sources

There are literally thousands of articles and papers which concern the *Archaeopteryx* and its relevance to science in general and bird evolution in particular. Many of these, whilst interesting, are not directly relevant to the issues examined in this book. Others simply duplicate points made by others. Thus, and to avoid an excessively long bibliography, I have only listed the more useful books, papers and articles used in general and for each chapter.

FURTHER READING (GENERAL)
Barthel, K.W., Swinburn, N.H.M., Conway-Morris, S., 1994, *Solnhofen: A Study in Mesozoic Palaeontology*. Cambridge University Press.

De Beer, G., 1954, *Archaeopteryx Lithographica, a Study based upon the British Museum Specimen*. British Museum of Natural History.

Desmond, A., 1982, *Archetypes and Ancestors – Palaeontology in Victorian London*. University of Chicago Press.

Feduccia, A., 1996, *The Origin and Evolution of Birds*. Yale University Press.

Hecht, M.K. *et al.*, 1985, *The Beginnings of Birds: Proceedings of the International Archaeopteryx Conference Eichstätt*. Jura-Museums.

Shipman, P., 1999, *Taking Wing – Archaeopteryx and the Evolution of Flight*. Phoenix.

CHAPTERS 1 TO 4: THE DISCOVERY OF THE LONDON *ARCHAEOPTERYX*
Darwin, C., 1859, *On the Origin of Species*. John Murray.

De Beer, G., 1954, *Archaeopteryx Lithographica, a Study based upon the British Museum Specimen*. British Museum of Natural History.

Desmond, A., 1982, *Archetypes and Ancestors – Palaeontology in Victorian London*. University of Chicago Press.

Feduccia, A., 1996, *The Origin and Evolution of Birds*, Yale University Press.

Lucas, J.R., 1979, 'Wilberforce and Huxley: A Legendary Encounter', *The Historical Journal*, 22(2), pp. 313–330.

Meyer, H. von, 1861, '*Archaeopteryx lithographica* (Vogel-Feder) und *Pterodactylus* von Solenhofen', *Neues Jahrbuch für Mineralogie, Geologie und Paläontologie*, 1861, pp. 678–679.

Meyer, H. von, 1862, '*Archaeopteryx lithographica* aus dem lithographischen Schiefer von Solnhofen', *Palaeontographica*, 10, pp. 53–56.

Ostrom, J.H., 1985, 'Introduction to *Archaeopteryx*', in *The Beginnings of Birds: Proceedings of the International Archaeopteryx Conference*. Hecht, M.K. *et al.*, pp. 9–20.

Viohl, G., 1985, 'Carl F. and Ernst O. Häberlein, the Sellers of the London and Berlin Specimens of *Archaeopteryx*', in *The Beginnings of Birds: Proceedings of the International Archaeopteryx Conference*. Hecht, M.K. *et al.*, pp. 349–352.

Wagner, A., 1862, 'On a New Fossil Reptile Supposed to be Furnished with Feathers', *Annals and Magazine of Natural History*, 9, pp. 261–267.

Wellnhofer, P., 1985, 'The Story of Albert Oppel's *Archaeopteryx* Drawing', in *The Beginnings of Birds: Proceedings of the International Archaeopteryx Conference*, Hecht, M.K. *et al.*, pp. 353–357.

Witte, O.J., 1863, 'Briefl Mitt Betreffend *Archaeopteryx lithographica*', *Neues Jahrbuch für Mineralogie, Geologie und Paläontologie*, 1863, pp. 567–568.

Y, 1862, 'The Feathered Enigma', *The Times* (London), 12 November, p. 9.

Y, 1862, 'The Feathered Enigma', *The Times* (London), 23 December, p. 4.

CHAPTERS 5 AND 7: HUXLEY, DARWIN, OWEN, *ET AL.*, AND EVOLUTION

Darwin, F., 1887, *The Life and Letters of Charles Darwin*. John Murray, 2 vols.

Dean, D.R., 1969, 'Hitchcock's Dinosaur Tracks', *American Quarterly*, 21, pp. 639–644.

Desmond, A., 1994–97, *Huxley*, Michael Joseph, 2 vols.

Desmond, A., Moore, J., 1992, *Darwin*, Penguin.

Foster, M., Lankester, E.R., 1898–1902, *The Scientific Memoirs of Thomas Henry Huxley*, 4 vols.

Guralnick, S.M., 1972, 'Geology and Religion before Darwin: The Case of Edward Hitchcock', *Isis*, 63, pp. 529–543.

Huxley, T.H., 1868, 'On the Animals Which Are Most Nearly Intermediate between Birds and Reptiles', *Annual Magazine of Natural History*, 4(2), pp. 66–75.

Huxley, T.H., 1868, 'Remarks upon *Archaeopteryx lithographica*', *Proceedings of the Royal Society of London*, 16, pp. 243–248.

Huxley, T.H., 1870, 'Further Evidence of the Affinity between the Dinosaurian Reptiles and Birds', *Quarterly Journal of the Geological Society of London*, 26, pp. 12–31.

Irvine, W., 1955, *Apes, Angels, and Victorians: A Joint Biography of Darwin and Huxley*, Meridian.

Owen, R., 1894, *The Life of Richard Owen*. John Murray, 2 vols.

Rupke, N.A., 1994, *Richard Owen – Victorian Naturalist*. Yale University Press.

Woodward, H., 1862, 'On a Feathered Fossil from the Lithographic Limestone of the Solenhofen', *Intellectual Observer*, 2, pp. 313–319.

Woodward, H., 1874, 'New Facts Bearing on the Inquiry concerning Forms Intermediate between Birds and Reptiles', *Geological Magazine*, 30, pp. 8–15.

Woodward, H., 1893, 'Sir Richard Owen', *Geological Magazine*, 10, pp. 39–54.

CHAPTER 6: SCIENTIFIC DEBATE ON THE FIRST *ARCHAEOPTERYX*

Agassiz, L., 1862, 'The Plan of Creation', *Scientific American*, 6(9), p. 133.

Agassiz, L., 1863, 'The Growth of Continents', *Atlantic Monthly*, 12(69), pp. 72–81.

Agassiz, L., 1874, 'Evolution and the Permanence of Life', *Atlantic Monthly*, 33(195), pp. 92–101.

Cope, E.D., 1867, 'An Account of the Extinct Reptiles Which Approach the Birds', *Proceedings of the Academy of Natural Sciences, Philadephia*, pp. 234–235.

Cope, E.D., 1871, 'Synopsis of the Extinct Batrachia, Reptilia and Aves of North America', *Transactions of the American Philosophical Society*, 17, pp. 505–530.

Dana, J.D., 1863, 'On Certain Parallel Relations between the Classes of Vertebrates, and on the Bearing of These Relations on the Question of the Distinctive Features of the Reptilian Birds', *American Journal of Science*, pp. 315–321.

Evans, J., 1865, 'On Portions of a Cranium and of a Jaw, in the Slab Containing the Fossil Remains of the *Archaeopteryx*', *Natural History Review*, 5, pp. 415–421.

Huxley, L., 1918, *Life and Letters of Sir Joseph Dalton Hooker*, Macmillan, 2 vols.

Mackie, S.J., 1863, 'The Aeronauts of the Solenhofen Age', *The Geologist*, 6, pp. 1–8.

Mivart, St G.J., 1871, *On the Genesis of Species*, Macmillan.

Owen, R., 1863, 'On the *Archaeopteryx* of von Meyer with a Description of the Fossil Remains of a Long-tailed Species, from the Lithographic Stone of Solenhofen', *Philosphical Transactions of the Royal Society of London*, 153, pp. 33–47.

Owen, R., 1878, 'On the Influence of the Advent of a Higher Form of Life in Modifying the Structure of an Older and Lower Form', *Quarterly Journal of the Geological Society*, 34, pp. 421–430.

Parker, W.K., 1864, 'Remarks on the Skeleton of the *Archaeopteryx* and on the Relations of the Birds to the Reptiles', *Geological Magazine*, 1, pp. 55–57.

Parker, W.K., 1864, 'On the Sternal Apparatus of Birds and Other Vertebrata', *Proceedings of the Zoological Society*, pp. 339–341.

CHAPTER 8: MARSH, COPE AND THE TOOTHED BIRDS

Anonymous, 1881, 'The Extinct Toothed Birds of North America', *The Manufacturer and Builder*, 13(5), p. 110.

Colbert, E.H., 1984, *The Great Dinosaur Hunters and their Discoveries*. Dover Publications.

Cope, E.D., 1873, 'On Some of Professor Marsh's Criticisms', *American Naturalist*, 7(5), pp. 290–299.

Davidson, J.P., 1997, *Bone Sharp: The Life of Edward Drinker Cope*. Academy of Natural Sciences of Philadelphia.

Gingerich, P.D., 1976, 'Evolutionary Significance of the Mesozoic Toothed Birds', *Smithsonian Contributions to Paleobiology*, 27.

Marsh, O.C., 1870, 'Note on the Remains of Fossil Birds', *American Journal of Science*, 2, p. 272.

Marsh, O.C., 1872, 'Discovery of a Remarkable Fossil Bird', *American Journal of Science*, 3, pp. 56–57.

Marsh, O.C., 1872, 'Preliminary Description of *Hesperornis regalis*, with Notices of Four Other New Species of Cretaceous Birds', *American Journal of Science*, 3, pp. 360–365.

Marsh, O.C., 1873, 'Fossil Birds from the Cretaceous of North America', *American Journal of Science*, 5, pp. 229–230.

Marsh, O.C., 1877, 'Introduction and Succession of Vertebrate Life in America: An Address Delivered before the American Association for the Advancement of Science, at Nashville, Tenn., Aug. 30, 1877.' Offprint held at London Natural History Museum.

Marsh, O.C., 1880, *Odontornithes: A Monograph on the Extinct Toothed Birds of North America*. US Geological Exploration.

Osborn, H.F., 1897, 'A Great Naturalist – Edward Drinker Cope', *The Century Magazine*, 55(1), pp. 10–15.

Osborn, H.F., 1931, *Cope: Master Naturalist*. Princeton University Press.

Schuchert, C., LeVene, C.M., 1940, *O.C. Marsh: Pioneer in Paleontology*. Yale University Press.

Stegner, W., 1954, *Beyond the Hundredth Meridian*. Penguin Books.

CHAPTER 9: THE DISCOVERY AND SALE OF THE BERLIN SPECIMEN

Anonymous, 1880, '*Archaeopteryx*, Rare Fossil Bird', *The Times* (London), 27 April, p. 4.

Dames, R., 1927, 'Werner von Siemens und der *Archaeopteryx*', *Nacher. Ver. Siemens-Beamt. E.V. Sportver. Siemens Berlin e.V.*, 19, pp. 233–234.

Gregory, F., 1977, *Scientific Materalism in Nineteenth Century Germany*. Reidel.

Häberlein, E., 1877, '*Archaeopteryx lithographica* v. Meyer', *Leopoldina*, 13, pp. 9–10.

Ostrom, J.H., 1978, 'A Surprise from Solnhofen in the Peabody Museum Collections', *Discovery*, 13(1), pp. 30–37.

Ostrom, J.H., 1985, 'What Might Have Been: The Bird That Got Away', *Discovery*, 18(1), pp. 26–29.

Ostrom, J.H., 1985, 'The Yale *Archaeopteryx*: The One That Flew the Coop', in *The Beginnings of Birds: Proceedings of the International Archaeopteryx Conference*. Hecht, M.K. *et al.*, pp. 359–367.

Viohl, G., 1985, 'Carl F. and Ernst O. Häberlein, the Sellers of the London and Berlin Specimens of *Archaeopteryx*', in *The Beginnings of Birds: Proceedings of the International Archaeopteryx Conference*. Hecht, M.K. *et al.*, pp. 349–352.

Vogt, C., 1880, '*Archaeopteryx macrura*, an Intermediate Form between Birds and Reptiles', *Ibis*, 4, pp. 434–456.

Wendt, H., 1968, *Before the Deluge*. Victor Gollancz.

CHAPTERS 10 AND 11: GERHARD HEILMANN AND THE ORIGIN OF BIRDS

Anonymous, 1940, 'An Interview with Gerhard Heilmann', *Socialdemokraten*, 24 October, p. 8 [translation provided by Ilja Nieuwland].

Broom, R., 1913, 'On the South Africa Pseudosuchian *Euparkeria* and Allied Genera', *Proceedings of the Zoology Society of London*, pp. 619–633.

Bryant, H.N., Russell, A.P., 1993, 'The Occurrence of Clavicles within Dinosauria: Implications for the Homology of the Avian Furcula and the Utility of Negative Evidence', *Journal of Vertebrate Paleontology*, 13(2), pp. 171–184.

Buffetaut, E., 1985, 'The Strangest Interpretation of *Archaeopteryx*', in *The Beginnings of Birds: Proceedings of the International Archaeopteryx Conference*. Hecht, M.K. *et al.*, pp. 369–370.

De Beer, G., 1954, '*Archaeopteryx lithographica*, a Study based upon the British Museum Specimen', *British Museum of Natural History*.

Heilmann, G., 1926, *The Origin of Birds*. H.F. and G. Witherby.

Jung, H.A., 1990, 'Der Buergermeister und der sechste Urvogel', *Kosmos (Stuttgart)*, 86(3), pp. 38–43.

Marshall, C.R., Raff, E.C., Raff, R.A., 1994, 'Dollo's Law and the Death and Resurrection of Genes', *Proceedings of the National Academy of Sciences of the United States of America*, 91, pp. 12283–12287.

Nieuwland, I., 'Gerhard Heilmann and the Artist's Eye in Science.' Talk given at the 1999 meeting of the Society for Vertebrate Palaeontology.

Salomonsen, F., 1946, 'Gerhard Heilman', *Dansk Ornithologisk Forenings Tidsskrift*, 40, pp. 146–149 [translation provided by Ilja Nieuwland].

CHAPTER 12: THE 1970s REVOLUTION IN BIRD EVOLUTIONARY STUDIES

Abbott, A., 1992, '*Archaeopteryx* Fossil Disappears from Private Collection', *Nature*, 357, p. 6.

Anonymous, 1985, 'Was *Archaeopteryx* a Dinosaur?' *New Scientist*, 106(1452), p. 23.

Anonymous, 1988, '*Archaeopteryx*: et de six', *La Recherche*, 203, p. 1210.

Bakker, R.T., Galton, P.M., 1974, 'Dinosaur Morphology and a New Class of Vertebrates', *Nature*, 248, pp. 168–172.

Benton, M.J., 1983, 'Paleontology – No Consensus on *Archaeopteryx*', *Nature*, 305, pp. 99–100.

Bock, W.J., 1985, 'The Arboreal Theory for the Origin of Birds', in *The Beginnings of Birds: Proceedings of the International Archaeopteryx Conference*. Hecht, M.K. *et al.*, pp. 199–207.

Buhler, P., 1986, '*Archaeopteryx* – a Discussion of Present Research on the Jurassic Birds', *Journal für Ornithologie*, 127, pp. 487–508.

Craig, H., 1971, 'New *Archaeopteryx* Found in Old Museum Collection', *NYPS Notes*, 2(2), pp. 3–4.

Dericqles, A., 1985, 'The Puzzling *Archaeopteryx* Fossil', *Recherche*, 16, pp. 394–397.

Eisenmann, E., 1974, 'Comment on Proposal to Suppress *Pterodactylus crassipes* Meyer, 1857 and Counter-proposal to Recognize *Archaeopteryx lithographica* Meyer, 1861, and to Fix its Type-species', *Bulletin of Zoological Nomenclature*, 31(3), pp. 114–115.

Gower, D.J., Weber, E., 1998, 'The Braincase of *Euparkeria*, and the Evolutionary Relationships of Birds and Crocodilians', *Biological Reviews of the Cambridge Philosophical Society*, 73, pp. 367–411.

Hecht, M.K., 1985, 'The Biological Significance of *Archaeopteryx*', in *The Beginnings of Birds: Proceedings of the International Archaeopteryx Conference*. Hecht, M.K. *et al.*, pp. 149–160.

Hinchliffe, J.R., 1985, 'One, Two, Three or "Two, Three, Four": An Embryologist's View of the Homologies of the Digits and Carpus of Modern Birds', in *The Beginnings of Birds: Proceedings of the International Archaeopteryx Conference*. Hecht, M.K. *et al.*, pp. 141–147.

Howgate, M., 1982, '*Archaeopteryx* in Hiding', *Nature*, 300, p. 469.

Lewin, R., 1983, 'How Did Vertebrates Take to the Air?' *Science*, 221(4605), pp. 38–39.

Lewin, R., 1985, 'How Does Half a Bird Fly?' *Science*, 230(4725), pp. 530–531.

Ostrom, J.H., 1970, '*Archaeopteryx* – Notice of a "New" Specimen', *Science* 170(3957), pp. 537–538.

Ostrom, J.H., 1972, 'Description of the *Archaeopteryx* Specimen in the Teyler Museum, Haarlem', *Proceedings of the Koninklijke Nederlandse Akademie van Wetenschappen, Series B*, 75(4), pp. 289–305.

Ostrom, J.H., 1974, '*Archaeopteryx* and the Origin of Flight', *Quarterly Review of Biology*, 49(1), pp. 27–47.

Ostrom, J.H., 1975, 'The Origin of Birds', *Annual Review of Earth and Planetary Sciences*, 3, pp. 55–77.

Ostrom, J.H., 1975, 'On the Origin of *Archaeopteryx* and the Ancestry of Birds', *Colloques Internationaux du Centre National de la Recherche Scientifique*, 218, pp. 519–532.

Ostrom, J.H., 1975, '*Archaeopteryx*', *Discovery*, 11(1), pp. 14–23.

Ostrom, J.H., 1985, 'The Meaning of *Archaeopteryx*', in *The Beginnings of Birds: Proceedings of the International Archaeopteryx Conference*. Hecht, M.K. *et al.*, pp. 161–176.

Ostrom, J.H., 1986, 'The Cursorial Origin of Avian Flight', *Memoirs of the California Academy of Sciences*, 8, pp. 73–81.

Ostrom, J.H., 1992, 'Comments on the New (Solnhofen) Specimen of *Archaeopteryx*', *Science Series (Los Angeles)*, 36, pp. 25–27.

Paul, G., 1984, 'The Hand of *Archaeopteryx*', *Nature*, 310, p. 732.

Thulborn, R.A., Hamley, T., 1982, 'The Reptilian Relationships of *Archaeopteryx*', *Australian Journal of Zoology*, 30, pp. 611–634.

Thulborn, R.A., Hamley, T. 1984, 'On the Hand of *Archaeopteryx*', *Nature*, 311, p. 218.

Vazquez, R.J., 1992, 'Functional Osteology of the Avian Wrist and the Evolution of Flapping Flight', *Journal of Morphology*, 211, pp. 259–268.

Walker, A.D., 1972, 'New Light on the Origin of Birds and Crocodiles', *Nature*, 237, pp. 257–263.

CHAPTER 13: ACCUSATIONS OF FRAUD

Anonymous, 1985, 'The *Archaeopteryx* – False Plumage', *Recherche*, 16, p. 638.

Anonymous, 1988, 'More Rock-Solid Evidence of *Archaeopteryx*', *New Scientist*, 118, p. 38.

Benton, M.J., 1987, 'Why *Archaeopteryx* Is Not a Fake but Suffers from Too Much Publicity', *Geology Today*, 3(4), pp. 118–121.

Chalupsky, J., 1987, 'Je *Archaeopteryx* podvrh?' *Vesmir*, 66(4), pp. 197–201.

Charig, A., 1985, '*Archaeopteryx* a Forgery', *Biologist*, 32, pp. 122–123.

Charig, A.J., Greenaway, F., Milner, A.C., Walker, C.A., Whybrow, P.J., 1986, '*Archaeopteryx* Is Not a Forgery', *Science*, 232(4750), pp. 622–626.

Clausen, V.E., 1986, 'Recent Debate over *Archaeopteryx*', *Origins*, 13(1), pp. 48–55.

Connor, S., 1987, 'Riddle of Missing Rock Resurrects *Archaeopteryx* Controversy', *New Scientist*, 115, p. 27.

Courtice, G., 1987, 'Museum Officials Confident *Archaeopteryx* Genuine', *Nature*, 328, p. 657.

Dickson, D., 1987, 'Feathers Still Fly in Row over Fossil Bird', *Science*, 238(4826), pp. 475–476.

Gee, H., 1988, 'Ruffled Feathers Calmed by Fossil Bird', *Nature*, 334, p. 104.

Gould, S.J., 1986, 'The *Archaeopteryx* Flap – Cardboard Histories Can Be Deceptive and Destructive', *Natural History*, 95, p. 16.

Gould, S.J., 1987, 'The Fossil Fraud That Never Was', *New Scientist*, 113(1551), pp. 32–36.

Hoyle, F., 1986, '*Archaeopteryx*', *New Scientist*, 111, p. 87.

Hoyle, F., Wickramasinghe, C., 1988, '*Archaeopteryx* Arguments', *Scientist*, 2, p. 10.

Hoyle, F., Wickramasinghe, C., 1986, *Archaeopteryx, the Primordial Bird – a Case of Fossil Forgery*. Christopher Davis.

Thomas, R.D.K., 1985, 'On Creationism: Reviewing the Issues and the Challenge', *Geotimes*, 30(9), pp. 8–9.

Vines, G., 1985, 'Strange Case of *Archaeopteryx* Fraud', *New Scientist*, 105, p. 3.

Wellnhofer, P., 1988, 'A New Specimen of *Archaeopteryx*', *Science*, 240, pp. 1790–1792.

Wellnhofer, P., 1990, '*Archaeopteryx*', *Scientific American*, 262, pp. 70–77.

Wellnhofer, P., 1990, 'Fraud and *Archaeopteryx* – Reply', *Scientific American*, 263, p. 10.

CHAPTER 14: NEW FOSSIL BIRD DISCOVERIES AND THE BIRD–DINOSAUR DEBATE

Altangeral, P., Norell, M.A., Chiappe, L.M., Clark, J.M., 1993, 'Flightless Bird from the Cretaceous of Mongolia', *Nature*, 362, pp. 623–626.

Anderson, A., 1991, 'Early Bird Threatens *Archaeopteryx*'s Perch', *Science*, 253, p. 5015.

Anonymous, 1978, 'The Oldest Fossil Bird: A Rival for *Archaeopteryx*?' *Science*, 199(4326), p. 284.

Anonymous, 1991, 'Early Bird Born Late', *Nature*, 351 (6329), pp. 677–678.

Barinaga, M., 1992, 'Evolutionists Wing it with a New Fossil Bird', *Science*, 255(5046), p. 796.

Cai, Z., Zhao, L., 1999, 'A Long Tailed Bird from the Late Cretaceous of Zhejiang', *Science in China Series D-Earth Sciences*, 42, pp. 434–441.

Chatterjee, S., 1987, 'Skull of Protoavis and Early Evolution of Birds', *Journal of Vertebrate Paleontology*, 7(3), supplement, p. 14.

Chatterjee, S., 1991, 'Cranial Anatomy and Relationships of a New Triassic Bird from Texas', *Philosophical Transactions of the Royal Society of London Series B*, 332, pp. 277–342.

Chen, P., Dong, Z., Zhen, S., 1998, 'An Exceptionally Well Preserved Theropod Dinosaur from the Yixian Formation of China', *Nature*, 391, pp. 147–152.

Chiappe, L., 1991, 'Cretaceous Avian Remains from Patagonia Shed New Light on the Early Radiation of Birds', *Alcheringa*, 15, pp. 333–338.

Chiappe, L.M., 1995, 'The First 85-Million Years of Avian Evolution', *Nature*, 378, pp. 349–355.

Chiappe, L.M., Shu'an, J., Qiang, J., Norell, M.A., 1999, 'Anatomy and Systematics of the Confuciusornithidae (Theropoda: Aves) from the Late

Mesozoic of Northeastern China', *Bulletin of the American Museum of Natural History*, pp. 3–89.

Dudley, R., 2000, 'The Evolutionary Physiology of Animal Flight: Paleobiological and Present Perspectives', *Annual Review of Physiology*, pp. 135–155.

Elzanowski, A., Wellnhofer, P., 1992, 'A New Link between Theropods and Birds from the Cretaceous of Mongolia', *Nature*, 359, pp. 821–823.

Feduccia, A., 1974, 'Endothermy, Dinosaurs and *Archaeopteryx*', *Evolution*, 28(3), pp. 503–504.

Feduccia, A., 1985, 'On Why the Dinosaur Lacked Feathers', in *The Beginnings of Birds: Proceedings of the International Archaeopteryx Conference*. Hecht, M.K., et al., pp. 75–79.

Feduccia, A., 1993, 'Aerodynamic Model for the Early Evolution of Feathers Provided by *Propithecus* (Primates, Lemuridae)', *Journal of Theoretical Biology*, 160, p. 159.

Feduccia, A., 1993, 'Evidence from Claw Geometry Indicating Arboreal Habits of *Archaeopteryx*', *Science*, 259, pp. 790–793.

Feduccia, A., 1996, *The Origin and Evolution of Birds*, Yale University Press.

Forster, C.A., Sampson, S.D., Chiappe, L.M., Krause, D.W., 1998, 'The Theropod Ancestry of Birds: New Evidence from the Late Cretaceous of Madagascar', *Science*, 279, pp. 1915–1919.

Gibbons, A., 1996, 'Early Birds Rise from China Fossil Beds', *Science*, 274(5290), p. 1083.

Hecht, J., 1997, 'The People's Fossils', *New Scientist*, 9 August, pp. 32–35.

Hou, L.H., Zhou, Z.H., Martin, L.D., Feduccia, A., 1995, 'A Beaked Bird from the Jurassic of China', *Nature*, 377, pp. 616–618.

Hou, L., Martin, L.D., Zhou, Z., Feduccia, A., 1996, 'Early Adoptive Radiation of Birds: Evidence from Fossils from Northeastern China', *Science*, 274(5290), pp. 1164–1167.

Ji, Q., Currie, P., Norell, Ma Ji, Sa, 1998, 'Two Feathered Dinosaurs from Northeastern China', *Nature*, 393, pp. 753–761.

Jones, T.D., Ruben, J.A., Martin, L.D., Kurochkin, E.N., Feduccia, A., Maderson, P.F.A., Hillenius, W.J., Geist, N.R., Alifanov, V., 2000, 'Nonavian Feathers in a Late Triassic Archosaur', *Science*, 288, pp. 2202–2205.

Martin, L.D., 1983, 'The Origin of Birds and of Avian Flight', *Current Ornithology*, 1, pp. 105–129.

Martin, L.D., 1985, 'The Relationship of *Archaeopteryx* to Other Birds', in *The Beginnings of Birds: Proceedings of the International Archaeopteryx Conference*. Hecht, M.K. et al., pp. 177–183.

Martin, L.D., 1991, 'Mesozoic Birds and the Origin of Birds', in *Origins of the Higher Groups of Tetrapods: Controversy and Consensus*. Schultze, H-P., Trueb, L. (eds), pp. 485–540.

Martin, L.D., Zhou, Z., Hou, L., Feduccia, A., 1998, '*Confuciusornis sanctus*

Compared to *Archaeopteryx lithographica'*, *Naturwissenschaften*, 85, pp. 286–289.

Morell, V. 1993, '*Archaeopteryx*: Early Bird Catches a Can of Worms', *Science*, 259(5096), pp. 764–765.

Norberg, R.A., 1995, 'Feather Asymmetry in *Archaeopteryx*', *Nature*, 374, p. 221.

Norell, M.A., Chappe, L., Clark, J.M., Perle, A., 1993, '*Mononykus olecranus*, an Unusual New Bird from the Cretaceous of Mongolia', *Journal of Vertebrate Paleontology*, 13(3) supplement p. 51.

Novas, F.E., Puerta, P.F., 1997, 'New Evidence concerning Avian Origins from the Late Cretaceous of Patagonia', *Nature*, 387, pp. 390–392.

Ostrom, J.H., 1987, '*Protoavis*, a Triassic Bird?' *Archaeopteryx*, 5, pp. 113–114.

Ostrom, J.H., 1991, 'The Question of the Origin of Birds', in *Origins of the Higher Groups of Tetrapods: Controversy and Consensus*. Schultze H-P., Trueb, L. (eds), pp. 467–484.

Padian, K., Chiappe, L.M., 1998, 'The Origin and Early Evolution of Birds', *Biological Reviews of the Cambridge Philosophical Society*, 73, pp. 1–42.

Shipman, P., 1997, 'Birds Do It . . . Did Dinosaurs?' *New Scientist*, 1 February, pp. 27–31.

Zimmer, C., 1992, 'Ruffled Feathers', *Discover*, 13(5), pp. 44–54.

CHAPTER 15: THE *ARCHAEOPTERYX* SAGA

Anonymous, 2000, 'Is It a Dinosaur? No, It's a Fake', *Guardian* (London), 7 February.

Anonymous, 2000, 'Fossil Ruffles Feathers', *Guardian* (London), 24 February.

Anonymous, 2000, 'Archaeoraptor a Composite, Panel of Scientists Determines', *NationalGeographic.com* (Internet), 7 April.

Anonymous, 2000, 'Unearthed: the Early Bird Held Together with Glue', *Independent on Sunday* (London), 2 July.

Gugliotta, G., 1999, 'Missing Dinosaur–Bird Link? Some Believe Fossil is Evidence of Ancestry; Others Have Doubts', *Washington Post*, 16 October.

Key, I., 1999, 'Turkey with Teeth That Was the First Dinosaur Bird', *Daily Mail* (London), 16 October.

Kurtenbach, E., 2000, 'Dino–Bird Link Disputed', *CNews* (Internet), 21 January.

Mazzatenta, O.L., 1999, 'Experts Talking Turkey about the Missing Link', *Daily Herald* (Scotland), 16 October.

Recer, P., 1999, 'The Turkeysaurus That Was First to Conquer the Skies', *Daily Express* (London), 16 October.

Simons, L.M., 2000, '*Archaeoraptor* Fossil Trail', *National Geographic*, 198(4), pp. 128–132.

Sloan, C., 1999, 'Feathers for *T. rex*', *National Geographic*, 196(5), pp. 98–107.

264   *Sources*

Tejada, S., 1999, 'Dinosaurs Are Not Extinct: Their Descendants Fill the Sky',
   NationalGeographic.com (Internet), 15 October.
Tejada, S., 1999, 'Dinosaurs Raise a Flap', *NationalGeographic.com* (Internet),
   18 October.

PICTURE CREDITS

The author and publishers would like to thank the following for permission
to reproduce illustrations: p. 3, Ian Bear; p. 6, Jura-Museum; p. 18, UCL
Watson Library; p. 28, *Neues Jahrbuch für Mineralogie, Geologie und Palaeontologie*;
p. 39, Heilmann estate; p. 47, *Transactions of the Zoological Society of London*;
p. 84, Heilmann estate; p. 103, *London Illustrated News*; p. 111, *Popular Science
Review*; p. 112, Heilmann estate; p. 118, *Science*; p. 126, *USGS*; p. 142, Jura-
Museum; pp. 149, 155, 158, 164, Heilmann estate; p. 176, R. Baxter; p. 177,
Neues Jahrbuch für Mineralogie, Geologie und Palaeontologie; p. 180, R. Baxter;
p. 202, Hunt Emerson; p. 212, Sankar Chatterjee; p. 224, R. Baxter; p. 225,
Larry Martin; p. 242, R. Baxter.

Index

Allosaurus, 132
American Museum of Natural
    History, 167, 169
Andrews, Roy Chapman, 167–9,
    219, 243
Anthropometric Society, 137
Apatosaurus, 132
Archaeopteryx (general references)
    Creationists and, 195–8
    Forgery, accusations of, 200–9
    Heilmann, Gerhard and, 157–9
    Naming of, 30, 32, 42–3, 95–6,
        179
    Scientific comment on, 24–44,
        83–6, 87–90, 157–9, 182
    Specimen from Guinea, 153
    Play about, 153
    World War Two and, 170–1
Archaeopteryx (London specimen)
    Arrival in London, 63–4
    Discovery of, 4–13
    Forgery, accusation of, 200–9
    Preparation of, 8–13
    Sale of by Carl Häberlein, 48–67
    Scientific comment on, 24–44,
        83–6, 87–90
    Study by John Evans, 97–8
    Study by Thomas Huxley,
        108–15

Study by Richard Owen, 65–7,
    82–3, 87–90
Archaeopteryx (Berlin specimen)
    Discovery of, 140–3
    Sale of by Ernst Häberlein,
        143–8
Archaeopteryx (other specimens)
    Eichstätt specimen, 208,
        214
    Maxberg specimen, 172–3
    Solnhofen specimen, 208, 210,
        214
    Solnhofer Aktien-Verein
        specimen, 214–15
    Teyler specimen, 177–9, 183
Archaeoraptor, 235–50
Argyll, Duke of, 89
Aulenback, Kevin, 243

Baird, Spencer, 145
Bakker, Bob, 186
Ballou, William Hosea, 134–5
Beer, Gavin de, 35, 171–2
Birds
    Anti a link with dinosaurs,
        187–93, 216–18, 221–34,
        245–50
    Chinese fossil discoveries,
        219–35

Birds (*cont.*)
  Crocodile evolution and, 181,
    184, 188
  Dinosaur evolution and, 105–10,
    159–63, 168–9, 177–8, 182,
    187–93, 223–34
  Evolution of, 29, 99–100,
    104–10, 112–13, 157–63,
    167–9, 177–8, 187–93,
    209–14, 223
  Flight, evolution of, 215–18,
    226–7
  Wrists of and evolution, 183–4
'Birds Are Not Dinosaurs' (BAND),
    187–93, 216–18, 221–34,
    245–50
British Museum (Natural History),
    see Natural History Museum
    (London)
Brontosaurus, 132
Broom, Robert, 154, 162
Brown, Barnum T., 160
Brush, Alan, 228
Buckland, William, 105
Buffetaut, Eric, 153

Carus, Karl Gustav, 72
Caudopteryx, 230
Chambers, Robert, 73
Charig, Alan, 204
Chatterjee, Sankar, 210–14, 234
Chen Pei-Je, 223
Chiappe, Luis, 222
Colonosaurus, 125
Compsognathus, 110–14, 175, 178,
    201
Conan Doyle, Arthur, 160
Confuciusornis, 221–2, 224, 237
'Convergent evolution', 190
Cope, Edward Drinker, 116–39,
    151, 167
  Archaeopteryx and, 116–17
  'Bone war' and, 131–9

Dinosaurs and, 121–2, 131–4
  Early life of, 117, 119–21
  Marsh, Othniel, feud with,
    121–31
Creationist Christians and evolution,
    194–8, 250
Cresswell, Richard 15, 16,
Crocodiles, bird evolution and, 181,
    184, 188
Crystal Palace, 101–3, 107, 133
Currie, Phil, 223–5, 239–50
Czerkas, Steven and Sylvia, 238–50

Darwin, Charles, 15, 16, 19, 21, 25,
    26, 33, 44, 56, 68, 73–6, 88,
    90, 116, 134, 151, 200, 203
  Archaeopteryx and, 90–3, 97
  Evolution, theory of, 74–6
  Huxley, Thomas, and, 74–7
Deinonychus, 174–6, 182, 189,
    190–1, 246
Desmond, Adrian, 112–13
Dinosaurs
  Birds evolved from, 105–10,
    159–63, 168–9, 177–8, 182,
    187–93, 223–34
  Discovery of, 100–1
  Gobi Desert and, 167–9
Diplodocus, 132, 159, 160
Dollo, Louis, 161
Dollo's Law, 161–2, 185
Dörr, Johann, 140–1
Draper, John W., 14–15, 19

Egerton, Philip, 96
Evans, John, 87, 96–8, 125, 148

Falconer, Hugh, 87, 88, 90–2, 94,
    96
  Comments on London
    Archaeopteryx, 90–2, 97
Feathers, 12, 13, 25, 28, 32, 216–18,
    223–6, 228, 229, 233–4

Feduccia, Alan, 187, 192, 214, 216,
    217–18, 221–2, 225, 233
Flight, evolution of, 215–18, 226–7
Footprints, fossilized, 95
Freie Deutsche Hochstift, 147

Galton, Peter, 186
Gee, Henry, 244
Geinitz, Professor, 145
Geneva, University of, 147
Geologist, The, 94, 97
Gray, John, 108–9
Griphosaurus, 42–4
Günther, Albert, 108

Häberlein, Carl, 5, 6, 7, 8, 9, 10, 11,
    12, 13, 14, 23–7, 29–44,
    48–65, 116, 140, 172, 200,
    203, 205
    Finds London *Archaeopteryx,* 5–9
    Life history of, 5
    Sale of London *Archaeopteryx,*
        33–44, 48
Häberlein, Ernst, 140–4, 146, 148,
    172
    Finds Berlin *Archaeopteryx,* 140–3
    Sale of Berlin *Archaeopteryx,*
        143–8
Hawkins, Benjamin Waterhouse,
    102
Hecht, Max, 191
Heilmann, Gerhard, 154–65, 175,
    179, 181, 184, 185, 213–16
    Archaeopteryx and, 157–9
    Bird evolution and, 157–63,
        181
    Early life of, 154–6,
    Origin of birds and, 156–65
Henslow, Robert Stevens, 14
Herbert, Hilary, 138, 196
Hesperornis, 124–9, 165, 206, 233
Hingkeldey, Friedrich, 35
Hitchcock, Edward, 95

Hoatzin, 184
Hooker, Joseph, 20, 21, 88, 90, 94
Horner, Jack, 218–19
Horse (evolution of), 129
Hoyle, Fred, 198–209, 250
Humboldt Museum, 148, 170
Huxley, Leonard, 129
Huxley, Thomas Henry, 17, 19–21,
    33, 69–81, 87–90, 98, 116,
    125, 140, 151, 159, 160, 203,
    227
    Archaeopteryx and, 87–90, 94,
        98–100, 108–15, 203
    Bird evolution and, 99–100,
        104–15
    Darwin and, 74–81, 94, 98
    Debate with Samuel
        Wilberforce, 19–21
    Dinosaurs and, 104–15, 132
    Early life of, 70–1
    Evolution and, 72–4, 95, 98,
        113–14
    Marsh and, 127–30
    Owen, Richard, and, 69–73,
        77–81, 88–90, 99, 101, 106,
        108, 114–15, 152
Hylaeosaurus, 102

Ichthyornis, 125–9
Ichthyosaurus, 102
Iguanodon, 100, 102, 103, 107, 160

Jarry, Alfred, 153
Ji Qiang, 228, 229
Jones, Terry, 233
Jung, Carl, 27
Jura-Museum, 35

Kowalevsky, Professor, 135, 136–7

Laelaps, 121–2, 131, 138
Lancaster, Ray, 160
Lemming, H., 146–7

Liaoning fossil quarries, China,
219–20, 237
Livingstone, David, 137
Longisquama, 232–4
Lütken, Christian, 154
Lyell, Charles, 91

Mackie, S. J., 94
Mantell, Gideon, 101
Marsh, Othniel Charles, 119–39,
151, 159, 196, 227
Archaeopteryx and, 120, 144–6,
147
'Bone war' and, 131–9
Dinosaurs and, 131–4
Early life of, 119–21
Huxley, Thomas, and, 127–30,
227
Newspapers and, 122–3
Toothed birds and, 124–39
Martin, Larry, 188–9, 216, 221–2,
227, 228–9, 233, 245
Martius, Karl von, 45, 51–3, 67
Megalosaurus, 100, 102, 105–6, 107,
160
Meyer, Hermann von, 27, 28, 29,
30, 36, 37, 42, 45, 95, 96, 98,
116, 178, 217
London *Archaeopteryx* and,
28–30, 45, 55
'Missing link' debate (see also
Creationist Christians)
London *Archaeopteryx* and,
24–44, 83–6, 87–90, 109–15
Toothed birds and, 125–7,
130–1
Mononykus, 220
Munich Bavarian State Collection,
24, 25, 32, 33, 35, 36, 37, 44,
45, 50, 55, 116, 143, 146,
170
Munster, Count, 23
Murchison, Roderick, 54, 59

National Geographic Society, 211,
213, 240–50
Natural History Museum (London),
46, 48–67, 96, 97, 106–7, 117,
170
Acquisition of London
Archaeopteryx, 46, 48–67
Forgery, accusations of against
Archaeopteryx, 200–9
New York Herald, 123, 134–7
Norell, Mark, 188, 229

Olsen, George, 168
Olson, Storrs, 216, 234, 246,
248
'Onondaga Man', 123
Opitsch, Eduard, 172–3
Oppel, Alfred, 37–40, 45, 51, 55,
116
Origin of birds, 156–65, 166, 185,
232
Origin of Species, The 15, 16, 17, 19,
21, 24, 26, 58, 68, 77–81, 92,
94, 97, 102, 103, 117, 122,
123, 138, 151, 154, 203,
206
Publication of, 77–81
Archaeopteryx and, 92
Osborne, Henry, 127, 167
Ostrom, John, 174–93, 197, 211,
215–17, 227
Archaeopteryx and, 178–90
Deinonychus and, 174–9, 181–7,
188–90
Early life of, 174–5
Ottmann Quarry 3, 5
Oviraptor, 168
Owen, Richard, 46–81, 94, 108–9,
116, 131, 134, 138, 145, 146,
151, 160, 190, 196, 200,
203
Darwin and, 77–81
Dinosaurs and, 100–3

Early life of, 68–9
Evolution and, 71–3, 101–2, 152, 190
Huxley, Thomas, and, 69–73, 77–9, 88–90, 99, 101, 106, 108, 114–15, 151
Purchase of London *Archaeopteryx*, 49–67
Study of London *Archaeopteryx*, 65–7, 82–3, 87–90, 97
Oxford University Museum, 14–21, 105–6, 107
Debate in, 15–21

Panizzi, A., 65, 67
Pappenheim, 5, 23, 24, 27, 32, 33, 38, 49, 51, 54, 55, 56, 58, 67, 119, 145, 177
Peabody, George, 119
Phillips, John, 105, 106, 107
Plesiosaurus, 102
Proavis, 162–3, 167, 213
Protoarchaeopteryx, 227–30, 232
Protoavis, 210–14, 234
Protoceratops, 168
Pterodactyls, see Pterosaurs
Pterosaurs, 4, 11, 23, 28, 35, 36, 37, 40, 52, 89, 141, 146, 152, 159, 177, 186

Queen Victoria, 1, 48, 115

Rowe, Timothy, 242–50
Royal Society, 87, 90, 94, 95, 96
Ruben, John, 233
Ruskin, John, 66

Scrotum humanum, 105
Seeley, Harry, 152, 159, 186
Siemens, Werner von, 148
Sinosauropteryx, 223–7, 228
Sloan, Christopher, 240–50

Smith Woodward, Arthur, 157
'Soapy Sam', see Wilberforce, Samuel
Solnhofen
Fossils from, 4–6, 10–11, 23, 27, 177
Quarries near, 1–5, 27
Somerset, Duke of, 54
Spetner, Lee, 200, 207
Sphenosuchus, 181
Spielberg, Steven, 166
Stanhope, Earl of, 54
Stanley, Henry, 137
Stegosaurus, 132, 160, 175

Tarsitano, Samuel, 191
Taunton, Lord, 54
Taylor, Ian, 207–8
Thecodonts, 153–4, 183–4
Times, The (London), 79, 83–6, 91
'Toothed birds', 124–39, 151, 196 (see also *Hesperornis* and *Ichthyornis*)
Tyler Museum, 177–8
Tyrannosaurus, 160, 175, 182, 245, 246

United States Geological Survey, 133, 134, 135

Velociraptor, 168, 182, 245, 246
Vestiges of the Natural History of Creation, 73
Vogt, Karl, 147–8

Wagner, Johann Andreas, 25, 32–45, 48, 51, 55, 58, 82, 89, 96, 116, 197, 206
Describes London *Archaeopteryx*, 40–4
Walker, Alick, 181, 188–9, 233
Walpole, Horatio Spencer, 54

Waterhouse, George Robert, 46–67, 97

Wellnhofer, Peter, 208–9, 214, 227

Westminster Review, 80

Wickramasinghe, Chandra, 198–209, 250

Wilberforce, Samuel, 16–21, 78, 80
   Debate with Huxley, 16–21

Wilhelm, Kaiser, 146

Witte, O. J., 23, 24, 25, 27, 29, 32, 37, 40

Woodward, Henry, 96

Xu Xing, 241, 247–8

Y., 85–7, 91

Yale University, 119, 139, 146